THE COMING PROSPERITY

THE COMING PROSPERITY

How Entrepreneurs Are
Transforming the Global Economy

Philip Auerswald

OXFORD
UNIVERSITY PRESS

OXFORD
UNIVERSITY PRESS

Oxford University Press, Inc., publishes works that further
Oxford University's objective of excellence
in research, scholarship, and education.

Oxford   New York
Auckland   Cape Town   Dar es Salaam   Hong Kong   Karachi
Kuala Lumpur   Madrid   Melbourne   Mexico City   Nairobi
New Delhi   Shanghai   Taipei   Toronto

With offices in
Argentina   Austria   Brazil   Chile   Czech Republic   France   Greece
Guatemala   Hungary   Italy   Japan   Poland   Portugal   Singapore
South Korea   Switzerland   Thailand   Turkey   Ukraine   Vietnam

Copyright © 2012 by Philip Auerswald

Published by Oxford University Press, Inc.
198 Madison Avenue, New York, NY 10016

www.oup.com

Oxford is a registered trademark of Oxford University Press

Library of Congress Cataloging-in-Publication Data
Auerswald, Philip E.
The coming prosperity : how entrepreneurs are transforming the global economy / Philip E. Auerswald.
   p.   cm.
ISBN 978-0-19-979517-8 (hbk. : alk. paper) 1. Globalization—Economic aspects.
2. Globalization—Developing countries. 3. Economic development—Developing countries.
4. Economic development—United States. 5. Developing countries—Population—Economic aspects.
I.Title.
HF1359.A927   2012
337—dc23   2011029789

1 3 5 7 9 8 6 4 2

Printed in the United States of America
on acid-free paper

For Cecelia, Helena, and Isabel

CONTENTS

PART FOUR: *The Next America*

THE COMING PROSPERITY

INTRODUCTION

> The prevailing world depression, the enormous anomaly of
> unemployment in a world full of wants, the disastrous mistakes
> we have made, blind us to what is going on under the surface—
> to the true interpretation of the trend of things.
>
> —JOHN MAYNARD KEYNES, *"The Economic Possibilities for Our
> Grandchildren"*

This is a book about the unparalleled possibilities of now. It takes as its backdrop an inescapable fact: the majority of the world's population is at last connecting with the global economy; billions of people are deriving benefits from the past five centuries of technological and institutional innovation from which they have previously been excluded. As a consequence, human well-being will likely improve to a greater extent in coming decades than at any time in history. But progress toward global prosperity is not inevitable. The choices we make today will determine the extent and reach of the coming prosperity, and the part we play in it.

There would be no need to write this book if a general appreciation existed for the scope of the coming prosperity, or the half millennium of historical momentum from which it derives its impetus. Yes, the ascendance of China, India, and Brazil is universally recognized. But, for some understandable reasons, this new reality still mostly inspires alarm rather than eager anticipation.

In the US, in particular, the economic ascent of the global majority is mostly either blamed for the nation's alleged decline or damned as the underlying cause for an array of global challenges—from climate change to water scarcity. Sure, Shanghai is suddenly full of whiz kids poised for dominance in the science fairs of the future, and villagers in Kenya can now receive money from a relative abroad on their cell phones. Great—that's good for them. But such changes aren't going to do much for veterans returning home from Iraq and Afghanistan who can't find work, or for families who lost their homes to foreclosure in the most severe recession since the Great Depression. Paychecks for most US workers have not reversed the downward slide they began when Richard Nixon was president—back when the most high-tech object in an average American household was a Casio calculator. The number of people on food stamps exceeds the population of California. Much of Detroit remains a wasteland, New Orleans is struggling to regain its former glory, and everywhere else different versions of the new American Nightmare—persistent unemployment, lost wealth, and exhaustion of technological possibilities—seem to be overtaking the American Dream. The coming prosperity? Nice try. A country headed down the tubes is more like it.

Let's be honest: There is truth here. America is not just a place in transition. It is, in too many homes, a place in pain.

But the immediacy of pain on our doorstep should not blind us to the epochal promise of prosperity that is evident on the horizon. That promise is every bit as tangible for Peoria as it is for Beijing. New pathways of progress are opening up more rapidly than old ones are closing. Never have more people had greater opportunity to create value for society, and for themselves, than we do today.

Of course, shared value is no more about profit than prosperity is about the accumulation of more stuff. While the search for economic profit and the desire for material wealth are, inarguably, very powerful human motivators, they do not constitute the totality of human interest. In the world's wealthiest places as well as the poorest, some of the most remarkable entrepreneurs and innovators will always be those who think less of how they will benefit, and more about what they will change. The efforts of such individuals to push back against entrenched incumbent interests are an essential element of the coming prosperity.

Without purpose, there is no progress. For individuals, companies, and nations alike, it's time to be what matters.

Before you read on, a few words of warning: I am an economist. I am also a father, a husband, and a teacher. I am a native resident of the District of Columbia, a half-Tunisian, and a fan of the original *Speed Racer* animated TV series (I didn't see the movie).

I am neither a scientist nor a venture capitalist, so you're not going to hear about how nanotechnology and biological computing will soon totally transform the world as we know it. No, I am not among those that doubt the continuing transformative potential of radically new technologies. That major waves of technological transformation lie ahead is, in my view, a near certainty. But this is not a book that delves into technology futures. Instead, this is a book about pathways of action for our time. It is a book about how to think of the three billion people who will join the global economy in the next quarter century as partners rather than competitors, as sources rather than sinks.

My own conviction concerning the powerful possibilities of our historical moment derives from more than a decade and a half of work, travel, and research related to innovation, entrepreneurship, and the complex dynamics of social change. In 1993, while a graduate student in economics at the University of Washington, I was subjected to an enlivening bit of intellectual shock therapy when I participated in the third annual (of the now more than twenty) Complex Systems Summer School organized by the Santa Fe Institute. There I collaborated with the evolutionary biologist Stuart Kauffman, a graduate student from Cornell named José Lobo, and, later, the economist theorist Karl Shell on the puzzle of how technologies and organizations coevolve with markets. After completing my doctorate, I went to Harvard's Kennedy School of Government, where I had the good fortune to work on the topic of innovation policy with Lewis Branscomb, an emeritus professor and former director of research at IBM, and John Holdren, currently President Obama's science adviser.

While at the Kennedy School, I met Iqbal Quadir, the founder of Grameenphone—the first company to bring cell phone service to a developing country on a large scale. Quadir and I spent many hours discussing the ways that entrepreneurship, innovation, and technology interact in the process of economic development. In the course of those conversations, I circled back to some eternal questions that had led me to study economics in the first place: How can the actions of one person affect the evolution of a society? How do economic decisions affect ecological outcomes, and vice versa?

I was also prompted to ask a major disconcerting question that hit closer to home: Why was a person whose work was singularly dedicated to finding entrepreneurial solutions to global challenges such an exception at the nation's most prominent educational institution? To be sure, many others on the Harvard faculty were also renowned for actively seeking practical solutions to society's most complex and intractable challenges— Holdren was one, and the remarkable Paul Farmer another. Yet (notwithstanding rhetoric to the contrary) so much of what occurred at Harvard, just as at most other leading research universities, was painfully distanced from problems of the present. (There is, actually, an explanation for this phenomenon—more on that in chapter 9.) At the same time, of the few successful "practitioners"—the term used in academic environments for pretty much anyone without a PhD who has done something—on the Harvard campus, fewer had Quadir's ability to describe their experiences and articulate their insights analytically and in a historical context, and thus his potential to inform academic and policy discussions.

These discussions and reflections led Holdren and me to invite Quadir to join us on the founding editorial team of the journal we came to call *Innovations*, dedicated to the understanding and the encouragement of entrepreneurial solutions to global challenges. Our aspiration at the outset was that the journal would not only advance thinking about practical innovations, but that it would also compel change in academic environments by offering entrepreneurs a space in which to describe their insights more analytically and academics in turn a space in which to think more practically.

Once we started to look for examples of outstanding innovations that were addressing global challenges, we were amazed at what we found. Why had I never before heard of Dr. Govindappa Venkataswamy, whose retirement project had resulted in two million people being cured of blindness? Or Victoria Hale, who left a lucrative job at a major pharmaceutical company to start the world's first not-for-profit pharmaceutical firm—a company which, within a few years, produced and deployed a cure for one of the deadliest diseases afflicting the people of South Asia?

During five years of coediting *Innovations*, I have become increasingly attuned to the fact that among the "chatterati" whose prognostications preoccupy the public, most tend to treat the big story of the twenty-first century—a global transformation enabled by entrepreneurship, technology, and innovation—as a side story overshadowed by scarcity-driven crises. To be sure, notable exceptions exist—among them Charles Kenny's *Getting Better*, Matt Ridley's *The Rational Optimist*, and the excellent and informative data visualizations produced by Hans Rosling and his team at Gapminder. But even among the best "big-think" books and blogs, the overwhelming majority clearly are deficient when it comes to paying attention to the entrepreneurial possibilities of the present—a positive insurgency on a global scale that is creating today's historically unprecedented era of prosperity.

Now I know what you're thinking: Optimists are nice to have around, but you don't want to take them too seriously. Let the optimists sing "Kumbaya" and gather for group hugs. But when they're done, please make room for the serious people to step in, roll up their sleeves, and get to work.

As for entrepreneurship and innovation, who isn't in favor of small businesses and clever scientists? No one. Yes, we mourn the loss of Steve Jobs and celebrate his total commitment to creativity and design excellence. But the fact is that entrepreneurs are not going to be the ones who solve the headline problems facing the human race in the twenty-first century. When a global pandemic breaks out, who is going to help us avoid calamity? The World Health Organization, the Centers for Disease Control, a few hundred scientists, and a few thousand doctors. Not a bunch of entrepreneurs. As nuclear power plants proliferate globally, who is going ensure that plutonium doesn't end up providing the energy to catalyze terrorist cells instead of recharging fuel cells? Not a bunch of entrepreneurs. When entire countries face decades-long droughts caused by climate change, who is going to step in to keep their populations from starving? That's right. Not the entrepreneurs. And what's more, didn't we just have a global financial meltdown caused by too much entrepreneurship and innovation? Wasn't the whole mortgage market collapse evidence enough that we need less disruption in society, not more?

I understand this perspective well. I have been the author of op-eds and essays on energy and national security, and have coedited a volume on the private sector's role in reducing the public vulnerability to catastrophic terrorism. A couple of years ago, after more than a decade of work, I published a 4,500-page compilation of documents chronicling the diplomatic history of the conflict in Iraq. As a lecturer at Harvard's Kennedy School of Government and then a faculty member at George Mason University's School of Public Policy, I have attended dozens of seminars about global threats of various types. Even further back, as an undergraduate in the mid-1980s, I had the good fortune to take a seminar with former CIA director Stansfield Turner on the topic of terrorism and democracy. The subject of my term paper? Islamic fundamentalist ideology.

What have I learned from this cumulative study? That the vast majority of alleged threats to humanity are, in fact, dwarfed by the magnitude of opportunities that exist in the twenty-first century. Furthermore, if anything is more naïve than an unquestioning belief in the transformative power of entrepreneurs, it is an unquestioning belief in the power of national governments, international organizations, and multinational corporations to address complex twenty-first-century challenges. In many parts of the world where change is most urgently needed, governments are as likely to be a part of the problem as a part of the solution. In such environments, all institutions structured to work through national governments face serious handicaps. The relevance, much less effectiveness, of the UN and the World Bank—the two institutions most clearly tasked in the post–World War II order with addressing global challenges—is less assured today than that of entrepreneurs.

While the stale dichotomies of the industrial age—top down versus bottom up, government controlled versus free market, and liberal versus conservative—continue to line the shelves of the marketplace of ideas, the distinctions on which they are based have increasingly collapsed. What matters most to the pathway of societal development isn't the share of resources dedicated to government as opposed to private business per se, but rather the share of resources dedicated to exploitation of known opportunities as opposed to exploration of new ones. This core trade-off—and the balance between order and adaptability it implies—is fundamental in any society. How that trade-off has evolved from the industrial age to ours, the age of entrepreneurship, is the key to understanding the productive power of populations in the twenty-first century.

I do understand specific concerns shared by many informed observers about particular population-induced problems; pandemics, climate change, and water scarcity are notable among them. In fact, I believe these three global threats deserve particular attention—a concern evidenced by the topics Quadir and I have chosen to feature in *Innovations*.[2] My strong conviction, however, is that these challenges related to the growth of human populations cannot be properly comprehended in isolation from the expansion of human opportunity, described above. Our era, it turns out, is one beset not by biblical plagues of divine provenance, but rather by paradoxes of prosperity that we ourselves have authored.

In every corner of the world, from Abu Dhabi to Zurich, just as in Washington and Wall Street, yesterday's power brokers can be counted on to paint opportunity as threat and dig in their heels against change. As a consequence, the work of making the most of humanity's moment will fall to those hundreds, thousands, or millions of entrepreneurs and innovators who dedicate themselves to discovering pathways to progress in the decade to come just as others did in the decade just past. People like Karim Khoja, who led the creation of the first mobile phone company in Afghanistan; Leila Janah, who is bringing digital-age opportunity to talented people trapped in refugee camps and other previously disconnected places; and Ibrahim Abouleish who, over three decades, transformed seventy hectares of desert land a quarter mile from the banks of the Nile into the site of a world-class organic products business—a literal oasis of social enterprise and education.

Progress? You ain't seen nothin' yet.

STRENGTH IN NUMBERS

On the surface, the relentless motion of humanity can appear turbulent and threatening. But beneath the surface flows a deep and steady current of positive change. Perceived impediments to future prosperity—large-scale unemployment, resource scarcity, and climate change among them—are in fact eddies in this larger current.

Contrary to a century's worth of predictions made by prophets of doom, ours is an era of unprecedented opportunity.

1 CAR TROUBLE

The price of progress is trouble, and I must be making a lot of progress.

—CHARLES ERWIN WILSON, *CEO of General Motors*

At the height of combat during World War II, as US troops were massing in England in anticipation of the Normandy invasion, the United States Congress engaged in a heated debate about a domestic issue of grave concern: how to avert mass unemployment when millions of servicemen came home after war's end. Only a dozen years earlier, at the nadir of the Great Depression, World War I veterans had converged on Washington demanding early disbursement of congressionally mandated payments. The result was an ugly confrontation in the nation's capital between the "Bonus Marchers," as they were dubbed, and US Army units led by none other than the chief of staff, General Douglas MacArthur. Wishing to avoid a repetition of this disturbing scenario, Congress enacted the GI Bill, signed into law by President Franklin Delano Roosevelt on June 22, 1944; it was a momentous piece of legislation credited with creating opportunity for a generation.

Returning veterans in numbers far exceeding congressional projections accepted the government's offer of free college tuition and zero-interest home mortgages. Yet the government's estimates pertaining to one contentious provision of the GI Bill turned out to be dramatically exaggerated: of the unemployment benefits available to returning veterans, only 20 percent were claimed.

This better-than-expected outcome did not end concerns over the potential for large-scale unemployment to cause economic calamity and political disruption. Almost exactly four years after V-J Day—on August 13, 1949, to be precise—an MIT professor named Norbert Wiener wrote a letter to Walter Reuther, president of the United Auto Workers (UAW). It contained a darkly prophetic message: within a decade or two, Wiener wrote, the advent of automatic automobile assembly lines would result in "disastrous" unemployment. The power of computers to control machines made such an outcome all but inevitable. As a creator of this new technology, Wiener wanted to give Reuther advance notice so that the UAW could help its members prepare for, and adapt to, the massive displacement of labor that Wiener saw on the horizon.

Now if anyone in 1949 grasped the disruptive potential of computing machines, it was Norbert Wiener. What Albert Einstein was to the nuclear age, Norbert Wiener was to the information age. Home-schooled until age nine by his demanding immigrant father, Wiener made headlines as the "Youngest College Man in the History of the United States" when he enrolled at Tufts University in 1906 at age eleven. In 1913, at only eighteen, he earned his PhD from Harvard in mathematical philosophy. By the time Wiener wrote to Reuther, he had grown round and renowned. ("Short, rotund, and myopic, combining these and many qualities in extreme degree" was one contemporary's description.) He had contributed to the development of the first modern computer, created the first automated machine, and laid the groundwork for a new transdisciplinary science of information and communication that he termed "cybernetics." His work would anticipate and inspire Marshall McLuhan's heralded studies of mass media, would provide the initial impetus for the explorations by James Watson and Francis Crick that led to the discovery of the double helix, and would spur science-fiction writer William Gibson to coin the term "cyberspace" in describing a type of virtual world that Wiener himself had envisioned two decades before the creation of the first web page.

As Wiener warned Reuther of the potentially dire consequences of automated production, he also had a plan to avoid calamity. The UAW, he advised, should "steal a march upon the existing industrial corporations" by taking ownership of the technology for robotics, and then using the returns from the production of robots to fund "an organization dedicated to the benefit of labor." He admitted the existence of another option: the UAW could undertake to keep the new technology from entering into industrial use. But having suggested this option, he immediately dismissed

MC22 F-105

CLASS OF SERVICE		SYMBOLS	
This is a full-rate Telegram or Cablegram unless its deferred character is indicated by a suitable symbol above or preceding the address.	**WESTERN UNION** JOSEPH L. EGAN PRESIDENT	DL=Day Letter NL=Night Letter LC=Deferred Cable NLT=Cable Night Letter Ship Radiogram	1201

The filing time shown in the date line on telegrams and day letters is STANDARD TIME at point of origin. Time of receipt is STANDARD TIME at point of destination

```
 BA050 DEC275
DE LLR283 PD=WUX DETROIT MICH 17 317P=
PROFESSOR NORBERT WIENER=
   =SOUTH TAMWORTH NHAMP=
```

DEEPLY INTERESTED IN YOUR LETTER. WOULD LIKE TO DISCUSS IT
WITH YOU AT EARLIEST OPPORTUNITY FOLLOWING CONCLUSION OF
OUR CURRENT NEGOTIATIONS WITH FORD MOTOR COMPANY. WILL YOU BE
ABLE TO COME TO DETROIT=
     =WALTER P REUTHER PRESIDENT UAW CIO=

                                    ε(352 PM AUG 17 49)

,THE COMPANY WILL APPRECIATE SUGGESTIONS FROM ITS PATRONS CONCERNING ITS SERVICE

Telegram from Walther Reuther, President of the United Auto Workers, to Norbert Wiener, August 17, 1949.
Source: The Institute Archives at the Massachusetts Institute of Technology.

it: since ideas forming the basis for robotics were already "very much in the air," they likely could not be suppressed.

Surprisingly, Reuther, the Big Labor kingpin, did not dismiss the portly professor's Cassandra calls. To the contrary, Reuther responded to Wiener promptly by telegram. "Deeply interested in your letter," he wrote. "Would like to discuss it with you at earliest opportunity following conclusion of our current negotiations with Ford Motor Company. Will you be able to come to Detroit?" For some months thereafter these two global figures sought to coordinate their schedules. When they met at last in March 1950, they pledged to work together to create a labor-science council to anticipate, and prepare for, major technological changes affecting workers. But then their paths diverged. The idea never came to fruition.

Now, why start a book about humanity's prospects for prosperity with an anecdote about an exchange sixty years ago between two forgotten giants seeking to avoid an economic disaster that never happened? After all,

1949—the year Wiener first wrote to Reuther—was also the year of the Berlin airlift and the Soviet Union's first successful hydrogen bomb test, and the year that Mao Zedong stood in Tiananmen Square and declared the founding of the People's Republic of China. Surely such events are more appropriate anchors for a tale about the arc of human history.

That is just the point. The story of the twentieth century is invariably told as a political and military narrative: first, the war to end all wars that did not; then, the democracies' world war to defeat fascism; and finally, the successful struggle to defeat Soviet communism. Far less well appreciated, but arguably more relevant to the present, is the economic subtext of this same history: the rise and partial fall of large-scale, centralized production. This economic subtext—the essence of the exchange between Wiener and Reuther—is the preamble to the coming prosperity. And so it is with that story that I begin.

At the start of the twentieth century, the economic landscape was transformed by the emergence of an entirely new form of business entity, larger and more complex than any that had existed previously. The major impetus behind this growth was what economists call economies of scale and scope: the ability to reduce costs per unit by (1) increasing the quantity of output and/or (2) integrating within a single business entity the different stages of production, from the acquisition of raw materials to the assembly of a finished product. At the core of this transformation were technological and organizational innovations spanning a century and a half—a familiar genealogy of industrial advancement including James Watt's steam engine, Edmund Cartwright's power loom, Thomas Edison's electric grid, Frederick Taylor's principles of scientific management, Henry Ford's assembly line, and, eventually, Norbert Wiener's automated robots. Economies of scale and scope proved so powerful that the individuals and companies able to exploit them at the turn of the last century succeeded in revolutionizing existing industries and building new ones in a matter of years. Wherever the chaos of haphazard private contracting had been the norm, large corporations stepped in to organize production for increased efficiency and lower cost.

The automobile is a particularly remarkable instance of the phenomenon. A consumer good that did not exist in 1900 became, by the 1930s (when Wiener was laying the groundwork for cybernetics), the dominant industry in the world's most rapidly growing economy. The River Rouge complex that Ford built in Dearborn, Michigan, in the mid-1920s was the epitome of the process of centralizing integration so characteristic of that era. At one end of the facility—which occupied over a square mile and employed over one hundred thousand people—barges unloaded iron ore, coal, and limestone. At the other end exited nearly all the components that made up the Model T; only the final assembly took place at another plant.

The River Rouge was quintessential Middle America of the time, yet in photographs taken from the air it resembles nothing more than the highest form of socialist realism: at once impersonal and heroic, gritty and majestic. The resemblance is no coincidence. The harnessing of the power of scale and scope was a global phenomenon. It found its most dramatic expression not in Standard Oil, Ford Motor Company, or Thyssen Steel, but rather in the Union of Soviet Socialist Republics. Absolute political control allowed the Soviets to undertake an unprecedented experiment: placing the entire productive apparatus of a nation under the control of what was, at least in theory, a single administrative authority. If, as appeared to be the case in the 1930s,

Aerial view of the Ford Motor Company's River Rouge complex, January 12, 1948.
© The Ford Motor Company. Reprinted with permission.

economic power was rooted in the ability to harness economies of scale and scope, then the decentralized market economies of the West seemed to have ample reason to worry. No one would be able to match the Soviets. The anti-communist panics of the 1950s—the real history of the United States at the time—followed directly from these economic realities.

In 1928, the same year that the River Rouge plant was completed, the not-yet globally renowned John Maynard Keynes gave a talk to a group of high school students at Winchester, one of England's elite public schools (what we in the United States refer to as prep schools). The title of the talk, which appeared in print in 1930, was "Economic Possibilities for Our Grandchildren." Keynes opened the print version with a statement that—with appropriate substitution of the US for Great Britain—could have come directly out of a speech by Federal Reserve Chairman Ben Bernanke in the midst of the 2008–2009 recession, or, for that matter, President Obama's inaugural address. ("History doesn't repeat itself," said Mark Twain, "but it does rhyme.") Keynes wrote:

> We are suffering just now from a bad attack of economic pessimism. It is common to hear people say that the epoch of enormous economic progress which characterized the nineteenth century is over; that the rapid improvement in the standard of living is now going to slow down—at any rate in Great Britain; that a decline in prosperity is more likely than an improvement in the decade which lies ahead of us.

Keynes continued by pointing to the error of focusing excessively on transient phenomena, at the expense of understanding longer-term trends. At the time he was writing, Keynes's "true interpretation of the trend of things" featured the miracle of capital accumulation: by saving and investing in productive machines, each successive generation could produce more output than the one before, thereby increasing both per capita consumption and (potentially) per capita savings over time. As such a process followed its natural course, Keynes predicted that "assuming no important wars and no important increase in population, the economic problem may be solved, or at least within sight of solution, within a hundred years." By this statement Keynes meant simply that within a century society would reach a point where it no longer placed enough value on increasing future consumption to spur additional growth in savings and investment. Thereafter the economy would cruise along a steady-state trajectory in which per capita consumption would be constant. In other words, writing more or less contemporaneously to Black October, Keynes envisioned a future in which good choices would be followed by bliss.

To the Keynes of "Economic Possibilities" (a notably different creature from the one generally associated with his masterwork, *The General Theory of Employment, Interest, and Money*), a bumpy ride along the way to the steady-state bliss point was to be expected, but not feared. In fact, in his essay he attributes the sudden increase in unemployment that marked the start of the Great Depression to just the sort of technological displacement of workers that, two decades later, would cause Norbert Wiener to fret. "For the moment the very rapidity of these changes is hurting us. . . . We are being afflicted with a new disease . . . namely, technological unemployment. This means our discovery of means of economizing the use of labor is outrunning the pace at which we can find new uses for labor. But this is only a temporary phase of maladjustment." In an era of disquiet and concern not unlike our own, Keynes looked about him and saw a world in which fundamentally positive trends were creating transitory challenges of adjustment. His greatest concern was, fundamentally, the same as Wiener's: that the increased efficiency of machinery would put people out of work.

The couple of decades that followed Keynes's talk to the students at Winchester did not exactly follow the script he sketched. The economic and political turbulence of the 1930s led to a global war that resulted in the deaths of sixty million people—a human toll that, in raw numerical terms, corresponds to one 9/11 attack every single day for half a century. Subsequently, even as market democracies gradually recovered from the war and socialist economies surged forward, the majority of the world's population remained on the sidelines of the global economy. As late as the 1980s, aggregate capital flows to poor countries averaged $1 billion per year. And when socialist economies (notably the Soviet Union and satellites in Eastern Europe) reached their steady-state consumption level, it turned out to be well below the still-growing standard in the West. Even if some countries were experiencing "the coming prosperity" as Keynes had envisioned it, most were not.

It turned out that Keynes's vision depended on two critical elements not present in most of the world until recently: (1) the *organization* of the economy attainable through large-scale investment, and (2) the *adaptability* of the economy attainable through entrepreneurship. Soviet socialist economies had the first, but the not the second; most of the rest of the world had neither. Outside of market democracies, few countries possessed the institutional structures that would allow new entrants to challenge entrenched economic and political interests. As a direct consequence, until the late 1980s the Soviet sixth of the world lagged and the two-thirds of the world allegedly in the process of development was left out altogether. Only the most fortunate sixth of the world (citizens of North America, Europe, and Japan, and of assorted enclaves of wealth elsewhere) benefited from the uneven march of progress.

That was the picture until the end of the 1980s. But then, as I will discuss further in chapter 6, the bottom finally fell out of the Soviet capital-accumulation machine. The Wall fell and communism crumbled. China turned a corner. Investment began to flow from rich countries to emerging markets—through the 1990s, at an average rate of $170 billion a year. At the turn of the millennium, the pace of global change accelerated. Over the decade that followed, the pace of investment in emerging markets—many of them, like South Korea and Taiwan, having already fully emerged—continued its astounding upward climb, averaging $400 billion a year. The most recent comprehensive data from the Bank for International Settlements show flows reaching $1.4 trillion in 2007—an increase by a factor of 1,400 in a quarter century.

Wealth spread accordingly. By 2010, as many billionaires were residing in previously poor countries as in all the advanced industrialized countries combined, with one significant exception: the United States alone accounts for 40 percent of the total. This success at the high end of financial success reflected a powerful, though obviously uneven, expansion of opportunities to create wealth. Fully two-thirds of global billionaires have made their own fortunes. Among them are a growing numbers of hugely successful emerging-market entrepreneurs—people like India's business services pioneer, Nandan Nilekani, China's Internet visionary, Jack Ma, and Mexico's telecommunications magnate, Carlos Slim.

Increased economic integration reflected in the surge of investment capital flowing to emerging markets has also created opportunities on a large scale for new small- and medium-scale enterprises to connect with global supply chains. International standard-setting bodies—successor organizations to institutions the British had created as mechanisms of colonial coordination—reversed their exclusionary function and became gateways of opportunity for hundreds of thousands of companies in over 170 countries around the world. In 2008 nearly a million companies sought certification from the International Standards Organization in quality management; of these, over a quarter were located in the People's Republic of China.

Of course, increased global economic integration has also led to a surge in illicit trade of various types—from human trafficking to drug smuggling and money laundering. For this reason, as I will point out in chapter 4, a fundamental prerequisite for prosperity in any given place is that the returns to productive entrepreneurial activities must be greater, on average, than the returns to unproductive and destructive entrepreneurship.

Bliss? Maybe not. But, on a global scale, we would be foolish to trade the economic possibilities within our reach in the twenty-first century for those of our grandparents. If that's not the single "true interpretation of the trend of things," as Keynes put it (see quote at the start of this book), it's pretty close.

Norbert Wiener's darker visions of the economic future of humanity have similarly been borne out in their own way. Robots do now perform much of the production-line work in auto factories that UAW members did sixty years ago; employment in the auto industry is also now far below the peak levels reached in 1995. More broadly, the manufacturing workforce in the United States has atrophied—from 35 percent of non-farm employment in 1960 to 10 percent today—primarily not, as is widely believed, because of "offshoring" to China and other parts of the world, but rather due to automation-driven increases in manufacturing productivity. (Evidence: Between 1995 and 2002 we in the US lost two million manufacturing jobs. China during the same time period? They lost fifteen million.)

In a twist even Wiener did not anticipate, the world of cyberspace that Wiener was among the first to have imagined has forced workplace transformations in places far from the factory floor—ones more rapid and more extensive than any caused by the advent of automated production. Phenomena as distinct and seemingly disconnected as the outsourcing of back-office functions by large corporations, the collapse of the newspaper industry, and the recent proliferation of options for online education are all manifestations of the fundamental trends that both Wiener and Keynes identified decades ago. First journalists and accountants, then X-ray technicians, artists, and photographers, among many others, have undergone the disconcerting experience of watching old market structures that previously would have guaranteed lifelong livelihoods crumble before their eyes.

The technology-savvy instigators of the fall 2011 "Occupy Wall Street" protests seem hardly comparable to the Luddites of the early 1800s who smashed mechanized looms to protest the transformations brought about by the Industrial Revolution. But underlying both movements is a sense of injustice at the repudiation of a social contract embedded in the institutions and expectations of a prior era. David Graber, a contributor to the thinking behind the Occupy Wall Street protests, expresses this frustration in its contemporary form: "One of the most abundant resources on earth is smart, creative, imaginative people. And yet 99.9% of the power of the human race is not being marshaled right now. . . . All we need to do is open that spigot a little bit and we could come up with endless ways to create and produce and distribute." In this generation as in generations past, people deprived of the possibility to realize their productive potential become frustrated in a hurry.

Yet Graber and those who share his particular variety of dissatisfaction generally acknowledge—just as Wiener did before them—that putting the genie of technological change back into history's bottle after it has been released is neither possible, nor particularly desirable: however appealing life in a distant, idealized, communitarian past might seem to those who conveniently blot out its "nasty, brutish, and short" essence, we can't get there from where we are now. So the interesting question—in fact, the only question—is ultimately this: How do we direct the inexorable movement of technology most effectively to enhance, rather than obstruct, the ability of people everywhere to realize their productive potential?

In this sense the disruption of work caused by technological advance exemplifies the general phenomenon that is the focus of the next chapter:

paradoxes of prosperity, that is, the adverse consequences of fundamentally beneficial trends. In the case of fears over large-scale unemployment, the real risk to the future is the understandable tendency to react to adversity by hanging on to the past rather than seizing the opportunities that the underlying causes of adversity create.

As longtime auto industry observer Alex Taylor noted at the time of the auto industry bailouts, "by clinging to the attributes that made it an icon, General Motors drove itself to ruin." In other words, the steady decline of GM over the period of decades that ultimately led to its implosion in 2008 was caused not by too many robots, but rather by too little innovation. In places far from Detroit, beneficial change is stalled for the same reason.

As we'll see again in chapter 9, car trouble is everywhere.

2 DEMOGRAPHIC DIVIDENDS

The problems of population are so great, so important, so ramified, and so immediate that only government, supported and inspired by private initiative, can attack them on the scale required.

—JOHN D. ROCKEFELLER III

Like most parents, I just love it when my kids do economic theory. You're just hanging out in the park, at the beach, or around the kitchen table, and boom! Out comes a great insight about the nature of human decision making in complex social environments. We all know what that's like.

OK, maybe I'm making that up. But I do remember one such moment ten years ago. I was in the car on Route 128 outside Boston with my oldest daughter, Cecelia, who was five at the time. As we inched forward through the rush-hour traffic I cursed at the congestion, oblivious to the obvious fact that my daughter was following my every word. After a while, Cecelia piped up from the back seat: "There's no reason to get angry about the traffic, Daddy, because we're part of the traffic."

That just stopped me right in my tracks. In the years since, I have avoided many potential episodes of road rage by recalling this simple insight. There is, in fact, no reason to get angry about the traffic because we are all, without doubt, part of it. The insight is obviously valid for congestion on the roadway. But it also holds for myriad other social challenges that are the consequence of millions of seemingly benign individual decisions.

Urban sprawl and the traffic it engenders is an example of a paradox of prosperity—a fundamental twenty-first century phenomenon that is the topic of this chapter. Think of the metropolitan regions in the United States, for example, where traffic is the worst— Washington, DC, Los Angeles, Chicago, and San Francisco. It comes as no surprise that these places are also among the desirable places in the country to live. Residents of these cities who complain about ever-worsening roadway congestion remind me of the joke where a woman says to her friend about a favorite restaurant: "Nobody goes there anymore. It's too crowded." The same is true elsewhere in the world: traffic today tends to be bad in precisely those places where life is otherwise good.

The phenomenon generalizes. In 1893 Henry Adams (grandson of John Quincy Adams) was already proclaiming that "two more generations should saturate the world with population and should exhaust the mines." Yet, since that time, global population has increased by a factor of seven, while global per capita income has increased at almost one and a half times that rate. While, as I will discuss in chapter 10, there are good reasons to be suspicious of per capita income as an indicator of human well-being, there is nonetheless strong evidence to support the claim that the world has become a better place for people to live at the same time that it has become increasingly crowded.

Whether that trend continues depends on which roads we choose to take, singly and collectively, in the future. Paradoxes of prosperity like urban sprawl—and, more seriously, water scarcity and climate change— cannot be resolved through the actions of government alone. They may ultimately not prove solvable by governments at all. Progress requires the combined and sustained efforts of citizens, communities, executives, and entrepreneurs.

We're all part of the traffic.

In the six decades since the end of World War II, concerns over the problems posed by the proliferation of potentially unproductive people have been a recurring theme for politicians, business leaders, and economists alike. Post–World War II initiatives to control global populations and 1970s-era arguments for measures to defuse the population bomb have, over this lengthy interval, coexisted uneasily with serious projections pertaining to potential demographic disasters. In some cases, like the GI Bill, sensible policies have resulted, leading to substantial social benefit; in other cases, population fears have been invoked to justify truly horrific acts.

The alleged problem of population poses a central challenge to the thesis of this book: that ours is an era of unparalleled prosperity, driven by a global positive insurgency of entrepreneurship. If the litany of calamities befalling the planet are the direct consequences of too many people trying to share a planet of finite resources in the first place, what difference can a handful of entrepreneurs possibly make? Human populations keep growing, but the planet isn't getting bigger. Sooner or later, disaster is sure to follow.

Welcome to the world of the Reverend Thomas Robert Malthus—Anglican minister, great thinker, and downer extraordinaire. Malthus, as he is known to those of us who majored in political science (including some, like me, who were not instructed on our choice of major by the coach of the football team) is the author of *An Essay on the Principle of Population*, one of the most influential books ever written on political economy—the antecedent to today's social so-called science. In case it has slipped your mind, the core thesis of Malthus's masterwork is neatly summarized in a line early in the book: "The power of population is indefinitely greater than the power in the earth to produce subsistence for man." The insight Malthus communicates in this sentence is a simple and enduring one. It is based on two undeniable facts.

Malthusian fact number one: Human beings like to have sex. (This is even true of economists.) In the absence of birth control—there were no condoms in 1796—this means that people will have babies. As a practical matter, this is a process that is difficult to stop: more babies means more people, and more people means more babies.

Logical.

The consequence of Malthusian fact number one is what those folks in the statistics department refer to as "exponential growth"—those upwardly sloping curves the financial advisers show you when they're trying to sell you life insurance or convince you to put more money into your 401K. There's nothing wrong with exponential growth, particularly when applied to savings. But one also has to take into account, Malthusian fact number two: All those babies, and babies of babies, need food in order to survive. Food comes out of the ground. And, so far, no one has figured out how to cajole an acre of land to couple with an adjacent acre of land to make more acres of land. Though it is possible to cut down forests and reclaim swampland, at the end of the day, the land humanity has at its disposal is pretty much the land we're going to have.

So, the Malthusian argument in a nutshell is that humanity consists of profligate procreators propelling themselves at an accelerating rate into a wall of finite resources. Or, as Malthus puts it in his own lighthearted idiom,

> The great question is now at issue, whether man shall henceforth start forwards with accelerated velocity towards illimitable, and hitherto unconceivable improvement; or be condemned to a perpetual oscillation between happiness and misery, and after every effort remain still at an immeasurable distance from the wished for goal.

The predicament that results from Malthusian analysis is what General William Henry Draper, Jr. (more on him later) endearingly and enduringly termed the "population bomb"—a phrase that lived on as the title of a hugely influential 1968 book by Paul and Ann Ehrlich and a sequence of subsequent publications, most recently a spring 2010 cover essay in *Foreign Affairs* magazine titled "The New Population Bomb."

What is the relevance of the Malthusian argument today? Is humanity destined for demographic doom?

Whatever present-day Malthusians may claim to the contrary, the answer is no. Malthus was brilliant, to be sure, and his insights were of lasting significance. But the core tenets of the argument for which he is celebrated have been vitiated by the sharp edge of history.

The first reason why Malthus has turned out to be wrong is contained in a tidy little paper written in the early 1990s by an economics graduate student at Harvard named Michael Kremer. In that paper Kremer explained the entirety of economic growth in human societies from one million BC to the present—no mean feat.

When Kremer wrote this paper, the most accomplished theorists in the profession were busy trying to fix an inconsistency between newly fashionable models of economic growth and a particular feature of economic reality at the time. The issue was this: the new and improved approach to studying economic growth that was then making the rounds predicted that large countries should grow more rapidly than small countries because they have more people to invent stuff. Now, back in the early 1990s, the world's most populous countries—China and India, most notably—were not growing faster than other countries. They had been growing more slowly than less populous countries for some time. So that created a puzzle.

Kremer's approach to addressing this puzzle was to situate the facts of the late twentieth century in a longer historical time frame. Much longer, actually. By considering the growth of human populations since more or less the beginning of time as it relates to human society, Kremer was able to look anew at the prediction that large populations actually drive economic growth.

What this exercise revealed was that the particular fact his fellow growth theorists were seeking with such vigor to explain—the slow growth of large countries such as China and India—was actually a historical aberration. Over the very long term, the evidence supports the claims that the creativity of individual people powers human productivity—and the improvements in societal well-being that follow. While eating and having sex are essential activities for all humans, they do not comprise the entirety of the human experience. In between meals and moments of procreative intimacy, people work. They invent. They build. As a consequence, every person born is not only a consumer, but also a producer. An inventor. A builder. A creator.

More people imply a likelihood of more ideas; more ideas, in turn, imply more of the great ideas that ultimately propel human societies toward increased prosperity.

I summarized the basic facts that provide the context for Kremer's long-term development model at the start of this chapter; in the charts on the facing page I present them in greater detail. The top chart represents human population from AD 1 to 2008. Growth in population is minimal until the start of the eighteenth century, at which point a steady increase begins. Population really starts to take off, though, after World War II. In the second half of the twentieth century, global population more than doubles, going from roughly 2.5 billion in 1950 to almost six billion in 2000.

Compare this trend with that presented in the bottom chart, which is a plot of global per capita GDP over the same interval. The data on which this chart is based were painstakingly compiled over the span of decades by Angus Maddison, a British economic historian who spent his career at the Organisation for Economic Co-operation and Development (OECD) and the

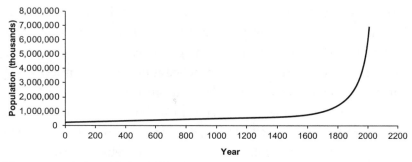

Human population, AD 1 to 2008.

Source: Angus Maddison, *Historical Statistics of the World Economy*, Organisation for Economic Co-operation and Development. For additional information see http://www.ggdc.net/Maddison/.

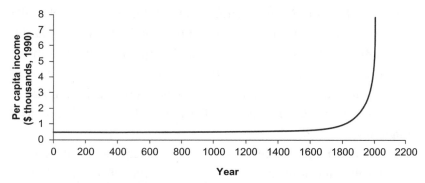

Per-capita GDP, AD 1 to 2008.

Source: Angus Maddison, *Hisorical Statistics of the World Economy*, Organisation for Co-operation and Development. For additional information see http://www.ggdc.net/Maddison.

University of Groningen. The data indicate that, in material terms at least, individual prosperity starts to take off at exactly the same time as population—at the beginning of the eighteenth century. This isn't to say that the observed increase in population directly caused the observed increase in per capita income, or the reverse for that matter. What these two charts demonstrate is simply that the two processes—increasing population and increasing wealth on a global scale—have been strongly correlated over the past two millennia. Kremer's model provided one coherent story as to how, and why, this might be: more people implies a likelihood of more great ideas.

In the two decades that followed Kremer's more-or-less lone stand in defense of scale effects—the implication that bigger populations can actually drive development—the position he took was vindicated in dramatic style as the world's two most populous countries, China and India, suddenly transformed themselves from basket cases to growth engines. With Brazil and Russia, India and China came to be identified as the BRIC countries, poised to propel the world's economy into the twenty-first century.

As Kremer found, the notion that the likelihood of great invention is pretty much a constant in all cultures, through all periods of time, fits the data on the long-term evolution of human society pretty well. For reasons I'll explore further, the aggregate creativity of humanity may actually increase with the number of people on the planet.

Call it the "population boon."

In 1974 the National Security Council in the White House concluded a major study, led by Henry Kissinger, titled *Implications of Worldwide Population Growth for U.S. Security and Overseas Interests*. The intention of the report was to raise to the level of national policy the concerns about global overpopulation that had been brewing in think tanks since the early 1950s, and even earlier among British and American academics.

From the start of the twentieth century, a wide variety of notables in the United States and Great Britain embraced the notion that certain human populations were prone to excessive procreation and should be systematically controlled. Eminent public intellectuals such as Margaret Sanger, Yale economist Irving Fisher, the aforementioned Gen. William Henry Draper, and an assortment of other great patriots with famous names—including Rockefeller, Carnegie, Gamble, and Bush—championed the idea that the growth of populations in Africa and Asia represented a clear and present danger to people of European descent. The name for this ugly ideology of human breeding was eugenics, and its own pedigree was impeccable— until 1941, when the United States was compelled by the attack on Pearl Harbor to join the war against the eugenics-embracing Nazis.

By 1974 the term "eugenics" was mostly shunned and the challenges posed by a growing global population were framed more in terms of economic choice than reproductive coercion. As stated in the Kissinger report,

> The political consequences of current population factors in the least developed countries (LDCs)—rapid growth, internal migration, high

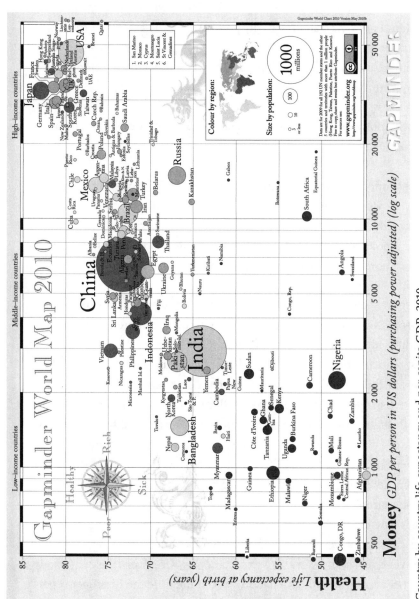

Country-by-country life expectancy and per capita GDP, 2010.

© Gapminder.org. Reprinted under Creative Commons (Attribution) License.

percentages of young people, slow improvement in living standards, urban concentrations, and pressures for foreign migration—are damaging to the internal stability and international relations of countries in whose advancement the U.S. is interested, thus creating political or even national security problems for the U.S. In a broader sense, there is a major risk of severe damage to world economic, political, and ecological systems and, as these systems begin to fail, to our humanitarian values.

This was not a problem that the National Security Council envisioned could be solved on its own:

We cannot wait for overall modernization and development to pro-duce lower fertility rates naturally since this will undoubtedly take many decades in most developing countries, during which time rapid population growth will tend to slow development and widen even more the gap between rich and poor.

The report spelled out alternatives to waiting for economic growth to solve the problem of population; they included such enlightened actions as providing education to women and expanding their employment opportu-nities, reducing infant mortality, and supporting the development of alter-natives to children as a source of security in old age.

The Kissinger report was correct with respect to the long-term trend in population growth: a shift in fertility on a global scale did take place, and it took decades. Mostly not as a consequence of US government policy, people nearly everywhere in the world became wealthier, and as they did so (admittedly to greater and lesser degrees) they had fewer children. A notable example is Vietnam—one country rather unambiguously and fa-mously outside of the US sphere of influence since 1975, the year that American forces were evacuated from Saigon. In Hanoi today, a young street vendor has the same life expectancy as Kissinger himself (or any other US citizen) would have had in 1974, at the time the Kissinger report was published. More to the point, the fertility rate in Vietnam, as in sev-enty other countries around the world today, is below the natural replace-ment rate of 2.1. This is a dramatic shift from the early 1970s, when only the world's wealthiest twenty-four countries had reproductive rates consistent with low or zero population growth. In the developing world as a whole, fertility rates fell by half—from six children per woman to three—in the second half of the twentieth century.

The second reason, then, that humanity has been liberated from the Malthusian trap is a fact of human behavior that Malthus himself either did not anticipate or failed adequately to appreciate. Think of it as the "iron law of modern parenthood," which goes as follows: the busier you are doing other things, the less time you have for sex. Of course, the availability of modern methods of birth control also factors rather importantly into humanity's escape from demographic doom. While couples the world over can attest to the importance of both preferences and technology as determinants of family, the most pervasive demonstration of its truth is at the level of entire nations. In every country, the evidence for the past fifty years has been the same: as incomes increase, rates of population growth decrease. How powerful is this iron law? Powerful enough that fertility rates have decreased to a significantly greater extent over the past fifty years in Hong Kong than in mainland China, despite the fact that people in Hong Kong have not been subject to the one-child policy with which hundreds of millions of their countrymen have been compelled to comply since 1978.

Granted, reproductive decisions are as personal as any that a woman (or a couple) makes. The factors that affect reproductive choices are many and diverse. The availability of socially acceptable and medically supported options is one significant dimension. So, despite their grim associations with the American eugenics movement, the family planning initiatives that originated out of concerns in the 1950s, 1960s, and 1970s about global overpopulation have had beneficial consequences.

That said, a very strong consensus exists that the primary drivers of the fundamental and historic shift in global population trajectories have been economic. At income levels of about $1,000 per capita, in today's terms on a national scale, reproductive rates begin to decline sharply. Above $4,000 per capita, fertility rates drop below the replacement rate of 2.1.

This makes perfect sense, of course. For one thing, children of wealthier families in poor places are more likely to survive to adulthood. Furthermore, as family income increases, children are actually worth less, in the sense that they are less likely both to provide labor and to be the sole source of care in old age. Children of wealthier parents also cost more to their parents, in absolute terms, than children of poorer parents, as expenses for children's schooling, clothing, and the like tend to increase with income.

Whether as a result of my conjectured iron law of modern parenthood or other fundamental factors, the fact is that we can wait for overall modernization and development to produce lower fertility rates naturally, since that is exactly what is happening around the world today—and what has been happening for nearly a half century now.

Dramatic as decreases in global fertility have been, they are unlikely to persuade die-hard neo-Malthusians that the population bomb is not still ticking. OK, human populations are growing less rapidly than experts generally envisioned when population panic was peaking forty years ago. That still doesn't mean that Malthus was wrong. The planet's resource base is still finite; as global population has now passed seven billion, the planet's ability to sustain life is being tested. As the fact of global climate change alone indicates, Malthusian specters of demographic doom are regrettably still very much with us.

Let there be no mistake: global resource issues are real. Water scarcity. Depleted fisheries. And more. Yet, it is precisely because resource issues are serious that we must think clearly about their nature and causes.

Yes, there are cheap thrills to be had in digging up neo-Malthusians of the 1960s and 1970s who have turned out to be completely wrong. Take this from *The Population Bomb*: "The battle to feed all of humanity is over. In the 1970s the world will undergo famines—hundreds of millions of people are going to starve to death in spite of any crash programs embarked upon now" (11). Um, say that again? What actually happened is this: in the two decades following the publication of *The Population Bomb*, technological and organizational innovation drove a surge in global agricultural production.

A 1972 report titled *Limits to Growth*, authored by an assemblage of academics and policy makers who called themselves the Club of Rome, is full of similar gems. *Limits to Growth* presented a model of the global economy— inspired by Norbert Wiener's cybernetics, though missing the learning in the system that was so central to Wiener's work—that extrapolated from trends in resource prices at the time to predict overshoot and collapse for human societies on a planetary scale. The mechanism for the collapse was that nonrenewable resource depletion was inevitably reflected in exponentially increasing commodity prices.

The reality over the quarter century that followed was not kind to the Club of Rome's predictions. Within a decade after *Limits to Growth* was published, global commodity prices began a long, steady decline that lasted over fifteen years. In other areas, however, the neo-Malthusians might argue that they have been closer to the mark. And, of course, the time frame for the Club of Rome report was one hundred years. It will not help us understand the phenomenon in question if we replace the Club of Rome's naïve extrapolation from an upward trend with an equally naïve extrapolation from a downward trend.

Upon closer examination, the real flaws in the arguments offered by demographic doomsayers have more to do with microeconomics—decisions made by individuals—than they have to do with macroeconomics. These flaws merit careful examination because they bear directly on the trends driving the coming prosperity.

First, neo-Malthusians see problems of resource scarcity as intractable because they ignore the one effective means humans have devised to solve them: the changes in behavior and inducement of innovation that result from changes in relative prices. Second, the most severe risks to humanity related to the depletion of natural resources—environmental challenges caused by human consumption in general, and climate change in particular—are caused by the overabundance of certain resources (oil and coal in particular), not their impending scarcity. In other words, along important dimensions, neo-Malthusian narratives of resource depletion get the problem exactly backward.

Consider prices first, in a US context. For three decades, the average number of miles driven by US motorists increased steadily. Then, in 2007, that steady climb was suddenly halted. For the first time since the Reagan era, Americans drove fewer miles that year than they had the previous year. What magic caused Americans to temper their long-standing love of the open road? Was the general public moved by the sight of Al Gore and Davis Guggenheim accepting the Academy Award for *An Inconvenient Truth*? Or was the public, perhaps, filled with indignation at the refusal by the Islamic Republic of Iran to disclose the nature and extent of its nuclear programs? (You know, "I'll show them. I'm going to walk to work!")

Cynical, market-obsessed economists have a different interpretation. They (we) tend to think that the nearly unprecedented drop in miles driven by US motorists had something to do with the fact that the price of gasoline crept to over four dollars a gallon. What we seem to have learned from this recent experience is that, once the price of gasoline gets beyond roughly that point, people in the United States actually start to adjust their behavior to do something previously unthinkable: keep their cars in the driveway just a little bit more.

Now this is just one example—offered minus the econometric studies and other accompanying empirics. (Check the endnotes if you're curious.) But the basic fact here, as in other markets for commodities, is that good old Econ 101—much maligned in its application to many other complex societal issues, and for good reason—actually does a pretty good job of explaining behavior when it comes to the consumption of natural resources. When connected to fundamentals, higher prices indicate a crowded market. And people do, in many circumstances, try to avoid the crowd—consuming less when prices go up. So, while markets in other respects and contexts can exacerbate adverse consequences of population growth, they do contain a built-in mechanism to deal with the scarcity of natural resources. What works isn't ignoring prices; it's getting them right.

The general refusal of neo-Malthusians to incorporate prices into their models of global dynamics (don't worry, we'll get to discussing speculative bubbles and other dynamic market distortions soon enough) is a partial explanation for their particular ineptitude in foreseeing pathways of technical change. In a 2008 essay assessing forecasts contained in *The Population Bomb*, Paul and Anne Ehrlich congratulate themselves on having correctly dismissed the potential for exploratory technologies to solve the global food crisis: "Similarly, our view of the panacea potential of novel food sources such as single-cell protein from bacteria or algae cultured on petroleum or sewage, leaf protein, or food production by nuclear agro-industrial complexes has proven entirely correct."

Economists have a term for the sort of technologies that the Ehrlichs dismissed four decades ago: they are known as "backstop technologies."

In the context of energy production, they are sometimes termed "alternative energy"—as in alternatives to conventional technologies. However, the term "backstop" is more accurate: it captures the notion that these technologies kick into production only when triggered by a sufficient increase in the price of the conventional technology—rice and wheat in the case of agriculture, or oil, coal, and natural gas in the case of energy. High prices in this version of the story are analogous to the roadway congestion mentioned at the beginning of this chapter: you only head off the main road and start to look for shortcuts when the traffic gets really bad.

Now, as noted just above, the overall trend in global commodity prices from the time that *The Population Bomb* was published until the end of the twentieth century was actually negative—prices went down. This was all quite contrary to the predictions made by the Ehrlichs and other neo-Malthusians.

In sum, the Ehrlichs were right about alternative technologies because they were wrong about prices. The calamity they foresaw never materialized, and as a direct consequence, neither did the potential solutions they dismissed.

In this decade, and into the foreseeable future, the trend has shifted. Neo-Malthusians will turn out to be right about prices after all. But, if the past is any precedent, they will prove wrong about solutions.

As I noted at the outset, the majority of purported twenty-first-century challenges that do matter fall clearly in the category of paradoxes of prosperity. These are the downsides—some dramatic, even potentially catastrophic—associated with the fact that, on a planet of indisputably finite resources, more people are living longer and more fully than ever before.

Among the paradoxes of prosperity, global climate change is a strong candidate to top the list. That climate change is the by-product of past increases in prosperity is inarguable. The first chapter of this book focused on automobiles—the very industry that, in the last century, most singularly defined American economic ascendancy (and later, decline) at the same time that it contributed significantly to the accumulation of carbon in the atmosphere with which we now must contend. Upsides and downsides of past progress are inseparable. Climate change is the cursed stepchild of the marriage between technology and innovation that also produced the Industrial Revolution and the substantial improvements in human well-being it ultimately engendered. The economies of scale that drove the Industrial Revolution literally derived their energy from coal and oil. The result is that, for the first time in human history, the weather itself has been reduced to an outcome of human decision making. What's more, the humans making the decisions relevant to climate change are distributed across the planet. This is not an easy pattern to change.

Yet the key point is this: climate change is a difficult problem to tackle not because it is caused by too many people, or even because coordination among those many people is exceedingly difficult. (It is.) While misguided policies and political gridlock at various levels certainly have played a role, the fundamental reason that climate change is challenging is that the two commodities most responsible for its occurrence—oil and coal—remain excessively abundant and inexpensive relative to alternatives. Oil and coal, the two fuels whose consumption contributes most to climate change, became the dominant source of energy in the twentieth century for one reason and one reason only: they are cheap. And, while generations of government subsidies certainly have played a role, they have remained cheap because they have remained abundant.

The implication is straightforward: real progress in avoiding the worst consequences of climate change requires oil and coal to become more expensive—or at least to appear more expensive to consumers. Sure, there are other causes of climate change, from rotting bogs to farting cows. And there are other credible approaches to dealing with climate challenges, from simple measures like high-efficiency building standards to exotic ones like geoengineering the climate in order to counteract adverse impacts of changes in atmospheric chemistry. But, if oil and coal remain cheap compared with lower-carbon forms of energy, the prognosis for serious progress in the mitigation of adverse impacts from climate change is going to remain poor.

In this context, the fact that commodity prices trended sharply upward in the decade that just passed is distinctly good news. (The spike in 2007–8 was not related to fundamentals of global demand, and can for the moment be disregarded. What is of interest is the long-term trend.) It's not just oil, of course. Iron, gold, zinc, and copper are all up by factors of three or more from their levels in 2000. The reason for this is straightforward: more people in more parts of the world are becoming prosperous than at any time in human history. Years of low prices (from the mid-1980s to roughly 2002) dulled incentives to use energy efficiently and develop new energy sources. Consequently, the capacity to produce, transport, and refine oil is now strained on a global scale. After decades on the sidelines, the world's two most populous countries and a number of other former developing nations are surging economically. Hundreds of millions of new entrants to the global middle class are seeking automobiles and other energy-consuming amenities. Although the manufacturing intensity of the US economy has declined significantly during the past twenty years, manufacturing in China has grown dramatically. China accounted for 40 percent of the growth in world oil demand during the past four years, recently surpassing Japan as the world's number-two oil consumer.

The point is that the fundamental forces driving global commodity prices pertain not to populations per se, but rather to increasing prosperity. Furthermore, the upward pressure on oil and coal prices created by this increased global demand—mostly from previously poor places—is also the single most promising force to counter climate change. The power of prices—determined in markets, pressured by global demand—has of late been ten times greater, for oil at least, than the most potent outcome achievable in the near term through the still-elusive goal of an economy-wide carbon tax. Contrary to the rhetoric that continues to dominate public debate in the United States, oil price increases have the power to succeed in transforming behavior where policy and polemic have failed: they can create powerful incentives to make the overdue investments that can, in the long term, increase firms' productive efficiency, lower costs for consumers, and limit the adverse impacts of global climate change.

Paradoxes of prosperity cast a long shadow over our hopes for a better world. If resource curses have bedeviled development for centuries, by what magic will they suddenly be lifted to permit the fulfillment of prosperity's promise? What's more, technologically induced unemployment, resource scarcity, and climate change are but three of many paradoxes of prosperity. What of water scarcity, decreasing biodiversity, cultural homogenization, and the erosion of traditional knowledge, to name but a few others?

Against all of this doom comes a single message of solace, not from scripture but from an economic theorist—Mancur Olson. In *Power and Prosperity*, he wrote, "No historical process that is understood is inevitable."

Economic calamities following World War II—anticipated respectively by members of Congress during the war and by the father of cyberspace in the war's aftermath—never took place. Instead, the United States underwent the most dramatic and sustained period of economic expansion that any nation had so far experienced—with associated improvements to the well-being of millions of Americans.

Contrary to widespread belief, the same prospect exists today for the world as a whole. The illustration on this page sums up the core quantitative conjecture of this book—because it pertains to the future, it can be nothing else than a conjecture. It presents a graph of the percentage of humanity that, in our lifetimes, is being liberated from the daily struggle for survival that was humanity's norm for the millennia prior to the eighteenth century—as Thomas Hobbes famously put it, lives that were "solitary, poor, nasty, brutish, and short." (Based on the life expectancy faced by humans for 99 percent of our existence as a species, I would have died seven years ago at age 39—like my paternal grandfather. No book writing for me.)

Reduced to quantitative basics, the story of improvements in human well-being over the period of millennia is a classic S-shaped adoption

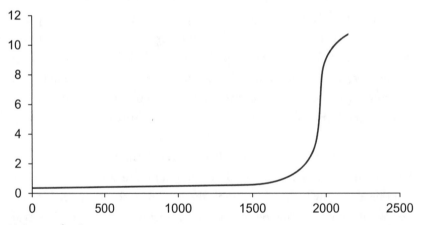

Living on the S.

Source: Author calculations; Angus Maddison, *Historical Statistics of the World Economy*, Organisation for Economic Co-operation and Development. For additional information see http://www.gddc.net/Maddison/.

curve, familiar to anyone who has studied the diffusion of technology. Only, in this case, what is being adopted is not a transistor radio or, as I will discuss in chapter 4, a mobile phone. What is being adopted is the state of being liberated from a subsistence existence, with the cognitive freedom that entails.

As Bob Litan, my colleague at the Kauffman Foundation, put it to me in discussing an early version of this manuscript, we—generations alive today—are living on the S of human history: the steepest part of the slope of human progress. Just a few decades ago, the average person in the developing world (or Appalachia) was more likely to see his or her child die from diarrhea than to make a phone call to a relative or turn on an electric light at home. On a global scale, prosperity was as much a function of the accident of birth, and the access to global networks that birth conveyed, as it was a function of ability or effort. The result was a persistent rift, not between rich and poor countries, but between a global majority destined for a highly localized and materially impoverished existence and a global minority blessed with the resources and freedom to travel without restriction in search of the best in education, career opportunities, and living environment. The result was, and is, a world sharply divided between the globally rich and the locally poor.

Yet now, after four centuries of sustained advance in science, innovation, and the organization of society, the frontier of technology is finally reaching the heart of the human community. Never before have more people had a greater opportunity to create value for society, and for themselves, than we do today. New technologies of communication and collaboration are enabling not just lone innovators, but entire populations, to connect and create at a scale previously unimaginable.

The consequence? Predictions of demographic disaster, consistently pushed back for the two centuries since Malthus, are finally reaching their expiry date. A combination of entrepreneurship, technological innovation, and broad societal transformation are giving even those children born in the most persistently poor places a chance to benefit from, and contribute to, the vitality of global markets and communities of social action.

To differentiate these places from the emerging-market economies—many of which, like South Korea and Singapore, have already emerged—I prefer to employ the term "ascending markets." As a result of rapid transformations under way in ascending markets, human well-being—the fundamental combination of capacities and opportunities that bounds each human experience—will likely improve to a greater extent over the next quarter century than at any other time in human history. All in all, it's a good time to be alive.

Looking for evidence more clearly grounded in lived human experience? How about the greatest episode of economic growth and national development in history? That's the story for chapter 3.

3 I'M SO BORED WITH THE PRC

Quantity has a quality all its own.

—JOSEPH STALIN (RUMORED)

The remarkable resurgence of the People's Republic of China is customarily traced back to the year 1979, when Premier Deng Xiaoping initiated the first of a sequence of economic reforms enabling his country to join the global economy. Deng abolished the communal system of agriculture, replacing it with a house-hold responsibility system, largely restoring farmers' traditional independence from external authority. He famously proclaimed that China should "let some people get rich first," removing the societal stigma that had existed around private wealth creation under Mao Zedong. He created the Special Economic Zones to accelerate the growth of China's trade with the rest of the world, seeding the creation of Shenzhen, a city whose unprecedented growth makes it an unheralded wonder of the world.

All the while, Deng held to a pragmatic worldview; long before assuming the leadership position in China he had pro-nounced, "I don't care if a cat is white or black. It's a good cat so long as it catches mice." By unleashing the potential of the world's most populous country and its oldest civilization, the story goes, this man who was less than five feet tall cast a shadow that has extended well into the twenty-first century.

Now I, for one, wasn't much interested in China or Deng Xiaoping in 1979. My own most treasured memory of that year is that of seeing The Clash in concert at the University of Mary-land's Ritchie Coliseum during their first American tour. They had just released their first album, an eponymously titled effort that featured such soon-to-be-classics as "Janie Jones," "Police and Thieves," "Clash City Rockers," and, of course, "I'm So

Bored with the USA." I was fourteen years old, and just that summer had spent three weeks in London with an old neighborhood friend from DC whose father was stationed at the US embassy there. In that short time, I discovered punks, mods, ska, and above all the incomparable joy of very loud music. The experience made an impression.

As a young American, I could really relate to The Clash, even "I'm So Bored with the USA." The fictionalized US that Joe Strummer and company were singing about was boring to me too—the kitsch of *Dallas*, the vacuous euphoria of *Grease* and *Saturday Night Fever*, the insipid sound of the Bee Gees. (No, I wouldn't have known or cared that Olivia Newton-John and the Gibbs brothers were, in actuality, British/Australian—or, more surprisingly, that the future Bee Gees were actually born in Beijing.) No surprise that a bunch of unemployed Londoners also were tired of hearing about the US.

I think back to that now because America today seems a bit to me like Britain in the late 1970s. Our empire, never quite so well-defined as theirs, seems to have evaporated with alarming rapidity. In our case, the upstart challenger is not across the Atlantic, but across the Pacific.

In much the same way that the US was boring to Joe Strummer and company, China seems fundamentally boring to most Americans. The reason for this isn't that China is a faraway place, or that Chinese is an inaccessible language—though both are true. The real obstacle is psychological. People who have experienced firsthand the change that has occurred in China over the past three decades find it hard to come up with comparisons that do justice to their impressions. People who haven't experienced China's transformation are left to wonder what all the fuss is about. Some—avid readers of Tom Friedman, Jim Fallows, and Fareed Zakaria, in all likelihood—are fully persuaded that a remarkable and unprecedented transformation is taking place. But the majority are just plain tired of hearing about this new China.

Yet, despite all the changes that have occurred both in China and in US-China relations over the past three decades, our views of the Middle Kingdom today are much as they have been in the past. Among the very few documents that my father saved from his thirty-year career at the State Department was the transcript of a 1987 reunion of former directors of the department's policy planning staff. That meeting brought together a who's who of US foreign policy in the post–World War II era: George Kennan, Paul Nitze, Walt Rostow, and George Shultz. Among them was former ambassador to Beijing Winston Lord, who characterized our nation's bimodal view of China as follows:

> American attitudes towards [China] have swung between romance and hostility. We have held wildly fluctuating images. The evil Fu Man Chu, the noble peasant of Pearl Buck. . . . The Chinese successively have been beleaguered allies and implacable foes. Yellow Hoards, Red Guards, and Blue Ants. . . . Budding capitalists adorning magazine covers and beastly Communists abusing intellectuals. We need a steadier vision.

Factual descriptions of historical processes occurring in China are inevitably pushed into one of the two modes of perception that Lord describes. Someone who is astounded by the changes occurring in China is, almost by definition, someone blind to the transgressions of which its government is variously accused—among them currency manipulation, Gmail intrusions, natural-resource trickery, and repression in Tibet. By the same token, someone concerned about the detention of political dissidents is automatically a person who underappreciates the scope of China's positive transformation over the past three decades.

You'll have figured out by now that I'm with Winston Lord. Any understanding of the twenty-first century must include a thorough grasp of the changes that have taken place in China since the death of Mao Zedong in 1976, and that will continue to occur in dramatic form for some time to come. This means getting past easy dichotomies like friend or foe, model of economic development or repressive throwback. We need a steadier vision.

It also must include a firm grasp of the global implications of those changes. Here's a prime example. In this decade far more US newspaper ink has been expended on tracking the upward trend in oil prices than the downward trend in other consumer prices. As I pointed out in the last chapter, those observers of energy markets not wearing 1970s-era blinders have been able to grasp that the reason for the upward trend in oil prices is almost entirely because previously poor places—China in particular—have entered the global commodity demand equation. The trend is not due to the actions of Hugo Chavez, Mahmoud Ahmadinejad, or any other oil bogeymen of the moment. Places like China demand more oil and other commodities simply because they are growing wealthier; they are growing wealthier in large part because they are making things for us. The consequence is that we pay less for prom dresses, bathing suits, and American flags produced abroad, and we pay more for gasoline because some of it is now going elsewhere to make our stuff.

So what has been the net effect of China's growth on US consumers? Have we lost more from increases in gas prices than we have gained from lower consumer prices? Just the opposite is true. Expenditures by American consumers on clothing alone have dropped in the past quarter century by an amount four times that of increased spending on gasoline. The specific numbers are worth highlighting: In 1984, a typical American household spent $200 per month on gasoline and $250 per month on clothing (at today's wage/price levels). By 2010 the same American family was spending an average of $225 per month on gasoline—$25 per month more than a quarter century earlier—but only $150 per month on clothing ($100 per month less). That's $75 less spending per month, per household, across the US, thanks to China's transformation. (Cable bill: paid.)

Why, then, are the newspapers not full of good news about this huge long-term drop in the cost of clothing? Why are they instead obsessing about the twenty-five bucks a month more we're spending now on gasoline than we did in 1984?

Granted, American bookstores and blogs are otherwise filled with tales of transformations happening in China, and their implications for the United States. As a consequence, most of the attention in this book is directed elsewhere. However, China's story is too big and too significant to ignore when it comes to understanding the global trends that matter most in this century. So this chapter is dedicated to the mostly still untold story of what the transformation in China has been about, what its effect has been on the rest of the world, and what China's experience over the past twenty years does, and does not, tell us about the coming prosperity.

In the summer of 1986, at the end of a year's leave of absence from college, I worked as a copyeditor at Beijing's Foreign Languages Press—the Chinese government's publisher of record in all languages other than Chinese. If you ever saw an English-language version of Mao's famed *Little Red Book*, it came from the Foreign Languages Press, or Waiwenju as it is known in China. During that time I lived in a dormitory at the press, shared breakfast, lunch, and dinner at the canteen with my Chinese colleagues, and partook in the subsidized cabbages and other perks periodically delivered to staff from flatbed trucks that backed into the courtyard.

My job at the Waiwenju—at least, as I initially understood it—was to correct the English in Chinese-language textbooks published for export. At first this seemed like an easy and rewarding assignment, since the errors in any given sentence were numerous enough not only to keep me occupied but also to make me feel like a major contributor to the work of my unit.

I had been at work for a week or so when my immediate superior, a gregarious British academic named Greg Lee, approached me at my desk. Greg, a scholar of Chinese poetry, was the only other foreigner and English speaker in the work unit. (Greg has himself since written an insightful volume on this era titled *China's Lost Decade*.) Greg informed me that there was a problem with my work: my edits were so extensive that they were creating havoc among the staff responsible for book production. The texts I was being given to copyedit were, in fact, deemed by the press to be final drafts, ready for publication. It turned out that if my changes to the proofs altered the number of characters in a particular line the entire page would have to be retypeset. Thus my diligent efforts were unmanageably time-consuming for others in the press.

This, of course, was disappointing news. Here I'd thought I was off to a great start. But now I found out that my colleagues were getting amusement from my Chinese name, Fei Li Pu, which sounded like "Philip" but also conveyed a northern Chinese folk adage: "Too much effort without real benefit." In my first real place of work, I wasn't a valued asset after all. I was a problem.

I asked Greg what I should do. "Well . . . you can go ahead and make edits," he said wryly, savoring the humor of his advice, as he stood up to leave. "Just don't change the number of characters in a line."

So that's what I did. What had been an easy, even trivial, copyediting assignment now became a devilishly complicated linguistic puzzle. How could I correct the English in these texts without affecting the immutable architecture of the page as printed? Not easily done.

I tell this story because it says something about what China was, and how it has been changing. Naturally, inflexibility in organizations is a global phenomenon. Such a scenario is hardly restricted to a country with a planned economy. In an era before electronic word processing and type-setting, this story could have played out in somewhat the same manner at a publishing house elsewhere in the world, even in the United States.

However, imagine the increase in quality, and productivity, that results from the removal of arbitrary restrictions such as "make edits to this text, but make sure not to change the number of characters in a line." The systemic changes formalized by Deng Xiaoping permitted individuals and business managers to make decisions outside of the most rigid dictates of central planning. In such a context it is not difficult to imagine how rapid gains to productivity and subsequent economic growth ensued.

Among the restrictions of the Maoist era, perhaps the most significant had to do with rural labor. In the power vacuum that followed the death of Mao, farmers who had formerly been tied to rural collectives—with truly catastrophic results—were left by the state to enjoy new autonomy. In 1979, under the leadership of Deng Xiaoping, the Chinese government yielded to these realities, enacting reforms that codified the return of fam-ily-based farming.

The consequence of increased autonomy at the household level was increased agricultural productivity. But the implications reached well beyond rural areas and grain silos. The practical impact of these reforms was to ini-tiate a long-term process in which roughly a fifth of the world's population might have the opportunity to seek and create opportunities for themselves. The consequence? Nothing less than a turning point in human history.

Twenty-one years before Y2K, the twenty-first century was under way.

After my freshman year in college, in the summer of 1983, I joined the small legion of college students then annually trekking to Alaska in search of the small fortunes reputedly to be made working on fishing boats. (Yes, this is true. Such a phenomenon existed. Millennials may not believe it, but only twenty-five years ago, working on a fishing boat consti-tuted a get-rich-quick scheme—as did teaching English in Japan.) I viv-idly recall landing in Anchorage late one July day. By the time I had hitchhiked to a campsite, it was midnight. The sky was clear and the sun was still up—a definite "you're not in Kansas anymore" moment. I pitched my tent and tried to sleep despite the disconcerting lack of darkness.

The next morning I hitched into downtown Anchorage to try to find some day work. (I ended up nailing boxes of salmon roe shut for a couple of days before heading down to Seward to find a spot on a boat.) As a city boy from the East Coast, I was struck by how the entire city seemed to have been built in the few weeks since the last snow melt. Everywhere the asphalt was fresh, black, and unconstrained by median lines or other conventional markings of the road. Buildings scattered through the newly tamed wilderness evinced a hasty functionality. I had been in Alaska one day; I felt as though the rest of the city had only gotten in the night before.

That trip to Alaska was my only preparation for the experience of visiting the city of Dongguan in southern China in 2005. Here was an old city—formerly an important regional capital—outgrowing its urban kernel at a positively cancerous rate. I went to Dongguan as a guest of a senior professor at Tsinghua University in Beijing (often described, in somewhat aspirational terms, as China's MIT), who had organized a set of meetings for me with local entrepreneurs. The brand new Dongguan airport was a sleek bit of construction that would have constituted a welcome upgrade had it taken the place of even the newer terminals at Washington, DC's National Airport. My hosts put me up in a five-star hotel that was one among half a dozen either just finished or under construction in fields on the outskirts of the city.

At a sumptuous dim sum lunch on the day of my arrival in Dongguan, I met my hosts: a smartly dressed young woman who worked as a consultant to local entrepreneurs, a gregarious gentleman from the local chamber of commerce, and a lanky teenager whose reason for being there was not entirely clear to me. Over the course of the lunch I realized that the seeming teenager was, in fact, a young entrepreneur by the name of Zhang Runbo. More to the point, we were all there as his guests: he was the one paying the bill.

At about the same time that I was slam dancing to "Clash City Rockers," China's comeback began when Zhang Runbo's father and uncle walked off of their farm in China's Guangdong Province in the direction of the city of Dongguan.

Freed by the fraying of state order that followed the death of Mao and the subsequent reforms to agricultural policy under Deng Xiaoping, the Zhang brothers had wasted no time in taking advantage of new opportunities to create better lives for themselves and their families. At first, construction provided the ticket that the brothers sought. They began as laborers. Within a few years they had created a small construction company of their own. As that business expanded, they glimpsed a bigger opportunity in southern China's export boom: printing—and not just any kind of printing, of course. The Zhang brothers decided to get into the business of printing boxes. How else were all those exports going to make it overseas, if not encased in cardboard? They named their company Chun Hing, "The Revitalization Paper Company."

They did not lack for customers. As their business grew, so did the sophistication of their operation. By 2005, when I visited their printing plant—an expansive operation concealed behind a modest entry on a dusty Dongguan byway—they were printing boxes for an array of corporate giants in consumer electronics. Their operations revolved around three German-made printing presses, purchased at a cost of over a million dollars apiece.

So far this story is familiar and easily understood. Humans have been moving in search of better opportunities for as long as they have been around to move. The great waves of transatlantic and transpacific immigration that took place during the nineteenth and early twentieth centuries enabled the United States to become a global economic and political power. The story of the Industrial Revolution is fundamentally nothing but that of labor being combined with ever more efficient machines to generate output of improving quality and decreasing cost, just as the Zhangs did with their printing operation.

But other dimensions of the Zhang brothers' story have a significance and universality that are particular to our own time. The Zhang brothers were able to create wealth for themselves, their children (including Zhang Runbo), and the region where they live through the simple act of joining the global economy. They did not develop a new technology. They did not implement a novel management strategy. They found a way to connect and contribute to activities occurring at a massive scale all around them, making use of the capacities at their disposal. They succeeded by finding a way to make the most of China's moment.

The Zhang brothers' story and comparable ones that could be told by tens of millions of people around the world comprise the core narrative of our time. More than climate change, more than global terrorism, more than the threat of pandemics, our historical moment is defined by the process by which people who were previously both isolated and impoverished are finding opportunities to connect and prosper.

In the next quarter century, the majority of the world's population still similarly trapped within circumstances of subsistence—hundreds of millions of them in China, others elsewhere in the world—will have their turn to create wealth by connecting and contributing to the global economy. The human potential released in that process shows every likelihood of generating a wave of increased global prosperity exceeding that propelled in the past two decades by China's reemergence, just as the magnitude of China has already eclipsed that of Japan and the formerly lauded Asian Tigers: South Korea, Taiwan, Singapore, and Hong Kong.

The primary impediments to the coming prosperity are the adverse consequences it generates: global financial crises (no, not simply caused by greed on Wall Street), extreme volatility in commodities prices (no, not simply caused by greed in Riyadh), and global climate change (no, not simply caused by greed at ExxonMobil). Smoothing the inexorable process of global transition under way and mitigating its adverse consequences will require astute and farsighted public policies—a core topic of the journal that I edit. Yet the reality, and even the potential severity, of impediments is unlikely to alter the fundamental trend of our age: up.

Home to scores of multinational organizations and the hundreds of small- and medium-sized companies like the Chun Hing printing and construction group, Dongguan is one of the key regional forces behind China's gigantic trade surplus with the United States. Little known outside of China, Dongguan has of late produced 40 percent of the tennis shoes sold in the US, two hundred million of the sweaters sold annually in US shops, and not a few other items lining the aisles in stores around the world. It ranks only behind Shenzhen and Shanghai among China's leading export cities. (Shenzhen, a story in itself, is a city the size of Los Angeles built over the span of thirty years out of a fishing village surrounded by farmland.)

However, Dongguan is also to Chinese what the Alamo is to Texans, or Wounded Knee is to Native Americans: the site of a decisive defeat with lasting and tragic consequences. From the standpoint of the quarter of the world's population that resides in the People's Republic of China, the upstarts in the global economy are the people from the "beautiful land," which is how the Chinese name for the United States, *Meiguo*, translates into English. Before us, the Japanese, the British, and to a lesser extent other Western powers, usurped China's role as the global economic leader. What every Chinese middle school student knows, but relatively few in the US recognize, is that for five hundred years, from the fourteenth century until the 1830s, China accounted for over 25 percent of world economic output. In 1820 the figure was 33 percent—more than the US economy at the height of its global economic dominance immediately following World War II—and China's moment lasted for half a millennium. As a point of contrast consider this: by the time Deng Xiaoping got to work in 1979, after a particularly destructive two decades of Maoist experiments in social and economic transformation, China's share of global GDP was barely 4 percent—a precipitous decline. Today, after nearly three decades of staggering growth, China accounts for about 13 percent of world output—impressive relative to 1979, but still far from its norm in centuries past.

Yet despite the raw size of its economy, China in the 1830s was evidencing clear vulnerabilities, the cumulative result of three prior centuries of foreign rule (under the Manchu dynasty), isolation, and institutional sclerosis. The British East India Company was aggressively developing markets in southern China for its most lucrative, albeit illicit, product: opium. (Yes, Queen Victoria was, by proxy, a pusher.) The Chinese imperial government issued edicts to block opium smuggling, but to no avail. The market was not one that the British were going to abandon lightly: as a consequence of British consumers' voracious appetite for Chinese exports, Britain was experiencing a severe trade deficit with China. (Sound familiar?) Opium sales helped to reverse the gap. (The US has been counting on exports of financial services and Boeing aircraft instead, but so far it isn't quite doing the trick.)

As Britain's illegal sales of opium in China continued to grow, the emperor appointed a senior civil servant, Lin Zexu, to act as the country's drug czar. From his headquarters in—guess where?—the city of Dongguan, Lin initiated a crackdown in June 1839, confiscating and later destroying over a thousand tons of opium. The British made the most of the incident, reacting swiftly and decisively to assert their commercial interests. Other Western countries—who, like Britain, did not recognize the illegality of the opium trade—were supportive. Stating commerce to be "among the natural rights and duties of men," John Quincy Adams would later criticize China for its "unsocial" refusal to trade on "terms of equal reciprocity"—rhetoric that would not be out of place in today's debates over China and trade.

A three-year war with Britain ensued. Another followed after a little more than a decade—and this one also involved France. The scientific and technological advantage of the Western nations was overwhelming. China was compelled to accept a sequence of unequal treaties pertaining to trade relations first with European powers, and then with Japan. The country's decline was under way.

Those who appreciate historical ironies thus have ample scope for enjoyment in visiting Dongguan today. It has taken 150 years, but the tables of global economic exchange have turned in a most dramatic way. What was once the site of a declining nation's last stand against foreign incursion is today the site of a rising nation's opening gambit in the game of foreign trade.

China's recent story is a powerful one, made no less compelling due to its many Dickensian subplots: remote factories where workers labor in conditions of indentured servitude, cities encased in smog, and pervasive corruption among public officials. If not for our inherited suspicion and fear of China and Chinese motivations, we might celebrate the distributed work ethic and determined thriftiness that have facilitated the transformation in process within the world's most populous country.

Before we move on to discussing the rest of the world for the remainder of this book, what lessons can we draw from China's remarkable growth? Can we expect similar surges elsewhere? Here are three takeaways, so far, from history's most massive turnaround to date:

The first point is that the spectacular growth of China is often misunderstood as a story of cheap labor. It is not. Cheap labor relative to Western standards existed in China for over a century before the recent surge in development: it was also known as poverty. The Chinese reservoirs of underutilized (a.k.a. cheap) labor are vast, but the talent to work with machines productively is limited, as it is everywhere else. What has changed since 1979—and in particular during the last fifteen years—is a combination of that underutilized labor with both huge infusions of capital and entrepreneurial adaptability—precisely the mix of factors driving development that I discussed in chapter 1.

The second point is that China is exceptional, not only in its scale, but also in the extent of its economic centralization. To be sure, the Chinese political structure is not nearly as monolithic as it is often portrayed as being; from a budgetary standpoint, the country is extremely decentralized, with considerable discretion in the hands of provincial authorities. Furthermore, in the places that have contributed most greatly to China's growth, a Wild West, anything-goes atmosphere reigns. A significant amount of decentralized decision making is at play. But the fuel behind China's transformation—savings earned from exports, invested in infrastructure for growth—is to a far greater extent than in other countries controlled by a central, nondemocratically elected government.

The third point is that China's current growth strategy is not sustainable—from the standpoint of either productivity gains or environmental losses. As China has grown, it has been compelled to dig ever more deeply into its reservoir of underutilized talent. As a consequence of a relative scarcity of labor and the fact that the employed workers are constantly using better equipment—a phenomenon that economists refer to as "capital deepening"—wages have risen. For China at some point in the not-too-distant future—just as for the Soviet Union in the 1970s—the time will come when old-fashioned capital accumulation is no longer an adequate strategy to sustain rapid growth. (More later in the book on the reasons for the Soviet collapse.) Will its growth come to a crashing halt as it runs out of labor capacity to match its ever-increasing capital base? Will China hit a productivity wall in the same dramatic fashion as occurred in the Soviet

Union? Recurrent labor unrest may suggest that some sort of turning point has already been reached.

China's advantage relative to the Soviet Union is that it possesses entrepreneurial adaptability to complement the advantages of scale that it derives from massive investments in physical capital. However, it is also hampered by a political system that continues to award positions of academic and industrial leadership on the basis of party loyalty rather than analytic acumen or business skill. China's further societal development depends on Chinese leadership's ability to grasp the insight that Joseph Schumpeter famously advanced decades ago: while political stability requires sustained growth, sustained growth actually requires a significant degree of economic instability. Will the necessary degree of economic instability end up being associated with more social and political instability than China's political leaders care to handle? Time will tell.

Addressing the adverse consequences of growth is another dimension that will challenge China in the next quarter century. To make the transition from economic growth to genuine societal prosperity, China will need to extend the dynamism that has been central to the country's transformation over the past three decades toward the search for, and implementation of, improvements in social services and coping with environmental degradation. In some domains, progress has been evident and rapid. China's newly prosperous captains of industry must develop a culture of philanthropy to pick up where government leaves off. Spurred on significantly by the national grief and widely distributed response to the Sichuan earthquake of 2008, China's businesses have shown signs of developing a type of social conscience that would have been unheard of a decade ago. To be sure, this trend is just getting started; it has a way to go even in the United States and Western Europe. For China's prosperity to continue, it will have to gain momentum.

Underlying all of these qualifications is the material fact that over a period of thirty years, three hundred million people in China—a number equal to the entire population of the United States—have been liberated from the desperation of extreme poverty and given the singular hope that economic opportunity can provide. As astounding as this achievement is, there is every reason to believe that, globally, it constitutes only a first wave. It has been nearly two centuries since Napoleon said, "Let China sleep. When she awakes she will shake the world." Well, China is wide awake now. And the rest of the world is following suit. The coming changes, as well as the challenges, will transform the lives of ten times as many people around the world as have so far been reached by China's turnaround.

The next chapter describes how the coming prosperity is reaching even the world's poorest, most conflict-ridden environments. While the details of this process are impossible to predict, we do know one thing about the coming prosperity: it won't be boring.

4 POSITIVE INSURGENCIES

When then there is a stronger incentive to take than to make—more gain from predation than from productive and mutually advantageous activities—societies fall to the bottom.

—MANCUR OLSON, *Power and Prosperity*

Afghanistan, land of opportunity.

OK, so maybe this isn't the image that first comes to mind when you think of one of the ten poorest countries on the planet. But look out at the world from the eyes of Karim Khoja for a few minutes, and your perspective might change.

I met Khoja in Cambridge, Massachusetts, in October 2008. He was among the speakers at the launch event for MIT's Legatum Center for Development and Entrepreneurship—a lineup that included five Nobel laureates in economics and Ben Cohen, cofounder of Ben and Jerry's. Khoja was there to talk about his experience as the CEO of Roshan, the Afghan cell phone company.

Now, speaking of preconceptions, when you envision world-class corporate executives based in Afghanistan, well, obviously, you don't think of anything, because until Khoja—who is originally from South Africa—there haven't been any. So, in this instance, picture a Liverpool rugby coach with a full head of jet-black hair that encroaches slightly on a menacing pair of eyebrows. Upon first glance he looks to be a guy ready to greet all comers with a crushing handshake. But the moment he's introduced, that effect is undone by the gracious smile that unfolds below his smoothly brushed mustache.

On the stage, Khoja is quickly on his feet when it's his moment on the agenda. "Have we pulled out our hair? Have we gone gray?" he asks, shaking his hands for emphasis, with reference to the challenges he has faced. "I was six foot four when I went to Afghanistan. I'm about five foot three now." One surmises that a sense of humor is among the characteristics that have been essential to his success in Afghanistan. That he has two decades of experience as a senior telecommunications executive in countries ranging from Pakistan to Croatia hasn't hurt either.

Before Roshan, which means "light/a new beginning" in Dari and Pashto, two of the country's primary languages, Afghanistan lacked a telecommunications infrastructure altogether. As Khoja says, "When I landed in Kabul, unless you were very rich, if you wanted to make a phone call you had to walk seven hundred kilometers to the nearest country." Yes, that would be the distance between Washington, DC, and Boston. "There was one cellular phone company which was charging $500 for the handset and $12 per minute, or $3 for local calls. You had to bribe their salespeople even to see you."

The country's mountainous terrain, with its few roads and minimal supplies of water and power, made building and maintaining cellular phone networks a formidable challenge. "To build a typical site, we have to clear land mines and then build an access road up to one kilometer long. The electricity and other power infrastructure are minimal, so we have had to install generators at each of our sites." About 10 percent of Roshan's budget is spent on security, primarily to protect its employees in the field. Even then, the company is able to operate safely in large parts of the country, including those beset by conflict, only by communicating openly with local leaders and actively seeking, according to Khoja, "to create jobs for individuals in villages by using local people to build sites, provide security, and run shops."

An additional challenge Roshan has faced is that 70 percent of the people in Afghanistan are illiterate. When Roshan posted its first help-wanted ad, ten thousand people responded, but few had even the most rudimentary qualifications. Khoja recalls his chief technology officer, Eric Chapman, announcing a week into the search, "We're going to choose engineers, and we're going to do it in a different way." Sounding totally exasperated, he continued: "If they can open up a PC, switch it on, and speak English, we're going to hire them." "Those [people] were our engineers," Khoja explained. Building an Afghan staff entailed a sustained commitment to on-the-job training that ultimately paid off. Khoja continues: "Today when you come to Roshan, you come to our network control center, you come to our call center, you will find not one single expatriate. It is those sixteen engineers we chose—the ones who could speak English and start up a PC—that today run a quarter-of-a-billion-dollar network nationwide."

Funded by the Aga Khan Fund for Economic Development, the for-profit arm of the Aga Khan Development Network, Roshan was always intended to be a money-making venture. "We're not shy about making a profit because that money then goes back into our agencies so that we can keep a sustainable loop."

Roshan set ambitious goals that turned out to underestimate the demand for their for its service? service rather dramatically. "When we put the business plan together for Roshan, we were looking at 150 thousand subscribers in five years, with a $50 million investment and with an internal rate of return of 15 percent," Khoja states. Today? Roshan connects more than 3.5 million subscribers in a service area that covers half the country, and the company has attracted over $440 million in direct foreign investment. It directly employs eleven hundred full-time staff members and indirectly provides thirty thousand high-quality jobs throughout the country.

Granted, the (war) stories we hear about Afghanistan and the (entrepreneurship) stories we don't hear are linked. Entrepreneurs don't get very far under conditions of totalitarian repression, and the founding of Roshan was made possible by the ouster of the Taliban. But there is a big difference between the systematic repression that existed under the Taliban (which is historically very rare) and the sort of everyday cronyism, neglect, or even anarchy that is far more typical of poor and poorly governed places around the world. Today's Afghan government ranks among the most corrupt in the world. However, it is precisely the failure of government to provide basic services, combined with a lack of formal regulatory constraints, that can create tremendous opportunities for entrepreneurs.

To claim, as many in development circles do, that an honest, stable government is a prerequisite for economic vitality is akin to claiming that a healthy, bountiful garden is a prerequisite for rainfall. Just ain't so.

Previous chapters have addressed threats to the coming prosperity by large-scale unemployment, resource scarcity, and climate change. In each of these cases I have argued that threats are either systematically overrated, inherently linked to larger and fundamentally positive trends in the global economy, or both.

But what of global terrorism? Surely the attacks of 9/11 demonstrated that advanced industrial economies are vulnerable to serious disruption from fringe elements hostile to progress and prosperity. Even if entrepreneurs can successfully create opportunities for millions of youth in ascending markets, deploy alternatives to carbon-based fuels, and develop market-based mechanisms for coping with resource scarcity, they aren't going to match up well against Koran-thumping, AK-47-toting sons of former mujahideen. The letters that spell "apocalypse" just can't be rearranged to form "prosperity." And an apocalypse—a definitive day of Final Judgment—is exactly what religious extremists are seeking to bring about.

Immediately following the shock of the attacks on the World Trade Center and the Pentagon, two schools of thought on how to respond defined the reaction from experts and ordinary citizens alike. The "let's go get the bastards" school of thought (what would become "shock and awe" when applied to Iraq) held that perpetrators of terrorist acts are fundamentally bad people who derive their support from other fundamentally bad people. The solution is, as a consequence, to find them and kill them. In sharp contrast, the "let's go help the bastards" school of thought (what would become "winning hearts and minds" when applied to Iraq and Afghanistan) conceded the existence of individuals and groups with interests antithetical to the values of the United States and other advanced industrial democracies, but argued that these misguided people were motivated by fundamental and ultimately fixable inequities on a global scale. The solution is to find them and help them.

Over the decade that has elapsed now since 9/11, which of these schools of thought has proven correct? As it turns out, neither. The so-called War on Terror prosecuted in Afghanistan, Iraq, and now Pakistan has confirmed lessons derived from decades of experience elsewhere in the world in societies under stress: patronizing people in poor places does little more to build prosperity in the long term than hunting the criminals that hide among them.

What does work? The key to transforming conflict-ridden, poor places—and a key to the coming prosperity—turns out to be far more straightforward than is usually portrayed. Fundamentally, it is not about building schools—though education is essential. It is not about building power plants—although infrastructure services are essential. It is not even about putting mobile phones in people's hands—although lowering the cost of communication can be a dramatic catalyst. Rather, the key to transforming conflict-ridden, poor places is facilitating an environment in which the most capable people in the society prefer to create rather than destroy. Specifically, it requires the (potentially assisted) emergence of a societal context in which the returns to productive entrepreneurship are at least as great as the returns to corruption and destructive entrepreneurship. Once that happens, true development can start.

In the Shomali Plains, about thirty miles north of Kabul, the issue is literally that grapes are rotting on the vine. There, losses in agricultural know-how are among the casualties of three decades of war; a seven-thousand-year history of growing grapes that was abruptly truncated by the Soviet invasion in 1979. Since then, those fields not rendered deadly by the presence of land mines (of which there are an estimated ten million) were neglected, as expertise atrophied and equipment decayed. With the expulsion of the Taliban, external groups—from nonprofit organizations such as Heidi Klum's Roots for Peace to the US National Guard—began to work with local Afghans to clear minefields and restore productive agricultural practices.

In 2008, the National Guard approached microirrigation pioneer Paul Polak for advice. Polak is a world-class entrepreneur who looks and sounds like your grandfather and possesses the rebellious spirit of your teenage daughter, the trustworthy smarts of a master mechanic, and the analytic acuity of your favorite college professor. Back in 1981, when most people of my generation were either listening to Bon Jovi or slam dancing, Paul Polak had already worked his way through one career as a psychiatrist and another running a venture in real estate and oil and gas. That's when he decided to get into the business of creating opportunity for farmers. He began with the observation that most smallholding farmers lacking access to a stream or pond can reach water by digging a five- to sixty-foot-deep well. Was it possible to design and successfully market irrigation technologies that would be both affordable to dollar-a-day farmers and efficient in irrigating small plots from shallow wells?

Over the next twenty-five years, through his company International Development Enterprises (IDE), Polak created a practical approach to building markets for microirrigation systems that has been successfully employed in South Asia and Africa and reached more than two million households. The microirrigation technologies developed and sold by IDE provide a mechanism for increasing labor productivity, expanding planting options, extending the growing season, and obtaining higher prices in the market. The result is increased income and improved well-being.

The National Guard sought Polak's assistance in addressing the following problem: 30 percent of the grape crop in the Shomali Plains was going to waste because the vines were not being tended properly. At the time, Polak recalled in a recent conversation, "their strategy for dealing with this was to create model farms to show off best practices. In my experience, that doesn't work very well. I asked, are there fence post materials available? Is there wire available? Why don't you cut a deal with some entrepreneurs to gather up the materials and sell them to farmers so that they can put the vines up on trellises?" Polak said that the Guard heeded his advice: "Some people in development have a hard time comprehending my approach because it's not about promoting big, shiny stuff. But these are farm boys from Missouri, so they get it right away."

In this case, making a new market required little more than the power of suggestion, combined with some coordinated mentoring and support. With assistance from the National Guard, new microenterprises developed and yields went up sharply. Bringing back the grapes also helped keep out the production of poppies (used in the production of narcotics) and marijuana. "You can trellis grapes and make ten times the profit that you can with poppy," said Col. Marty Leppert of the National Guard's Agribusiness Development Team.

Can such small-scale efforts really form the basis for the development of a nation? As I will discuss in detail in chapter 8, a better question is this: On what else can the development of a nation possibly be based?

The reality that entrepreneurs—whether founders of mobile phone companies or farmers—can thrive in environments rife with violence and corruption should come as no surprise. Ample evidence exists of entrepreneurial initiatives thriving in failed states or regions beset by anarchy. The examples that come to mind most readily are in the category of destructive entrepreneurship: the production and sale of narcotics, human trafficking, and the like. However, the recent growth of mobile telecommunications has created many powerful counterexamples of productive entrepreneurship flourishing in places with weak or nonexistent governments. The leading Somali cell phone company is a notable example; it was founded in 1994, exactly a year after US Marines evacuated the country, having been defeated in Mogadishu by a local warlord (an ignominious event memorialized in the film *Blackhawk Down*). The company has not only survived but thrived ever since, even in the absence of a stable, formal government.

How can we counter a destructive insurgency? With positive insurgencies led by entrepreneurs.

If there is a place outside of Africa where the challenges of development appear even more overwhelming than they do in Afghanistan, it's Afghanistan's southern neighbor, Pakistan. With a population of 180 million people, the majority under the age of sixteen, Pakistan is the world's sixth most populous country. It is the only country in Asia to suffer from the sort of artificially imposed boundaries and random demography so typical of countries elsewhere born of the postcolonial era. Pashtuns, Balochs, Sindhis, and Punjabis coexist uneasily, their shared nationality still—more than sixty years after the country's independence—more a theory than a deeply felt reality.

Compounding these challenges is a legacy of corruption and political instability (Pakistan has yet to accomplish a single democratic transition of government), an ongoing border war with India, and a sequence of natural disasters—most recently the flood of 2010 that displaced twenty million people.

It is against this backdrop that I was surprised to receive a message in July 2010 from Nadeem Ul Haque. I had come to know Ul Haque over the previous year via exchanges on Twitter. He and I shared an interest in the role of entrepreneurship in development—and a corresponding frustration with the lack of attention paid to this topic by the global amalgam of development experts. At the time of our initial correspondence Ul Haque had, for over twenty years, been an economist at the International Monetary Fund (IMF). In this role Ul Haque had come to view with skepticism the role played by official development assistance (ODA) in Pakistan and elsewhere. I had been particularly impressed with the tone of Ul Haque's scholarly work. Where economists tended to employ euphemisms to describe the corrosive impact of corruption, cronyism, and waste on national development, Ul Haque addressed these ubiquitous phenomena clearly and directly.

In May 2010 I heard from Ul Haque. He had decided to return to Pakistan to see what he could do more directly to help advance the development of his native land. We tried to connect in person during the forty-eight hours before his departure, but were unable to find a time that could work. Soon after, his Twitter feed went cold.

Then, at about 11:30 p.m. that July night, I received a direct message from Ul Haque (again, via Twitter) that said simply, "Call me," providing a number in Pakistan. A few minutes later I reached him in Islamabad, where it was 8:30 a.m.

"Ah, Phil. Good. I'm in a meeting now, so we should talk more later. But look, I'm the minister of planning now . . . whatever." Ul Haque is not a man who takes too seriously the fleeting importance conveyed by a title. "Can you come to Pakistan soon? I could use your help." Moments later the conversation concluded, and I was left wondering what had just transpired.

Over the coming weeks I was able to put the entire picture together. It turned out that Ul Haque had been appointed deputy chairman of the Planning Commission in Pakistan, a position functionally similar to the chairman of the Council of Economic Advisers in the White House. He arrived to find on his desk an economic plan that had been put together at considerable expense by a leading US consulting firm (not to be named), advocating for the sort of high-value, export-led growth strategy favored by development professionals worldwide. Pakistan's future, the consultants advised, lay in bouquets of roses. They may as well have said "plastics." Ul Haque was not amused. However, dissatisfied as he was with the plan sitting on his desk, he had little time to update and clarify the details of the alternative approach to development—emphasizing entrepreneurship and innovation—that he had patiently been working out during his years at the IMF. He needed to articulate his alternative approach quickly, and he was looking for some people to do background work in support of that effort.

So that was the reason for the call. Now, at that time, I admit I was a bit apprehensive. For one thing, I was under pressure to complete a book (this one), so it wasn't the best moment to take on a major new project.

But even more to the point, I wondered, as the father of three children, if I might not be taking an unnecessary risk in traveling to Pakistan.

My eighty-three-year-old mother certainly thought so. "The government says it isn't safe! Don't go to Pakistan, Philippe! DON'T GO!" was her suggestion to me at the time. I told her that the travel advisory the State Department had just issued was actually for Europe, not Pakistan. I wasn't going to Europe. Furthermore, I noted, the State Department's standing notice to US citizens traveling in Pakistan actually made reference to only five American deaths as a consequence of terrorist attacks since 2006. For a vast country with 180 million citizens, that is not a big number—even if it actually understates the total by a factor of five or ten. As I persuaded my mother, I persuaded myself. Images issuing from the cable channels notwithstanding, there would be little danger to me in taking this trip.

In any event it quickly became apparent to me that I would be not be saying no to Nadeem Ul Haque. A solidly built, almost burly man with a square jaw and heavy eyebrows set below a barely restrained white mane, Ul Haque can be as charming as a diplomat or as direct as a sledgehammer. If he wanted me to assist him with his new challenge, that's what I was going to do.

So sure enough, ten weeks later, I landed in Islamabad to start a three-city, one-week tour, meeting with over a dozen entrepreneurs, business leaders, and government officials—all with the aim of helping articulate an approach for Pakistan other than bouquets of roses.

The first thing that struck me when I arrived in Islamabad was literally one of the first things I saw. My two colleagues, Sara Shroff and Elmira Bayrasli, and I had no sooner stepped off the dark, warm tarmac into passport control at the Islamabad airport when we were confronted with three signs overhead: Unaccompanied Women and Children to the left; Pakistani Nationals in the middle; and Foreign Passport Holders and Diplomats to the right. Taped on either side of the sign indicating Foreign Passport Holders were two plain sheets of paper that read "Welcome Honored Donors."

Now, even accounting for the devastating floods whose effects were still very much a reality at that time, you know you're in trouble when you arrive in a country and the first thing you see are signs that read "Welcome

Honored Donors." Pakistan's history of external dependence—or, put differently, the outside world's insistence on influencing Pakistan—was cap-
tured in those two plain, white, 8½" x 11" sheets of paper, taped up over
the heads of the passport control officers.

The meetings that followed both reinforced and defied the initial impression made by those disconcerting twin signs of welcome. On one hand,
the twin cultures of business—dependency of business on government
and dependency of government on external assistance—were both very
much in evidence. We met with the scion of a major industrial family who,
in the course of a generously allocated two hours, conversed with us and
recapped the engaging history of the family business, only to close with a
request: Could we please convey to the Planning Commission his plea that
they more effectively regulate the sale of low-cost, allegedly shoddy Chinese
products? The competitors, he complained, were denying the family access
to their own market. (If this sort of request for special treatment in the
marketplace sounds backward, think back to when autoworkers in Detroit
staged events to smash cars imported from Japan and auto executives similarly sought action from government to restrain trade. The tendency of
incumbents to seek protection from government is a universal one.)

Yet the entrepreneurs Elmira, Sara, and I met were another story.
Building a successful business is a challenge anywhere; in a place like
Pakistan, that challenge is aggravated by unreliable electric power, arbitrary and incomprehensible government regulations, and a widespread
external perception that the risks of doing business in the country out-
weigh opportunities. So, in a sense, it comes as no surprise to find that the
most successful Pakistani entrepreneurs are truly exceptional people.

Shamoon Sultan was a design student, expected to take up the reins in
the family business when he found his calling in the course of a research
project on the state of the country's embroidery industry. What he found was
that an entire community of master weavers resided in Karachi, but they
were dispersed and, as a consequence, deprived of an opportunity to use
their talents. He decided he had to change that. So he created Khaadi, a high-
end fashion label, with the dual objectives of building an internationally
recognized brand and providing master weavers in his native city with a
chance to practice their craft. "In order to save craft you have to create a market," he observes in his soft-spoken but self-assured manner. His experiment

worked. "My first weaver, a master weaver, was working as an assistant at a butcher shop. I got him out of there, got him to my place, and got him started. He is now the head weaver, owns two cars, [and] his son goes to a super college."

Monis Rahman was hired by Intel after graduating from college. He ended up on the microprocessor team as the youngest member of the group developing the Itanium chip. Working for Intel was Rahman's dream job. But being in Silicon Valley at that time, he felt a strong pull to create his own company. He left Intel, started a consulting firm, and then launched his first venture. Within thirteen months, he sold the company. After that experience, Rahman decided to return to Pakistan. His idea was to build a matchmaking site for Muslim singles. "I decided to do something that I felt I had a competitive advantage on—a matchmaking site for a Muslim niche market," the suave but intense Rahman recalls. "I was unmarried. I understood the market," he says matter of factly. A few days before he was due to leave Palo Alto, Rahman had Reid Hoffman, the founder of LinkedIn, over for a lunch of grilled *tikka*. In the course of their conversation, Rahman described the venture he had in mind. Hoffman, whose own first start-up (SocialNet) was also a matchmaking site, was interested. He offered to invest. He then called two friends, Excite founder Joe Kraus, and Zynga founder Mark Pincus, who were also interested. By the time Rahman boarded his flight back to Lahore in May of 2003, his new venture, which he ultimately called Naseeb Networks, was funded sufficiently to launch. (*Naseeb* is an Urdu word, derived from Arabic. It means "destiny.")

The site was an instant success. "We got hit like a truck. The response was overwhelming. We got ten thousand people. Fifteen thousand. Twenty thousand people. Every night the server would go down." Clearly, the concept met a need. To keep his costs down, Rahman ran the entire operation, involving eight staff, from a single room in his mother's house. "The room was so small that when one person had to use the bathroom everyone had to stand . . . not out of respect but because there was no room to get behind them." When the site converted from a free site to a partially paying site, its users stayed with it. With that success to back him up, Rahman launched a job-matching site—now one of the most heavily trafficked sites in the country.

And then there is Seema Aziz, who must be one of the world's most remarkable women. Twenty-six years ago, she and her brother decided to start an embroidery business. Through their father, they had access to two European-made embroidery machines. "We were young enough and stupid to say, 'We have the same machines as the Swiss. Look at what they do, look at what we do! We will create a product equal to the best in the world and it will be made in Pakistan.' This was the entire dream, the entire concept." The pair struggled with designs and tinkered with the embroidery machine for nine months to come up with their first product. They rented a base-ment shop in a foreign-goods market. "From day one we got a reputation: 'There's a shop that sells imported fabric and calls in Pakistani,'" she recalls of the launch with a laugh. With Seema Aziz as the CEO and the lead de-signer, the company Bareeze grew to become one of Pakistan's most respected textile brands, with retail outlets throughout Pakistan as well as in London, Delhi, Dubai, and Malaysia.

For a woman with no formal training in business or design, to reach the pinnacle of an industry entirely dominated by men was certainly a substantial accomplishment. However, it turns out to be only half of the story. Little more than two years after she and her brother launched Bareeze, Pakistan was hit with a severe flood—not unlike the one that struck the country in the summer of 2010. Aziz went out with two friends to some of the areas outside Lahore hardest hit by the floods. "At that time it was not very fashionable to go out and help," she recalled. Soon recognizing that essentials—food, water, and medicine—were reaching those displaced by the floods, Aziz and her friends directed their efforts toward a longer-term need: helping villagers to rebuild their homes. Once the novelty of the experience wore off, however, the friends dropped out, and it was just Aziz. "I couldn't let go. I'd never seen so much tragedy or so much poverty at such close quarters." Over the period of months of assisting the villagers with their reconstruction effort, she came to a realization: "'The flood will come again,' I thought. 'Will they wait for someone like me to come and help them rebuild? What's the difference between them and me?' I realized, clearly in a minute, 'I'm educated, I can plead the cause, and they can't.' Working with those people made me understand that education is the only real empowerment."

So Seema Aziz redirected her efforts to starting a school. "We have a two-language system in this country—English medium and Urdu medium. It used to bother me a lot. I think it's like apartheid. I was determined to make the school an equal education: English medium, exactly what I had." She built an elementary school. It grew. She built a secondary school. It grew. Under the umbrella of the organization she founded, the Care Foundation, Seema Aziz raised more money, and trained more teachers. She launched a second school, and a third—all while building Bareeze. Twenty years later the Care Foundation directs a network of two hundred schools in which 145 thousand children—one out of every two hundred young Pakistanis currently in school—today receive their education.

As our conversation with Seema Aziz drew to a close, my colleagues and I thanked her for her time. She reacted less with humility than with surprise at how the afternoon had turned out. "I didn't know anyone cared," she said, half to herself.

Three weeks after I got back from Pakistan a bomb destroyed a police headquarters next door to the hotel where I'd stayed in Karachi. Early the following morning I set out for a meeting at the Washington, DC, offices of the Council on Foreign Relations (CFR) at which the Independent Task Force on US Strategy for Pakistan and Afghanistan was releasing its just-completed report. Among the more than a hundred attendees at this meeting, less than a block from the White House, I noted with interest that not a single one was affiliated with an Afghan or Pakistani organization. The Embassy of Estonia? Present. But representatives of the Afghan or Pakistani diaspora organizations, much less leaders from business or government, were nowhere in sight.

Looking at the Task Force report itself, I saw the same pattern. Among the twenty-five members, only one was of Afghan or Pakistani descent.

The content of the report, much like the other major reviews of Af-Pak policy that had been released in prior months, was situated firmly at the center of the conceptual box that the political leadership of the United States constructed in the days following 9/11. Premise: Islamic fundamentalist terrorism constitutes an existential threat to the United States. Options: Either go get the bastards, or go help the bastards.

The intellectual inertia evident at the CFR event left me uncharacteristically pessimistic about the prospects for change—not in Pakistan so much as in the United States. These leading national security experts appeared to have not yet grasped the key takeaway from over six decades of aid-based development work: patronizing people in poor places does little more to build prosperity in the long term than hunting the criminals that hide among them. A fundamental rethink was needed.

I thought back to the conversations I'd had with my mother before my brief trip to Pakistan. Yes, eighteen people had been killed in an attack next to the very hotel where I'd spent the night just a few weeks earlier. But another eighteen million residents of Karachi hadn't been killed. Those eighteen million people were going about their business, one way or another. Moreover, as I looked into the numbers further, I realized that the five thousand fatalities from terrorism in Pakistan during the past three years did not constitute even one-fifth the toll of Mexico's ongoing drug war during the same interval—a criminal insurgency which is taking place less than an hour away by black SUV from Disneyland. What's more, Pakistan tends to rank below both Sri Lanka and India when it comes to incidence of terrorism. Yet such a ranking—and a decades-long civil war—did not prevent Sri Lanka from making remarkable strides in its development; for example, achieving a plateauing of its population growth rates comparable to that achieved in China, but (like Hong Kong) without a coercive one-child policy. And India, of course, has surged forward to compete with China for the distinction of being the country most indicative of the coming prosperity.

(Later on I determined that the present murder rate in Karachi—Pakistan's largest city, currently caught in a spiral of gang-related killings—is one-fourth that which my hometown of Washington, DC, experienced in 1991, at the height of its own murder epidemic. I also came to the horrifying realization that more people were killed in a single day of the Rwandan genocide than have died in the past decade of terrorism and gang violence in Pakistan. Though Pakistan may be a dangerous place, it hardly merits the reputation is has acquired in the decade since the start of the "War on Terror.")

Less than a week later, however, the apprehension I'd felt following the event at the CFR was dispelled, not by a different blue-ribbon panel of security experts, but rather by Erik Malmstrom and Jake Cusack, a pair of twenty-something former military officers then working toward master's degrees at Harvard.

These two guys had done exactly the thing in Afghanistan that I (like the majority of external experts) had mostly failed to do in my first visit to Pakistan: get out of the hotel and hit the road in search of the story. The story they told of their experiences over the summer of 2010, speaking with entrepreneurs in Afghanistan, suggested the kernel of exactly the sort of strategic rethink that had been so notably absent from the conversation at the CFR.

Discussing the findings in their reports, Cusack remarked, "Our image of Afghanistan is of a soldier standing in front of a mud hut. That's not what's going on. . . . Businesses are functioning, even thriving, in a very difficult environment." The entrepreneurs with whom Malmstrom and Cusack spoke didn't identify conflict as their primary problem: "Our perception going in was that physical insecurity would be the number-one concern of business. . . . But we found that Afghans were generally more concerned about the uncertainty in the business environment than they were about security." Malmstrom noted that, to the extent that businesses did feel insecure, the Taliban weren't the only ones responsible: "Businesses feel very threatened by the Afghan government. . . . One entrepreneur had this to say: 'Insecurity is caused by the government and the Taliban. They are the same.'" Though genuine opportunities were present, they were obscured by the overlay of large-scale external assistance. "We frequently found international organizations trying to help but actually distorting the system." His conclusion: "War should not be an excuse to resurrect failed policies, such as that centrally planned growth is necessary in a chaotic environment."

As Cusack correctly observed, "There's a certain mythology built around conflict, as if the laws of physics or economics somehow don't apply." Citizens at large, and the entrepreneurs among them, tend not to wait for the optimal condition of a stable supportive state in order to function. On the contrary, by beginning where they are, they are the ones most likely to compel the state to change.

Back in Pakistan, that is exactly the approach that Nadeem Ul Haque has been taking from within government. Less than a year from the time he assumed a leadership role, the Planning Commission had secured cabinet approval for an alternative approach to building a future in Pakistan that pushed state-led projects to the side and instead aimed for an economy-wide upgrade of the "software" of development—the incentives, institutions, market environment, and practices of governance which, in combination, either nurture or impede productive entrepreneurship. Granted, the existence of a single document, no matter how enlightened, does little to alter daily existence in a complex country of 180 million people. But taken in combination with the reality of entrepreneurial excellence embodied in Shamoon Sultan, Monis Rahman, and Seema Aziz, this "unplanning" approach to national policy making indicates a pathway by which Pakistan might—sooner than is generally imagined possible—assume a role in the economic affairs of the twenty-first century commensurate with its productive potential.

Part 1 of this book was about overcoming outdated narratives of threat—from population pressures, to resource crises, to massive unemployment and climate change—to grasp the powerful momentum of progress in our lifetimes. The core point was that, in nearly all cases, threats to global prosperity in the twenty-first century are inherently linked to opportunities. It is on that basis that this book is titled *The Coming Prosperity*.

Part 2 of the book, beginning with the next chapter, is about the fundamental economic trends and processes that have driven the growth of global prosperity over the past four hundred years—and the prospect for those processes and trends in the future.

Positive insurgencies, it will turn out, are not only the key to progress in postconflict societies. They are also at the forefront of beneficial change in other places where societal stability requires the constant generation of new opportunities, but entrenched interests resist change—that is to say, everywhere.

THE ANIMATING ELEMENT

All societies have entrepreneurs, but not all entrepreneurship is productive. Productive entrepreneurs create a space for the future by innovating new combinations of economic activity and pushing back against entrenched interests. In so doing, they realize the dynamic balance between order and adaptability that is essential to social vitality.

Productive entrepreneurship is the animating element of the coming prosperity.

5 MOBILIZING THE MASSES

Far away beyond her myriad coming changes earth will be
Something other than the wildest modern guess of you and me.

—ALFRED LORD TENNYSON, *"Locksley Hall Sixty Years After"*

Remember learning in school about the Black Friday financial panic of 1869? Few people do. That was another time in our nation's history when the financial system buckled. In that instance, a pair of speculators by the names of James Fisk and Jay Gould tried to corner the market for gold. (It's easy to imagine the headline: "Fisk Takes Risk on Gold with Gould!") Their angle was that they had insider access to President Ulysses S. Grant. When their artificially created bubble of assets popped, a bunch of people lost lots of money—though not, incidentally, Goldman Sachs . . . I mean, Fisk and Gould. Demands to reform the financial system followed.

Now I know that the past is full of financial panics, each of them in some way or another reminiscent of the one we recently experienced. But I bring up this one in particular because of another event that occurred in 1869: the completion of the first transcontinental railroad in the United States. I bet you do remember learning about that. Why? Because in the long run the railroad mattered and the financial panic of 1869 didn't.

Well, as we are all by now aware, another (metaphorical) transcontinental railroad is being completed today. It is wireless and global. Instead of connecting one-half of a country to another, it is connecting one-half of the world's population to each other, and everyone else. Is this global revolution in mobile communications a bigger deal than the recent financial crises? Well, was Cornelius Vanderbilt, railroad baron, a bigger deal than James Fisk, crooked financier?

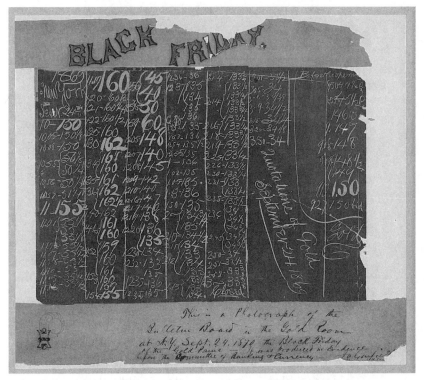

Photograph of the blackboard in the New York Gold Room, September 24, 1869, evidencing the collapse of the price of gold. A handwritten caption by James A. Garfield indicates it was used as evidence before the Committee of Banking & Currency during hearings in 1870. Caption: "This is a photograph of the bulletin board in the Gold Room at N.Y., Sept. 24, 1870 [i.e., 1869] the Black Friday of the Gold Panic. It was produced in evidence before the Committee of Banking & Currency - J. A. Garfield Chair[. . .]of the Com[. . .]." Library of Congress note: Black Friday was September 24, 1869. The hearings were in 1870. Damage to the lower right corner has removed a portion of the photo caption.

Source: Library of Congress. See http://hdl.loc.gov/loc.pnp/ppmsca.12856.

It's this simple: no technology in history has spread more quickly than the mobile phone. Not writing. Not the printing press. Not the personal computer. And no, not the railroads. Nothing even comes close.

The story of Roshan, with which I opened chapter 4, illustrates a broader, global phenomenon. Once they became available in ascending markets, mobile technologies have in general spread roughly five times as quickly as they did in mature economies. It took twenty years to sell the first one billion mobile handsets (mostly in the developed world), but only four years to sell the second billion (mostly in the developing world) and only two years to sell the third billion.

In sub-Saharan Africa, the number of cell phone subscribers jumped from 11 million in 2000 to 184 million in 2007 and 500 million in 2010. Growth in previously poor places elsewhere in the world has been comparable. China Mobile, an entity that did not exist fifteen years ago, was by 2008 the world's fifth-largest company, just ahead of Microsoft. In 2010, well over half the people on earth had mobile phones.

When it comes to technologies that have made it all the way to the village level on a truly global scale, the previous success was the radio. And before that? Fire.

This much we all know. When it comes to stories of gadget proliferation, the mobile revolution is the mother of them all. Hooray for the handset. We've all seen the ads for G3 networks and G4 networks. What's next? Let me guess. Could it possibly be G5 networks? No doubt telecommunications companies are excited. But, is anything else going on here? What difference will all this newly deployed technological capability make in the lives of human beings in the next quarter century? That is the question for this chapter.

The mobile revolution does more than illustrate how massive change can happen in a short period of time. Far more significantly, it illustrates specific technology-driven transformations that are carrying the United States and the rest of the world inexorably into the twenty-first century:

(i) For the first time in history, the frontier of technology is reaching the majority of the world's population.

(ii) Technology at a human scale is democratizing personal productivity as never before.

(iii) Previously closed networks of production and knowledge are now open and accessible to creative and determined people everywhere.

(iv) Open networks of production and communication are, in turn, enabling globally distributed collaboration and innovation on a massive, unprecedented scale.

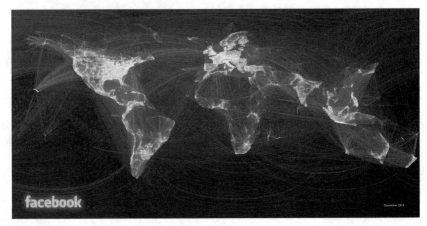

Facebook™ map of human connections.
© Paul Butler. Reprinted with permission.

These trends, taken in combination, comprise the storyline of the coming prosperity.

In chapter 1, I discussed how the history of the twentieth century was, fundamentally, about the rise and partial fall of economies of scale in production. The dominant technologies of the twentieth century were, correspondingly, those defined by their superhuman scale: the sky-scraper, the jumbo jet, the mainframe computer, the hydroelectric dam, the power grid, the particle accelerator, and the nuclear reactor. Sure, some paradigmatic twentieth-century technologies are at a human, rather than a superhuman, scale—the automobile, the television, and the transistor radio notable among them. But each of these functions only in the context of large-scale, centralized infrastructures: the car requires high-way and fossil-fuel infrastructures, and radio and television need broad-cast infrastructures.

In 1965, Intel cofounder Gordon Moore famously predicted that com-puting capability would double every eighteen months. He was right. And in the past forty-five years, Moore's law has brought technology down to a human scale. Today, everyone with a mobile phone holds in their palm a thousand times more computational power than was available to the NASA engineers working mission control on the day in 1969 when Neil Armstrong took humankind's first step on the moon. As owners of the initial round of smartphones discovered in the past decade, and as most of the rest of the world is discovering now, computational power in the palm translates into the capacity to do much more than talk. We have only to scroll through the thousands of applications that can run on a smartphone to get a glimpse of the possibilities. But the offerings in today's app stores will be to the applications of the near future what Pong was to World of Warcraft: no comparison.

In its human scale, the mobile phone shares a characteristic with many emerging twenty-first-century technologies that are or will be transformative—foot pumps for small-farm irrigation, 3D printers, and low-cost distributed power generators among them. But what sets the mobile phone apart from the other three is exactly what separates the iPhone from the iPod. Connectivity is the difference.

So what? Didn't we have communications networks and social networks in the twentieth century? Yes, of course. But in the twentieth century the most powerful networks were exclusive. In the twenty-first century, networks are explosive. (Tunisia? Egypt? Not exceptions—the rule.)

This point is important enough to merit a couple of minutes to address the fundamentals. First, what is a communications network? It is people linked by connections. A closed network is a bunch of people with connections only to each other, but not to anyone else; connections from the outside are not accepted. Think secret societies or cells of intelligence operatives. An open network is accessible to anyone who wants to initiate a connection with anyone else. Think the Internet.

In closed networks, membership is exclusive. Such networks do a great job of conserving information, since deviation from the rules of membership can be punished by expulsion, but they are less effective in creating new information. Medieval guilds, for example, famously managed to preserve (and incrementally advance) techniques for making widely treasured products such as crystal, glass beads, and porcelain over the span of generations. But successful as it was in perpetuating past techniques, the guild system was not well suited to innovating new approaches for the future. In other words, it was great for maintaining market order and ensuring economic returns, but not so good for fostering adaptability to changing circumstances. Consequently, when the Industrial Revolution surged, the guilds mostly faded.

What of open networks? In open networks, access is free—or, as in the case of a SIM card to power a mobile phone, close to it. No premium exists on membership in and of itself. Members in an open network contribute by adding value internally, rather than by enforcing exclusivity at the boundaries. Contributions by network members can take one of three fundamental forms: creating, communicating, and recombining. Each of these ways of adding value in networks is affected differently by increases in network size. The raw creative power of a network grows at a one-to-one rate (that is, linearly, because it looks like a line when graphed) as new members are added: one more person, one more potential creator. For any single message, the power to communicate similarly decreases linearly as new members are added. Think of the children's game telephone, in which a message is whispered from person to person around a circle. The more people in the circle, the less chance that the message will make it around without serious distortion.

In contrast, the number of conversations possible within a network (as opposed to the efficiency of the communication of one single, specific message) grows at a far greater rate than a one-to-one pace as new members are added. Add one person to a network of ten people and you've added the potential not for a single person-to-person conversation, but for ten of them: each of the existing group members now has one more person to talk to.

But the real power of large open networks, like those enabled by mobile communications, is in the third dimension of network participation: recombination. Think of each person in the network as the producer a different type of Lego block. With two people in the network and the two types of Lego blocks they produce, only one combination of blocks is possible (disregarding order): A + B. Now think about adding just three more members to the network. How many unique creations are possible with five different types of Lego blocks, rather than two? Over 120. Double the network from five to ten people, and now over six million combinations are possible. In this manner the possible combinations and recombinations of Lego blocks increase more than exponentially as the network grows in size.

As Joseph Schumpeter first articulated, the power of recombination is the single greatest force driving increases in societal prosperity over the long term. (More on recombination in the next chapter.) Only when enhanced by the power of recombination does the increased efficiency achievable by specialization—heralded by Adam Smith in *The Wealth of Nations*—yield TiVos, Mini Coopers, camera phones, and all the other complex outputs of twenty-first-century global supply chains.

In the long run, large, open networks overwhelmingly tend to win out over smaller, closed ones. This tendency is so strong that it extends to closed networks that encompass entire countries. I clearly remember visiting my cousins in France in the mid-1980s, the heyday of a device launched in 1982 by Poste, Télégraphes et Téléphones (PTT, the French national telephone company), called the Minitel. The Minitel was a marvel. It consisted of a small keyboard and monitor with myriad uses: you could buy things, book seats on the train, check the market, find a phone number, and even chat with friends. As it was France, pretty much everyone in the country eventually had one. It was a pre-Internet Internet that was connected by phone lines through a centralized system.

Now if there had been any way to save this Gallic innovation from its inevitable demise once the Internet rolled into town, I am sure that the good folks at the PTT (now France Telecom) would have teamed up with this or that minister to find one. They tried. But a national network, operated through a centralized carrier, could not compete in any way, shape, or form with the global, almost organic, architecture of the Internet. The Minitel limped along, but today it is nothing more than a glorified phone book.

Such battles happen all the time. Almost invariably, open networks beat closed networks, and larger networks beat smaller ones, in that order. Next up for closed-network obsolescence? The spy side (or human-assets directorate) of the US Central Intelligence Agency would seem to be one candidate. As the *9/11 Commission Report* communicated clearly, effective intelligence work in an age of information overload is less a matter of picking up hidden signals (as has been the traditional task of clandestine services) than it is one of sorting the signals that matter from all the noise that doesn't. (Spies aren't the only ones at risk in this manner. In the absence of reforms both to academic peer review and to the standard criteria for tenure in universities, self-referential cliques of academic experts may similarly end up losing out to open systems of knowledge creation and validation.)

To be sure, counterexamples exist. At the forefront of design and innovation, detail-oriented visionaries working in relatively closed systems can achieve a level of elegance and coherence in their work that open-system insurgents have a hard time matching. Think Steve Jobs. But even Apple has consistently proven vulnerable to open-architecture competitors. And, aside from Apple, finding closed-system innovators who have managed to remain viable is a challenge. Even the Pentagon has succumbed. When President Dwight D. Eisenhower coined the term "military-industrial complex," the US Department of Defense represented the apotheosis of closed-system technology development—a massive guild equipped with $5,000 hammers. Today it buys 80 percent of its technology from commercial, off-the-shelf vendors.

All of this leads to the following questions: What will happen when global information networks and opportunities to create continent-spanning collaborative relationships are finally within reach for the majority of the world's population? What new combinations will be possible then? We can only wonder.

Make no mistake: the mobile revolution is not, in reality, just a story of gadget proliferation. The mobile revolution is daily transforming people's lives in ways that are not easily comprehended to those of us in technology-rich, politically open environments.

"Asked to name the single biggest benefit of America's invasion, many Iraqis fail to mention freedom or democracy but instead praise the advent of mobile phones, which were banned under Saddam Hussein," the *Economist* reported in November 2009, more than five years after US and British forces removed Saddam Hussein from power. "Many Iraqis seem to feel more liberated by [cell phones] than by the prospect of elected resident government." Given that before this survey was taken the Iraqi people had endured a quarter century of dictatorship followed by five years of civil war, this testimonial—finding mobile phones to be even more liberating than ballot boxes—is not trivial.

In the tool-saturated environment that we in developed countries take for granted, the cell phone is a wonderful convenience but by no means the core driver of societal advancement. It's a different story for the majority of people worldwide. In the many parts of the world where roads are poor, libraries antiquated, health infrastructures inadequate, and banks nonexistent, mobile phones are simultaneously reducing the need for transport, providing access to current information, supporting medical care, and enabling access to financial services. In different places and to differing degrees, mobile phones have demonstrated the ability to function as virtual taxis, powerful diagnostic tools, computer terminals, and ATMs.

Let's start with banking. Have you ever been in a situation where you needed cash unexpectedly but couldn't find an ATM? Well, what if you couldn't find that ATM *ever*—as in not at all? Oh, and you have no checks, no credit cards—in fact, you have no bank account. Just the cash you have stashed under your mattress.

Still doesn't sound too bad? Well, what if you now have to make a big purchase—one worth, say, three months' salary. More cash than you usually feel comfortable carrying around? And what if you're in a neighborhood as safe as, say, Helmand Province in Afghanistan or Kinshasa in the Congo?

Welcome to everyday life until very recently for the majority of people on earth.

Now enter mobile banking. Suddenly, you are able to store value on the SIM card in your phone. The card is password-protected, so even if you lose your phone or it gets stolen, you won't lose your money. What's more, you don't need to go to a bank to turn the stored value into ready cash. Street-side mobile banking, or M-banking, vendors are everywhere.

Even better, you can now send and receive money transfers to and from friends and relatives—including people overseas—substantially more cheaply than via Western Union or other previously available alternatives. And did I mention that remittances—the money expatriate workers send to relatives back home—total over $440 billion per year, nearly three times the total of all government-to-government foreign aid sent to developing countries? And that total only includes money sent through formal banking and money-transfer channels. Here's what this means: if the reduced costs to consumers associated with M-banking were to increase remittances by 25 percent, it would be the equivalent of more than doubling foreign aid to the developing world . . . except, of course, that the increase in remittances would be preferable to the increase in aid, since 100 percent of remittance money (net of commissions) goes directly to the desired beneficiaries, whereas aid flown out to national governments in many places is as likely to end up exiting the country on the next flight out to a Swiss bank account as it is to land in the intended village or household. (Arithmetical analysis of the global economy more generally reveals that foreign aid—whether increased or decreased, effective or not—is at most a sidebar when considered in the context of the epic global narrative that is the coming prosperity.)

Ease and availability aren't the only considerations: safety is another significant benefit of mobile, as compared with conventional, banking. When mobile banking customers travel, they can store cash through the phone before they leave and pick it up when they arrive, thus eliminating the risk of loss or theft in transit. Bill Barhydt, founder of a pioneering company focused on international remittances reports that "in our interviews in Mexico, 100 percent of people—100 percent—could tell a theft story" related to cashing a conventional remittance check. "People were crying in our arms. The more often you're a target, the more likely you are to get hit again." With mobile banking, funds sent from relatives or other large money transfers can be sent and stored securely—converted to cash only when needed.

Now, given the increased security and freedom that mobile banking offers, you would expect it to be quite popular with people who once had no access to financial services or had to depend on the expensive and inconvenient services offered by conventional banks. And, of course, you would be right. In Kenya alone, M-PESA, the mobile banking initiative provided by Safaricom, the Kenyan cell phone service, has registered over 14 million customers since its launch in 2007. That's over 50 percent of Kenya's adult population.

Even from the very outset, the societal impact has been dramatic. During the postelection violence in Kenya in 2007–8, many M-PESA agents reported a reverse in the direction of remittances, as rural relatives sent money to urban family members fleeing the turmoil. Despite the disruption, those who evacuated affected areas could maintain access to their accounts. And M-banking services allowed international organizations to get emergency aid through to some of the communities hardest hit by looting and violence, and to do so far more quickly than in the past.

Mobile banking is, of course, just one of dozens of mobile phone applications that are now being developed and deployed in ascending markets.

A few of these applications are well advanced. CellBazaar, an eBay for cell phones in Bangladesh, serves over a million users daily. Esoko, which provides farmers with real-time information on market prices, is available in seventeen countries in sub-Saharan Africa.

Additional applications with potential for deployment over the planet's mobile infrastructure arise on an almost daily basis. Jana (formerly TxtEagle), a company (like so many others) started by an MIT graduate student, is working to create employment by linking workers with small-scale jobs via mobile phones. (In chapter 12 I describe Samasource, another microwork venture.) In the West Bank, a fantastic partnership of young entrepreneurs has developed a job-matching and job-training service for Palestinian youth—valuable anywhere, but indispensable for young people with high aspirations whose most significant source of job opportunities is on the other side of a maze of checkpoints; they're now exporting their model to other countries.

Yet the greatest changes coming through the growth of mobile telephony, and especially mobile banking, may be those that pertain to individual and political identity. For many people in the world today—in both mature economies and ascending markets—the cell phone number is now the single fixed point of social contact. The difference in ascending markets is that for many mobile phone users, their phone number is the first fixed point of contact they have ever had. This point of contact becomes a new identity when it is used to gain membership and access into previously inaccessible social domains—in the case of M-banking, the global club of people engaged in electronically enabled financial transactions. Because M-banking allows people to create a formal identity, it is a potentially powerful driver of developmental progress in that the financially excluded now have a way to document their trustworthiness, even though they lack the documentation provided by property rights (a listing of collateral) or by social capital (a listing of references) that providers of financial services have traditionally required.

Finally, and significantly, mobile phones are the political organizing tool of the twenty-first century—redefining what Bismarck dubbed "the art of the possible" in politics. In January 2001, Filipinos took to the streets—and to their keypads—to dump their disgraced president,

Joseph Estrada. In the week known as People Power II, they sent nearly seventy million text messages—55 percent more than the week before. As Reuters reported at the time, while the popular expression of discontent played out in other media as well, "it was cell phones that best illustrated the power that technology literally put in Filipino hands." Since then, mobile phones have been a tool of choice in public protests from Tehran to Tunis, and from Casablanca to Cairo.

Increasingly in this and other contexts, mobile phones are becoming an extension of the Internet. Shortly after the Jasmine Revolution in Tunisia in January 2011, newly appointed Tunisian communications director Sami Zaoui cited the fact that more than 40 percent of the Tunisian population is online—many through their mobile phones. "What we have lived in Tunisia is a peaceful and democratic revolution, and YouTube, Twitter, and Facebook were a great contribution to that—in addition of course, to all the demonstrators who were in the field." An opening of full media freedom is fundamental to the county's further development. Under the Ben Ali regime, "any initiatives that were not controlled were not accepted. [What is more] we didn't know what we could have after Ben Ali. The lack of confidence in the future blocked everything. By giving freedom of the Internet we give much more than freedom of the Internet. We are giving freedom of initiative."

To be sure, communications technologies are also used—and always have been used—as instruments of control, repression, and even violence. Radio Télévision Libre des Mille Collines (RTLM) in Rwanda famously broadcast racist propaganda directed at Tutsis before, and during, the genocide there. And even in Egypt, whose revolution has been being held up (and I agree) as an example of the beneficial impact of mobile technologies on governance, the Mubarak regime compelled Vodafone to send mass short message service (SMS) text messages as part of the infamous February 2, 2011, campaign of attacks on protesters in Cairo's Tahrir Square.

Furthermore, it is also true, as Malcolm Gladwell has noted, that

People protested and brought down governments before Facebook was invented. They did it before the Internet came along. Barely anyone in East Germany in the nineteen-eighties had a phone— and they ended up with hundreds of thousands of people in central

Leipzig and brought down a regime that we all thought would last another hundred years—and in the French Revolution the crowd in the streets spoke to one another with that strange, today largely unknown instrument known as the human voice.

Along similar lines, Sir John Millar, a contemporary of Adam Smith, described over two hundred years ago how the agglomeration of people in cities and the shared interests created through "the advancement of trade and manufactures" allow citizens to communicate "all their sentiments and passions . . . with great rapidity":

> The strong encourage the weak; the bold animate the timid; the resolute confirm the wavering; and the movements of the whole mass proceed with the uniformity of a machine, with a force that is often irresistible.

Mobile technologies dramatically lower the cost of communicating and of identifying shared spaces of interest. In this way they continue a process begun centuries ago with large-scale urbanization and the printing of the first political pamphlets. While autocratic regimes—particularly the one in the People's Republic of China—have become adept at filtering content on the Internet, the genie of open expression via the mobile phone is another form of technological change which, once out of the bottle, has so far proven very difficult to put back in.

Two summers ago I spent a week traveling in Tibet with my oldest daughter. Few if any places in the world are more dramatically on the front line of globalization—a phenomenon of which "Chinafication," like Americanization, is a subset. Contrasts there between tradition and transformation were so ubiquitous that they very quickly began to blur together. Many elements of that transformation are as troubling as they appear to be inevitable—the marginalization of the Tibetan people and the degradation of the natural environment foremost among them. Yet juxtaposed with stark images of a people quietly insisting on their own cultural and religious survival are equally dramatic images of personal empowerment and hope. One in particular has stayed with me. It is a fleeting portrait, caught from the window of a Toyota Land Cruiser while driving across an expansive plateau five hours from Lhasa and more than two miles above sea level. A motorcycle approaches. As it draws nearer, I see that it is driven by a Tibetan nomad woman. Her richly colored robe is snapping in the wind behind her. The intense brown of her complexion reflects a life lived in close proximity to the sun. Racing across the open space at sixty miles per hour, her eyes are intent on the road before her. She grasps the handlebar with one hand—and with the other, holds her cell phone to her ear. She is talking and she is laughing. Then she is out of sight.

Bringing networks within reach means extending the capabilities of billions of people around the world. The mobile phone as we know it may lead this trend, but, as I'll argue in the next chapter, countless other devices and innovations will follow almost inevitably.

Thanks to this new age of technologies at a human scale, we among the world's haves can at last welcome the world's have-nots. It's not hard to do: They have cell phones.

6 YOU ARE WHAT YOU VENTURE

He was a bold man that first ate an oyster.

—JONATHAN SWIFT

The prior chapter may have incorrectly conveyed the impression that I think the promise of the future is all about phones. This is not the case at all. Actually, I think it's all about recipes.

If you want to understand why humanity might not be doomed—despite the daily drumbeat of declarations to the contrary—I'd say you're more likely to get an answer from glancing at the last cookbook you purchased than from either pondering the possibilities of your iPad or diligently rereading your college economics textbook. Seriously. In part that's because the economics of the twentieth century was overwhelmingly about how best to share existing "pies" of human well-being, rather than how to bake more, new, and better ones. But your cookbook will also be instructive because recipes are actually a very useful metaphor for, and even direct illustrations of, how practical creativity creates prosperity; mobile-based innovations are one further example of that phenomenon. So before we get back to how entrepreneurs are essential to societal adaptability and thus long-run prosperity, let's first consider the remarkable fact of contemporary culinary innovation.

What ingredients go into twenty-first-century recipes? Basil. Eggs. Flour. Meyer lemons. Cornish hens. Grasshoppers (from northern Thailand). Whatever. The list goes on and on. But does that global list of ingredients differ significantly from that of inputs into recipes a generation ago? A century ago? A millennium? Not really. Even the consumption of oysters dates back to prehistory. At a global scale, the reality is that the range of ingredients used to put dinner on the table today is—due to the advent of large-scale agriculture—actually narrower than it was a few generations back.

Second, consider the fact that the earliest recipes that have been found are about as old as the earliest evidence of writing itself. Roughly a hundred billion people have lived since that time, each one requiring meals on a daily basis. In the process of creating those meals they (we) experimented with new techniques; occasionally they recorded their most inspired creations for future reference or to share with others. The result? The richness of global cuisine—everything from sole meunière and Peking duck to Krispy Kreme doughnuts and Jell-O molds.

Third, and most importantly, consider the fact that, after all this time, not only are human beings still creating new recipes, but they actually manage to sell those recipes to other people, and even, occasionally, get famous in the process. (A Google search for Julia Child, for example, yields about the same number of hits as one for Dwight D. Eisenhower, suggesting that superlative soufflés are on par with leadership of the Free World—at least so far as the Internet is concerned.)

Now pause for a moment to reflect on the improbability of these three facts, considered in combination. How can it possibly be that, after the trillions of meals that human beings have prepared and consumed over millennia out of essentially the same fundamental set of ingredients, individual people not only come up with new recipes, but can in fact become famous doing so? A new recipe here and there, sure. But entire cookbooks full of culinary novelty? Or even, as is the current reality in the United States, a $500 million per year market for cookbooks? Such a thing would seem to be a statistical impossibility. Yet new cookbooks aren't only possible, they're ubiquitous. That is because there is no demonstrated limit to humanity's appetite for novelty, just as there is no limit to humanity's potential for creativity.

At the same time, it is equally evident that novelty and creativity aren't sufficient for societal advance any more than they are for cooking. Anyone who has let their small children loose in the kitchen to create Harry Potteresque concoctions—or anyone, for that matter, who has attempted to conjure up a bit of their own of culinary magic—knows that not all recipes are created equal. For one thing, it helps if your newly invented dish is edible. Even better if your new creation is actually better than, or at least

The oldest known recipe book. This tablet from the Old Babylonian period (ca. 1750 BC) includes twenty-five recipes for stews; twenty-one are meat stews, and four are vegetable stews.

© The Near East Collection, Yale University (YBC 4644). See http://www.library.yale.edu/neareast/exhibitions/cuisine.html. Reprinted with permission.

comparable to, a favorite recipe of yours out of a cookbook and the average output of another member of your household.

But culinary recipes are also an example of a far more general category that Karl Shell (a founder of modern growth theory), Stuart Kauffman, José Lobo, and I have termed "production recipes." Production recipes are the *how* of economic life—the repeatable steps that allow individuals or, far more often, groups of people, to turn raw materials into useful products. Most production recipes, like most culinary recipes, are unwritten. Most managers, like most cooks, are not hugely inventive. The creation of new forms of economic activity, like the creation of new culinary forms, falls disproportionately to a few people. In the kitchen we call these culinary innovators chefs (or, if your family is like mine, Grandma). In economics we call them entrepreneurs.

Economist Martin Weitzman has put it this way: "Can we imagine a world in which we'd run out of new ideas?" Almost inconceivable. The reason is that most new ideas are generated as new combinations of old ideas, and the number of new combinations is almost limitless:

> Edison invented the electric light explicitly, you notice from his writing, as a kind of a cross between a candle and electricity. The whole electric distribution system, in Edison's mind, was patterned on then-existing gas distribution systems, where you plugged in electricity for gas. Once you have nuclear power and you have a submarine, it's almost inevitable you're going to have a nuclear submarine. A spreadsheet is, in a sense, a cross between personal computers and double entry accounting. It runs very, very deep in the human soul to investigate and to play with combinations. It's not an accident that we continually circumvented scarcity problems in the past.

True economic novelty is the equivalent of a new ingredient, one never used before; new economic combinations are equivalent to new recipes. For most of the twentieth century, the bulk of societal advance accordingly was attributable to one of two categories of activities. The first was the search for genuine novelty, that is, undertaking basic scientific research that yielded new technological possibilities. The second was bringing the most successful new combinations to as many people as possible—for example, McDonald's serving billions upon billions . . . of the same thing. As a consequence, until the very end of the twentieth century, if economists or management gurus focused their attention on economic novelty at all, they overwhelmingly emphasized the role of basic research and big business, not entrepreneurship. That was understandable because, for the bulk of the twentieth century, basic research and big business were the primary vehicles of economic growth and prosperity. This was true both in the rich world (large-scale, science-based agricultural production; highly processed, mass-produced foods; and multibillion-dollar franchised-restaurant chains) and in the developing world (research into higher-yielding plant varieties, industrial production of fertilizer, and the Green Revolution, which both of those enabled).

But in the twenty-first century, prior trends toward basic and big are reversing. Sure, basic science is still important. Big corporations—for example Walmart, whose exemplary response to Hurricane Katrina I discuss in the next chapter—are still doing a huge share of the heavy lifting of getting goods and services to people on a daily basis (and, as a general rule, their shareholders are benefiting accordingly). But on the frontiers of the economy—in terms of both technology and geography—entrepreneurs are back in the lead. They are the ones creating, testing, and on occasion bringing to scale the literal and metaphorical recipes of the future.

Part 1 of this book was mostly about the macro–story line of the coming prosperity: that, contrary to the predictions made for over a century by various prophets of demographic doom, ours is an era of unprecedented opportunity for people everywhere. Ever since Oswald Spengler and Arnold Toynbee produced their monumental studies of Western civilization, such macronarratives have been a publishing staple. Today that book category is filled by Thomas Friedman, Niall Ferguson, Fareed Zakaria, and Parag Khanna, among others.

Such part-journalistic, part-historical narratives are helpful in clarifying the trend of global change. Yet, as a rule, they say little of its fundamental origins. "Yes, I get the idea," says the skeptical reader of the Friedman-Ferguson-Zakaria-Khanna-style macronarrative, as well as the version thereof I advanced in Part 1. "The rest is rising and everyone will be better off. Or, if you believe the story the *Limits to Growth* crowd was peddling forty years ago, human populations are exploding and we're soon going to run out of everything. Either way it's punditry. Grand theorizing. Current events taught at the doctoral level, perhaps. But doesn't mean anything."

What is lacking in macronarratives of coming prosperity (or doom) is any indication of exactly how decision making by human beings on a day-to-day basis causes society as a whole to proceed forward (or backward) toward greater (or diminished) prosperity. In other words, what neither upbeat nor downbeat assessments succeed in addressing is the role of people in bringing about prosperity—or not. That human-scale story line is the focus of this chapter, and the remainder of part 2.

Why this deficiency? Well, for one thing, macronarratives are mostly authored by journalists, historians, and the occasional macroeconomist; as a consequence, a bias toward journalism, history, and macroeconomics is to be expected. But there is another reason, which is a bit thornier: standard microeconomic theory has little more to say about the process of growth and development than does standard macroeconomic theory.

Now, before I go any further with this, let me say that contrary to the norm among book-writing economists, I simply love neoclassical economics. OK, maybe not "love." But, after twenty years of doing my best to go at the edifice of neoclassical theory (and witnessing the attempts of many others to do the same), I grudgingly have come to the conclusion that standard economic theory is actually very good at doing what it does best: explaining the aggregate importance of intrinsically inconsequential individual decisions, in a world of surprising certainty. Where the standard theory (specifically, the tools of marginal analysis) gets bogged down is when it tries to cope with genuine novelty in the environment, or decisions that can't be reduced to inconsequential choices. And it caves in when it tries to explain entrepreneurship and innovation.

To understand why this is, let's get back to recipes, which are the best way to illustrate what standard theory can, and can't, tell us about entrepreneurship, invention, and innovation.

What goes into a recipe? Well, first, there's the list of ingredients—the inputs, the four eggs and two cups of flour. Next, there's usually some indication of what the recipe produces—the output, the "makes two dozen cookies."

Is that it? No, of course not: a recipe is incomplete without a description of what you are supposed to do with the ingredients—the instructions. "Combine flour, baking soda and salt in small bowl. . . ."

Now standard microeconomic theory is very sophisticated when it comes to two of the three essential elements of a recipe: specifically, the inputs and the outputs. Given a particular level of technology, the standard theory provides extremely precise guidance on how to pick the balance of inputs (in generic terms, capital and labor) that most efficiently will produce a desired level of output. In some cases a production recipe may even specify the precise proportions in which the elements must optimally be utilized.

The key here, of course, is the level of technology. What the standard production theory keeps in the background is what specifically the producer does with the inputs to generate the output. In other words, it connects inputs to outputs, but doesn't have a means of specifying the instructions—the process by which production happens.

Now, to be clear, in a world that's all about finding the right scale at which to undertake a well-known, more or less unchanging set of economic activities, leaving out the instruction from the recipe may not be a big deal. Say I own a pizza factory. I know what I can get paid to produce twelve-inch frozen cheese pizzas. I know what it costs me for flour, mozzarella cheese, and tomato sauce. The only thing left for me to figure out is how many ovens and other machines to buy and how many workers to hire. Then my problem is solved.

All of this is fine for the twentieth-century world of mass production driven by economies of scale—the world that economists developed the standard theory to describe. And even in the twentieth century, it does a good job of describing 99 percent of economic activity. But the 1 percent that matters most—entrepreneurship, invention, and innovation—it more or less leaves out altogether.

Very good cooks may be able to profit from their skill by, for example, charging for the meals that they prepare. (Ergo, restaurants.) Alternatively, they may painstakingly document their techniques so that others can duplicate their skill. (Ergo, recipes.) Yet, even when a recipe is well spelled out, dimensions of discretion that inevitably fall to the cook can lead to very different outcomes. As Joseph Schumpeter observed a century ago in *The Theory of Economic Development,*

The necessity of making decisions occurs in any work. No cobbler's apprentice can repair a shoe without making some resolutions and without deciding independently some question, however small.

In economic life, managers are cooks. Some are better, some are worse. Good ones can make money from their skill. Bad ones botch even the easiest recipes. Variance among managers makes it difficult to sort out, when assessing a project (as when eating a meal) whether any shortcomings experienced are due to a chef's lack of skill or due to the recipe employed.

The remarkable persistence of markets for cookbooks suggests that nourishment depends on much more than ensuring that existing recipes are properly prepared—as important as that can be. It also, and perhaps more fundamentally, depends on the creation of new recipes.

Or, to get past the metaphor, sustained prosperity depends on more than capable managers. It depends on more than blueprints, manuals, and franchises. It depends on more than projects with goals, targets, and timetables.

It is obviously the case that society can subsist without both culinary and economic innovators. Depending on one's approach to measuring human well-being, the sum total of organizational and technological advance since the time of the first writing—and the first recipes—has at some level been unnecessary. Arguably, we were fine in Bablyon. Antibiotics, air travel, and modern methods of agriculture may be delightful along some dimensions, but they have, each in their own way, also contributed to increasing humanity's vulnerability to climatic, viral, and ecological disasters.

Yet the fact of the matter is that six millennia following the advent of writing, humans have more options on the menu than just meat Assyrian style and Sumerian beer. Human progress—by which I mean sustained and *sustainable* prosperity—is fundamentally not about routines, but about novelty. It depends on invention in the face of change. It depends on creativity with limited resources. It depends on entrepreneurship.

"Blah, blah, blah," says the skeptic, with renewed vigor. "Talk is cheap. If you've got an improvement to the neoclassical model of production—which, by the way, has withstood three-quarters of a century of analytic scrutiny—why don't you (1) put it on paper, (2) send it to a peer-reviewed journal in economics, and (3) sit patiently in your office and wait to hear back? But don't try to snow people with your dime-store versions of economic theory."

Ouch. Well, to be honest, that is my reaction to most of the quasi-economics that circulates in popular discussions. And that's partly why I've spent much of the last fifteen years on a quixotic quest for a new and improved economic theory of production—one that would explicitly account for the instructions in a recipe, and not just the inputs and the outputs. Regrettably, that quest has (so far) not done much to change the contents of textbooks in economics. But it has resulted in some interesting discoveries, including some that have significant implications for the coming prosperity. Those discoveries are the topic of chapter 7.

7 THE WAY OF THE EMPTY HAND

Between the idea
And the reality
Between the motion
And the act
Falls the Shadow

—T. S. ELIOT, *"The Hollow Men"*

On the third night after Hurricane Katrina made landfall just south of New Orleans, Louisiana, Gov. Kathleen Babineaux Blanco arrived at the state's emergency center in Baton Rouge in a fury. "Does anybody in this building know anything about buses!" she called out. A serious situation was about to become calamitous. Citizens were stranded throughout the city, with no way to get out. Going into the disaster, a quarter of households did not have access to a car. To evacuate them was going to require other forms of transportation. But there weren't enough buses around to get them out.

The transportation shortage was felt particularly acutely in the city's nursing homes, where ambulatory evacuation was, in general, simply not an option. In the end, of the more than one thousand people who died during Katrina, over 150 were nursing-home residents. The multiple deaths that occurred in St. Rita's Nursing Home in St. Bernard Parish, east of New Orleans, prompted Louisiana Attorney General Charles Foti Jr. to charge its owners, Sal and Mabel Mangano, with negligent homicide. "They did not die of natural causes; they drowned," Foti told reporters at the time. "Thirty-four people drowned in a nursing home where they should have been evacuated." For their failure to evacuate the senior citizens under their care, the Manganos were faced with sentences of up to 175 years.

The after-action investigations that followed Katrina, in the context of the Manganos' trial and in other settings, detailed how the hurricane had exposed a fundamental flaw in the state's emergency-management guidelines for nursing homes. The state did require each nursing home to prepare an emergency plan; the state further required that the plan include both a signed contract with a bus company and a preset location to which residents would be taken in the event of a disaster. St. Rita's and other nursing homes that experienced disaster-related fatalities during the hurricane were in compliance with this requirement. Then why the breakdown? The reason was simple: The nursing homes' contracts were all with the same handful of bus companies operating in New Orleans. Once those few companies were out of buses—an inadequate number for the totality of commitments they had made—they could not honor their contracts. Thus, no evacuation.

In other words, this was a situation where the emergency plan was good for every potential scenario except for a real emergency. The special case not foreseen by the planners turned out to be the one for which planning was most needed.

Two years after they were first charged, the Manganos faced their day in court and were acquitted of all charges. Jurors ultimately attributed the deaths at St. Rita's to systemic, rather than personal, negligence. As one juror put it, "I went back and forth for sure, and when it came down to it, the Manganos were not criminals, but that's what they were being charged with."

At more or less the same time the Manganos were celebrating their freedom, I happened to be at a social event in Washington, DC, with a senior executive at Fannie Mae (the government-supported mortgage-lending giant) who offered a report from ground zero of the subprime mortgage crisis: "The paper just isn't moving." What that meant was that a different sort of hurricane was hitting the southern tip of the island of Manhattan—a locale better known as Wall Street. There financial wizards were being confronted with a direct analogue to the calamity that had befallen nursing-home owners in Katrina, though in this case it was mortgages, not senior citizens, who were being left stranded due to an inadequate evacuation plan. Instead of buses, it was buyers who failed to show up. Finely tuned to an era of stability, the financial system as a whole was set to function normally—as long as it actually functioned normally. Once the system didn't function normally, it came very close to not functioning at all.

In the aftermath of the collapse of the market for subprime mortgages in the late summer of 2007 and the financial crisis that followed in 2008, market analysts and policy makers expended a great deal of energy assessing the culpability of financial models. Was the market crash a consequence of mathematically rationalized groupthink? Was the trouble in the new risk-management techniques that gained widespread acceptance prior to the crash—notably the infamous value at risk, or VaR, models developed at J. P. Morgan in the 1990s? Did they have the perverse effect of making the financial system as a whole more vulnerable to extreme disruption? Testifying before Congress in 2008, longtime Federal Reserve Chairman Alan Greenspan argued that overreliance on data from a sustained era of macroeconomic calm and market exuberance—an era that Greenspan himself had been instrumental in engineering—contributed to the onset of the crisis:

> The whole intellectual edifice [supporting financial markets] collapsed in the summer of last year because the data input into risk-management models generally covered only the past two decades, a period of euphoria. Had instead the models been fitted more appropriately to historic periods of stress, capital requirements would have been much higher and the financial world would be in far better shape today, in my judgment.

In a world of complexity and uncertainty—the world we inhabit—a key determinant of the long-term viability of any entity is its ability to cope with the unexpected. Whether a single nursing home or an entire city, a single investment bank or the entire financial system, success depends both on ordered functioning under standard operating conditions and on the ability to adapt when faced with truly novel circumstances.

This idea turns out to be a very general and very powerful one—and even more so when we understand that adaptability includes alertness to opportunity as well as response to disaster. The advance of human societies fundamentally requires that they continuously attain a balance between order and adaptability. Entrepreneurs are vital to the attainment and maintenance of prosperity because they are, by definition, the ones who push back against incumbent interests and, in so doing, maintain that balance.

On the surface, the claim that prosperity depends on the attainment of a balance between order and adaptability may seem an innocuous one. It is anything but. For one thing, it implies that the ideological framing of the second half of the twentieth century—domestically, as organized labor versus big business, or globally, as central planning versus free markets—was a confusing distraction, as is the dichotomy between liberals and conservatives, that has lingered into the twenty-first century. What drove the trajectories of the industrialized countries since World War II was not the ideological tug-of-war between Left and Right, but rather the extent to which Soviet versus capitalist economic institutions succeeded in balancing order and adaptability.

How does this work? Let's go back to the story of the mid-twentieth century with which I opened this book. Innovations in the organization of production created a revolution in scale—the Industrial Revolution on steroids. The apotheosis of progress through scale was the Soviet Union, where from the mid-1950s to the 1960s, economic growth was dramatic. The launching of Sputnik in 1957 was a symbolic achievement when juxtaposed against the daily grind of Soviet production that made it possible, but nonetheless it was one that confirmed profound fears in the West that totalitarian efficiency was in the ascendancy. In response, Eisenhower initiated new programs of military research and development (R&D) so massive that, by the early 1960s, the US Department of Defense accounted for fully one-third of all R&D in the world.

By the end of the 1960s, however, the Soviet productivity miracle was starting to run into trouble. A young Harvard economist, Martin Weitzman (mentioned in the last chapter) documented in 1970 the structural flaws in the Soviet economy that were beginning to undermine its development. To identify sources of growth in the Soviet economy, Weitzman applied the techniques of aggregate production function estimation that Robert Solow used in his seminal studies of technical change in the US economy. The results were striking. In 1957, Solow had found that 87 percent of the growth in the US economy over the first half of the twentieth century was a residual. That is, the majority of US economic growth could not be accounted for as the natural outcome of simply having more people and machines to make stuff—in "econ speak," the accumulation of capital and labor. Solow attributed this growth residual to technological and organizational innovation. Studying the Soviet economy during the two decades from 1950 to 1969, Weitzman found that nearly all technical change could be explained by the accumulation of capital and labor; only 15 to 25 percent of growth could be attributed to technical change.

Why was this? For the Soviet economy, output growth through the 1950s and 1960s had been driven almost entirely by the absorption of surplus labor. In general, the mechanism for this type of economic growth is a simple one, illustrated by the story of the Zhang brothers, whom I described in chapter 3—simply giving underemployed workers the tools they need to be productive. Why is such a strategy for growth inherently limited? Imagine an economy comprised entirely of lawn-mowing services. At its starting point, there is one lawn mower for a hundred thousand people. However, for each new lawn mower produced, another worker is brought into the economy. Through this process of capital accumulation, people are rapidly paired up with equipment that dramatically raises their productivity. However, in this simple example, growth comes to a sudden halt once the last idle worker is paired with a lawn mower. At that point further improvements can only come with technical change and innovation. In the Soviet model, these were not forthcoming. Weitzman noted:

> There has always been a suspicion that Soviet emphasis on yearly, quarterly, and monthly plan fulfillment leads to a fear of uncertainty which has discouraged innovation at the local level. Does this mean that a greater degree of local autonomy on issues of innovation and risk taking would help increase the growth of the residual? . . . With their demonstrated commitment to rapid economic growth, the Soviet leaders may well continue their recent policy of hammering out those pragmatic organizational compromises considered necessary to secure future growth.

Like Schumpeter in *Capitalism, Socialism, and Democracy*, Weitzman was kind enough to allow that the Soviet planners understood that continued innovation would be required for growth. But the verdict of history is that they did not; such a fundamental change to the Soviet system was not forthcoming. The reality, as glimpsed by Weitzman and experienced daily by residents of the Eastern Bloc countries, was that disruptions caused by technical change and innovation were as toxic to Soviet planning as they had been to medieval European guilds four hundred years earlier. The evidence of such technical stagnation is seen readily in the Trabant and other artifacts of Soviet production that, once in the market, changed little, if at all, over several decades. The capability of Soviet scientists to generate world-class inventions was juxtaposed against the incapability of the Soviet economy to permit disruptive innovation. As a direct consequence, the Soviet system was, as early as 1970, headed slowly but inevitably toward collapse.

If the notion that sustained, and sustainable, development depends upon success in managing the trade-offs between order and adaptability sounds more like evolutionary biology than economics (as conventionally taught), that's because it is. After all, what permits the survival of a species: its genetic structure or its behavioral flexibility? The answer is, of course, both. Furthermore, the relative importance of genetic structure (that is, order) versus behavioral flexibility (that is, adaptability) depends on the environment. In entirely unchanging environments, organisms can afford to trade off some degree of adaptability for greater specialization to a particular environment. The magnificently bizarre creatures that inhabit the world's most inhospitable environments—extremophiles, as they are called—provide living illustrations. One such organism, the soft-shelled, single-celled protist called foraminifera, thrives on the ocean floor at depths of nearly seven miles, where the pressure is over a thousand times greater than it is at the surface. That arrangement seems to be working out pretty well for the foraminifera: fossil records indicate that they have been around for over five hundred million years. Adapted perfectly to their environment and undisturbed by change, the foraminifera can endure indefinitely where they are—but they would not survive for long anywhere else.

However, while the stable-niche strategy is a good one for a single-celled organism, it's not much use to human beings. After all, it has been about 1.5 million years since our first ancestors ventured beyond the Rift Valley in Kenya, and now we're a widely dispersed clan. So, where in the animal kingdom can humans seek edification on survival strategies that work? Yes, we would all like to soar like eagles, run like cheetahs, and see through the night like owls. But, when it comes to finding institutional arrangements to support prosperity, the ultimate example is the one stuck to the sole of our shoe: the ant.

Ants are social. They are organized. They are adaptable. And they are resilient. They thrive on every continent and in every environment, from apartments in midtown Manhattan to the rainforests of Irian Jaya. While a worker ant is one-millionth the size of a human, the total body mass of all ants on earth equals that of all human beings. Yet while we human beings have, so far, only managed to endure for roughly a hundred thousand human generations, ants have been around for ten million of their generations. Plenty of reason then to respect the ants.

But how have ants accomplished all this? The world's preeminent authority on myrmecology—the study of ants, of course!—is undoubtedly the famed biologist, Edward O. Wilson, who once said of ants: "Karl Marx was right, socialism works. It is just that he had the wrong species." The difference between humans and ants, according to Wilson, is in the extent to which people, unlike ants, act to advance their own interests rather than the interests of society as a whole: "The behavior of the individual social insect evolved with reference to what it contributes to the community, whereas the genetic fitness of a human being depends on how well it can individually use the society. We have become insect-like only by extreme contractual arrangements." I'll devote an entire chapter to the notion of interest—understood in its various meanings, including "acting out of self-interest," "earning interest in the market," and "that's very interesting." For the moment, however, what is of greatest interest is the precise manner in which ants—which, after all, are discrete living beings—accomplish their feat of collective intelligence.

When it comes to the precise mechanisms of coordination, it turns out that ants and humans have a lot in common. The reason that ants have been so amazingly successful, Wilson and coauthor Bert Hölldobler state in their 1994 book, *Journey to the Ants*, is quite simple: "Ants, like humans, succeed because they talk so well."

Ants are superlative communicators. The problem-solving strategies of ants are so effective that they inspired an electrical engineer and a social psychologist—James Kennedy and Russell Eberhart—to work together in the mid-1990s to develop techniques of particle swarm optimization (PSO) to solve particularly knotty problems. An early version of the program was intended "to graphically simulate the graceful but unpredictable choreography of a bird flock." To get close to the mark on this initial program was not difficult: the pair wrote a program in which each simulated bird mimicked the behavior of its neighbors. The result was adequate from the standpoint of coordinated movement, but disappointing from the standpoint of aesthetics: "Unfortunately, the flock quickly settled on a unanimous, unchanging direction." How did the team deal with this inadequacy? The authors added a variable they dubbed "craziness." At each step in the model, a completely random change was added to the movement of the flock. This adjustment "introduced enough variation into the system to give the simulation an interesting and 'lifelike' appearance, though of course the variation was wholly artificial."

Is ordered rule following plus a dose of craziness thus the secret formula guiding both the evolutionary success of ants and the ephemeral beauty of a flock of birds in flight? Close. To get to the heart of the matter, the best reference is a little-known but fundamentally important paper—itself also an inspiration to the developers of particle swarm optimization—by Mark Millonas, a brilliant physicist and occasional myrmecologist whom I met at the Santa Fe Institute in 1993 while I was a student at the Complex Systems Summer School there.

Millonas, an inspiring person who himself knew something about resilience and tenacity, having established himself as a world-class scholar in spite of chronic illness, distilled the behavior of ant and other swarm communities displaying collective intelligence into four principles.

First, members of the group must have some ability to assess and communicate quantitative costs and benefits involved in exploiting various opportunities—in the case of ants, distance to a particular food source, and thus the energy required to get there.

Second, members of the group must be able to compare and communicate qualitative characteristics of different opportunities—the quality of the food, and the safety of its location.

Third, members of the group should distribute their efforts, dividing resources "along many modes as insurance against a sudden change in any one of them due to environmental fluctuations. . . . A clearly ordered response to the environment, even if possible, may not even be desirable."

Finally, and most interestingly, members of the group should seek a balance between order and adaptability in their response to changes in the environment:

> When the rewards for changing a behavioral mode are likely to be worth the investment in energy, the group should be able to switch. The best response is likely to be a balance between complete order, and total chaos, and therefore, the level of randomness in the group is an important factor. Enough noise will allow a diverse response, while too much will destroy any cooperative behavior.

What Millonas found to be true of swarm behavior turns out to be true of many other complex systems. At the same time that Millonas was completing his draft on the principles of collective intelligence, Stuart Kauffman, a founding member of the Santa Fe Institute and one of the principal protagonists in the development of complexity theory, was similarly finding that organizations functioned best when poised at the cusp separating order from chaos.

Kauffman, an evolutionary biologist and early recipient of the MacArthur Fellowship (a.k.a. "genius grant"), constituted the decidedly chaotic but indisputably brilliant element in a collaboration also involving an imperturbable young Canadian named Bill Macready and a skilled programmer named Emily Dickinson. Together, this trio looked at how effectively an organization could solve a difficult computational problem depending on how it was structured. On one end of the spectrum, the organization was modeled as being entirely centralized, with no decision accepted unless it improved current performance for the organization as a whole; Kauffman and his team dubbed this the "ordered regime." On the other end of the spectrum, the organization was modeled as being entirely decentralized—an every-man-for-himself world in which decisions that benefited each smallest-scale operational unit within the organization were accepted if they benefited that unit alone, without consideration for the interests of the aggregate; the team dubbed this the "chaotic regime." What did they find in the end? "The best solution for the [organization], as for an ecosystem, is found at this point between the two extremes, poised in the transition between order and chaos," Kauffman summarized in a later paper. "By analogy, a hierarchical company with too much control at the top is likely to freeze too rigidly into poor compromise solutions. A company broken into too many small selfishly optimizing departments may churn chaotically."

Kauffman employed the term "edge of chaos" to describe the knife-edge balance between order and adaptability that an organization characteristically needs for sustained innovation and long-term survival. Millonas encapsulated the same concept within his principles of swarm behavior, which resulted in collective intelligence. Weitzman found expression for it within the language of neoclassical economics. In each of these cases the fundamental principle is the same: the basic challenge faced by any species, community, or organization is achieving the right balance between order and adaptability, given inherent variations in the environment and the near certainty of wholly unforeseen events.

However, when it comes to applying this insight to the dynamics of human societies, credit for the earliest and most incisive articulation goes to the great Austrian economist Joseph Schumpeter.

For a man who became the world's leading authority on societal disruption, J. A. Schumpeter could not have had a more stable family history. For over four centuries the Schumpeters had resided in, and dominated, the small Czech town of Triesch. For the four-year-old Joseph Schumpeter, this stability came to a sudden end in 1887, when the death of his father prompted his mother to move with him to the Austrian city of Graz. With his mother as his tireless promoter, Schumpeter ultimately received his education in the best schools of the Austro-Hungarian Empire—at that time, among the best anywhere.

From there, his ascent was more uncertain and halting than one might have expected given the eminence he ultimately achieved, a function of the tremendous upheavals of the times. After he finished his doctoral studies at the University of Vienna, a sequence of teaching appointments led ultimately to a faculty position at Harvard, fortuitously timed to remove him from Germany just before the rise of the Third Reich. It was at Harvard that Schumpeter built his reputation as one of the most expansive and incisive thinkers of his era; there he wrote what is regarded as his greatest work, *Capitalism, Socialism and Democracy*.

Schumpeter's career as an economist coincided with the birth of modern corporate capitalism. Schumpeter could directly observe the emergence of the world's first large-scale companies and the corresponding ascendance of the first great captains of industry (Carnegie, Thyssen, Ford, and other legends to-be). The advent of capitalism-at-scale induced major social and economic dislocations, but at the same time drove a tremendous increase in the availability of low-cost consumer products, substantially enhancing workers' quality of life. To describe the process by which new and innovative firms and industries displaced old and outmoded ones, Schumpeter coined the phrase "creative destruction."

The contrast between John Maynard Keynes and Schumpeter on this point could not be sharper. Their disagreement echoes loudly in the debates over economic policy today. To Keynes, as to Norbert Wiener (see chapter 1), technological unemployment was an affliction to be avoided if at all possible. To Schumpeter, the same phenomenon—the disruption of existing modes of business through linked processes of technological and organizational innovation—was the definitive dynamic of prosperity in a democratic society. What concerned Schumpeter in 1928 was not the alleged specter of transitory unemployment, but rather the potential vitiation of capitalism as large corporate entities moved, inexorably, toward managed stasis. What Keynes saw as society's ultimate bliss Schumpeter viewed as nothing else than rigor mortis.

To be clear—and this is important to what follows—Schumpeter had no antagonism toward big business. Among economists of the time, he was singularly insistent on the benefits of large-scale production for consumers and society in general. In the address he delivered as president of the American Economic Association in 1949, he chastised the profession for systematically failing to distinguish monopoly from big business: where the former could harm consumers by restricting output to increase prices, the latter had, in fact, generated most of the cost reductions that consumers had enjoyed over the prior century. That offending monopolies were also big businesses did not imply that the inverse was true.

Yet, for Schumpeter, capitalism contained within it a fundamental contradiction. The very power of economies of scale that allowed large firms to grow and that motivated the process of creative destruction also could allow some successful firms to render the process of innovation routine and thereby displace entrepreneurs. In his 1928 *Economic Journal* paper titled "The Instability of Capitalism," Schumpeter concludes:

> Capitalism, whilst economically stable, and even gaining in stability, creates, by rationalizing the human mind, a mentality and a style of life incompatible with its own fundamental conditions, motives, and social institution, and will be changed, although not by economic necessity and probably even at some sacrifice of economic welfare, into an order of things which it will be merely a matter of taste and terminology to call it Socialism or not.

Over a decade later, Schumpeter revisited this theme in *Capitalism, Socialism, and Democracy*:

> Since capitalist enterprise, by its very achievements, tends to automatize progress, we conclude that it tends to make itself superfluous—to break to pieces under the pressure of its own success. The perfectly bureaucratized giant industrial unit not only ousts the small or medium-sized firm and "expropriates" its owners, but in the end it also ousts the entrepreneur.

Given Schumpeter's finely tuned appreciation for the beneficial role played by entrepreneurs and his antipathy to planned economies, these two paragraphs represent an indisputably bleak vision of the future. The very success of capitalist economies in directing investment toward high-growth enterprises was, as he saw it, destined to create an economic savanna populated by lumbering elephants—which might easily be confused with dinosaurs. With the resources to fund innovation in large corporate resource labs, these corporate giants were in the process of stomping out the entrepreneurs whose capacity for "creating new combinations" was the true source of capitalist vitality.

"Hurricane Katrina provided many lessons for us to learn," former House Speaker Newt Gingrich offered in his 2006 testimony before Congress. "The most important lesson is that bureaucratic systems do not and cannot work. In Katrina we witnessed bureaucratic failure at every level: the city of New Orleans failed, the state government of Louisiana failed, and the government of the United States failed." Gingrich and others at the time contrasted the evident failures of the city of New Orleans, the state of Louisiana, and the Federal Emergency Management Agency in the immediate aftermath of Katrina with the widely reported effectiveness of Walmart's response to the disaster.

In arguing that Katrina taught us that "bureaucratic systems do not and cannot work," Gingrich was close enough to the truth to be persuasive, but not close enough to be correct. To be sure, Walmart's response to Katrina was exemplary. Even before the hurricane made landfall, Walmart had prepositioned supplies and initiated a response plan; as it rolled out over the coming days it ultimately involved delivering 2,500 truckloads of supplies. The $20 million that the company donated in needed goods in the course of the dis-aster set a new bar for corporate giving. The message that went out from Walmart CEO Lee Scott to employees in the area was simple: "A lot of you are going to have to make decisions above your level. Make the best decision that you can with the information that's available to you at the time, and, above all, do the right thing."

However, Walmart was not the only large-scale institution to distinguish itself during Katrina. Another organization to gain widespread recognition for its effective response was the Coast Guard—not a private corporation—which rescued more than 24,000 people in the two weeks after the storm. According to its own reports, immediately after the storm the Coast Guard mobilized a total of almost 5,300 personnel, 62 aircraft (a third of its entire air fleet), 30 cutters, and 111 small boats. The sheriff of St. Bernard Parish stated at the time that "the Coast Guard was the only federal agency to provide any significant assistance for a full week after the storm."

Furthermore, as we saw from the story of St. Rita's Nursing Home, with which I began this chapter, failures were not restricted to government. The private sector—in this case, nursing homes and private bus companies—failed magnificently as well.

So what were the actual lessons learned from the greatest domestic calamity experienced by the United States since World War II—and the only disaster in the last century to seriously jeopardize the future of a major American city? The lessons were clear, but they do not fit neatly into twentieth-century ideological bins.

What the Coast Guard and Walmart have in common that made them effective responders at the time of crisis is that both organizations deal with disasters of varying types and magnitudes on a daily basis. As economist Steven Horwitz noted in an essay written for the *Innovations* journal,

> Operating in a highly competitive environment on a global scale has forced Wal-Mart to improvise effectively in the face of constant competitive threats and routine environmental "surprises," such as shifts in seasonal demand that occur earlier or later than normal. This improvisation depends heavily on achieving the balance between operational scale and decentralized organizational structure that permits employees to use local knowledge effectively.

Walmart brought to bear its world-class logistics capability—a set of ordered practices developed through daily "learning by doing" over the span of more than three decades—but at the same time encouraged adaptability by entrusting decision making to individual store managers. Similarly, of the Coast Guard, Horwitz states:

> The Coast Guard's success depended critically on its everyday practice of providing lower-level personnel both the discretion and the information they need to improvise in response to particular situations. A single-minded focus on operational effectiveness at the Coast Guard has resulted in the evolution of an organizational structure that is, like Wal-Mart's, decentralized in time of crisis and responsive to local information.

The Coast Guard was able to deal with large-scale disaster not only because it had the resources to respond, but also and importantly because it possessed an adaptive capability born from responses to thousands of smaller-scale disasters.

Maurice Nizard, my grandfather on my mother's side, was the absolute definition of a curmudgeon. For the last thirty years of his life, after leaving his native Tunisia, he lived in a third-floor walk-up apartment just a block away from the Old Port in Marseille. He was suspicious, to the point of paranoia, about his many neighbors of Arab descent.

Though I had few opportunities to meet him during the time I was growing up, he did leave me with a bit of advice that stayed with me.

We were on an outing one afternoon and I was helping him carry some packages home. I managed to fill both my hands with bags. He threw a reproachful glance my way. "Always keep one hand free," he instructed me, "in case you have something else to carry."

Now, I admit, at the time I was underwhelmed by this bit of folk wisdom. What was the point of keeping one hand free if you never actually used it to carry anything? The inherent illogic bothered me.

But, like a pesky kōan, the advice stayed with me. When my grandfather died just a few months after this last afternoon I'd spent with him, it gained outsize significance—one of a handful of phrases culled imperfectly from recollections of a few encounters that substituted for those richer lessons obtainable only through a habit of a daily acquaintance.

The imperative of balancing order and adaptability is a universal one. It applies to personal affairs just as it does to business strategy and corporate policy. Whether packaged by a MacArthur genius as "managing at the edge of chaos" or offered up on a Marseille street corner as a homespun lesson from grandfather to grandson, the meaning is the same.

The empty hand is the gap between idea and reality, between motion and action. It is the cognitive space for the truly unexpected. It is the habit and practice of creative preparedness. It is the boundary between order and adaptability. And, when put into use, and yet at the same time kept empty, it is entrepreneurship.

Entrepreneurial adaptability was important to the development of human societies long before Hurricane Katrina, and long before the collapse of the Soviet Union. The most critical phase in the development of Western, market-based democracy occurred generations before those watershed events we most often associate with its origin—the United States' declaration of independence, for one, or the publication of Adam

Smith's *Wealth of Nations* (both of which, interestingly, occurred in the same year—1776). We take that nascent phase in the development of our own society for granted to such an extent that that we have all but forgotten it occurred.

That epoch, before Adam Smith, is the subject of the next chapter.

8 BEFORE ADAM SMITH

And it is fortunate for men to be in a situation in which, although
their passions may prompt them to be wicked (*méchants*), they
nevertheless have an interest in not being so.

—BARON DE MONTESQUIEU, *De l'esprit des lois*

One of the most fascinating attractions in Beijing is the Clock
Museum in the Forbidden City—the grand imperial palace at
the center of the city, immediately north of Tiananmen Square.
As its name suggests, the museum houses a collection of magnificent clocks that were gifts to the emperors of the Qing dynasty from European nations in the seventeenth and eighteenth
centuries. The clocks are a remarkable combination of technical
and aesthetic artistry. The most impressive among them is an
automaton built by Joseph Williamson of London and presented
in 1780 to Qianlong, the sixth Qing emperor. This robotic creation predates by two and a half centuries the work on cybernetics by Norbert Wiener, which is mentioned in chapter 1. The
lifelike robot writes beautifully fluid calligraphy with a brush
dipped in ink. With untiring perfection, the automaton com-
poses the characters for the usually auspicious but, in this context, somewhat haunting phrase, *wan shou wu jiang* (boundless
longevity).

Elsewhere in the Forbidden City are exhibits that display the
standard measures for commerce—official weights and
lengths—which were set by the emperor and held in the imperial palace. These artifacts are reminders of the fact that, in
dynastic China, the very nature of time was under imperial
control.

The first mechanical clocks, constructed under imperial
commission in the tenth and eleventh centuries, were designed
primarily to make astrological calculations. The fact that they

Automaton at the Clock Museum, Forbidden City, Beijing, China. The automaton was built by Joseph Williamson of London and presented in 1780 to Qianlong, the sixth Qing emperor. The phrase the automaton is composing is *wan shou wu jiang* (boundless longevity).

© *Eli Novin. Reprinted with permission.*

kept time was a secondary consideration. The reason for this was that in China, as in Europe during the millennium preceding the Renaissance, calendars—more like farmers' almanacs in terms of the richness of information they contained—were a direct reflection of the emperor's being in harmony with nature. At a time when the proper alignment of the stars had approximately the same significance that the proper alignment of data does today, failure to foresee major natural events was an indication of discord with the cosmic order. Therefore, calendrical calculations and astrological divination were essential instruments of what we would today call public policy.

The most celebrated among these earliest mechanical timekeeping devices—the third clock ever made—was two stories tall and built of wood and bronze by Su Sung, a diplomat and administrator turned scientist. Su Sung's clock was an imperial tool built on an imperial scale. A masterwork of craftsmanship and ingenuity, it nonetheless quickly fell into disuse; within fifty years of its construction, the clock no longer functioned. As it was essentially a technology of imperial control rather than commercial coordination, the secret (one might say the recipe) of its manufacture lay with the few individuals responsible for its design. When they died, the secret died with them.

In contrast, when mechanical clocks were invented independently in Europe two centuries later, they were used more for regulating commerce than for administrative purposes. Their production was therefore decentralized and, in today's language, responsive to market needs. Admittedly, the first medieval town clocks were employed to mark the hour for prayer, but their primary social function was to establish a commonly defined workday for laborers of different types, thereby creating a standard that facilitated the first labor-management negotiations. The word "clock" itself signifies a bell, from the French word *cloche*. As the brilliant economic historian David Landes observes in *Revolution in Time: Clocks and the Making of the Modern World*, "Something new had arrived on the scene. Seen . . . functionally, these timekeeping machines began as automated bells."

The clock bells originally coordinated activity in monasteries, which were the hub of medieval economic life, and then in villages and towns. When the Black Death created a sudden and dramatic scarcity of labor, workers had more leverage in labor negotiations. Employers, on the other hand, were interested in regularizing the workday. Mechanical clocks literally provided a mechanism for resolving the early labor-management conflicts that ensued. As Landes recounts,

> It was not the work bells as such, then, that were resented and mistrusted [by workers], but the people who controlled them; it is here that the chiming tower clock made its greatest contribution. It provided regular signals—at first on the hour, later on the halves or quarters—which necessarily limited opportunities for abuse.

Standardization of time at a very local level—that is, within earshot of the tower clock—inevitably led to attempts to standardize time in villages:

> As new clocks were built, discrepant time signals gave rise to new issues of discord: Why are we obliged to work earlier than they? Or to stay later? Perhaps it was with this kind of conflict in mind that Charles the V of France decreed in 1370 that all clocks in the city should be regulated on the one he was installing in his palace on the Île de la Cité.

As it turned out, these early clocks were not accurate or reliable enough to be synchronized effectively. However, the attempt reflects the fundamental role clocks played as standard-setting devices that supported the distribution of economic power and social development in medieval Europe.

As Europe advanced, so did Europe's clocks, which became progressively smaller and more intricate. When, in the eighteenth century, European monarchs sought to curry favor with China's emperors, clocks were the gift of choice. But these gifts were anything but the harmless toys that courtesans of the Forbidden City took them to be. By their very existence, portable mechanical clocks implicitly took the authority for setting time-keeping standards away from the emperor; soon thereafter, the insurgent technological and economic prowess of European democracies would bring an end to imperial power itself.

You've probably heard the one about the old fish who calls out to the young fish swimming by, "How's the water?" The young fish replies, "What's water?"

So it is with prosperity in market-based democracies. Old fish: "How's the capitalism?" Young fish: "What's capitalism?"

Now, regardless of what my kids think, I'm not a particularly old fish—at least not if "old" is defined in relationship to the development of modern institutions of market-based exchange and democracy. I refer to the institutions upon which we rely to achieve and maintain the vital balance between social order and adaptability that I discussed in the previous chapter. However, the perspective of the old fish regarding the institutional arrangements of market-based capitalism in which we are today immersed is at least partially accessible thanks to a brilliant book written forty years ago by famed Yale economist Albert O. Hirschman: *The Passions and the Interests: Political Arguments for Capitalism before Its Triumph.*

Long before Schumpeter, Keynes, Malthus, or even Adam Smith undertook their respective analyses of the nature of capitalism, multiple generations of political philosophers engaged in a spirited and thoughtful debate about the deep relationship between entrepreneurship and governance. The participants of that debate are the protagonists in *The Passions and the Interests.* Many are long forgotten, among them Giambattista Vico, Sir James Steuart, John Millar, and Bernard Mandeville. Others, such as

David Hume, the Baron de Montesquieu (Charles Louis de Secondat), and Francis Bacon, are mostly remembered for contributions to political philosophy other than those featured in Hirschman's book.

To set the stage, keep in mind that the era in question is not only remarkable for its rich history of ideas. It was also the historic point of origin for the current era of global prosperity. Yes, of course, humans had been exploring and inventing for centuries before the Renaissance in Europe. The famed Chinese Admiral Zheng He launched the age of exploration in the China Sea and the Indian Ocean nearly a century before Vasco da Gama first set sail. At that time, the Europeans were just getting over the effects of the Black Death, whereas the Arab world was making advances in science and technology that it would take centuries for Europe's scientists to match.

Clearly commerce, discovery, and invention are thoroughly global phenomena and not in any way subject to Western primacy. Consequently, whether or not the heroes of *The Passions and the Interests* can fairly be characterized as the intellectual architects of the world we currently inhabit is highly debatable. Nevertheless, it was in Europe that the particular institutional arrangements for entrepreneurial (rather than imperial) exploitation of inventions first emerged. Once the social scaffolding for market-based democracy was in place, mankind's attainments began to soar. The major developments were centered first in Europe, then in North America and Japan, and now are distributed globally.

To return to the metaphor with which I began, the current carrying humanity toward the coming prosperity thus flows from a source more than five centuries in the past. We can begin to appreciate the flow of history only after we fully grasp the existence of the water.

Hirschman's starting point is lust—or, more precisely, early medieval thinking about lust. Writing in the fifth century, Saint Augustine denounced lust for money, power, and sex as the three principal sins of fallen man. (Well, what do you expect a saint to say?) In a world thus corrupted by sin, Augustine concluded that the best that a sovereign can do is to use his overwhelming powers of coercion to keep the three lusts, or passions, in check.

While unambiguous in his condemnation of the passions, Augustine does leave a bit of an opening for redemption through one of them: the passion for power. Specifically, he praises the early Romans for their "civic virtue" as they succeeded in "suppressing the desire of wealth and many other vices for their own vice, mainly, the love of praise." Augustine's elevation of "the love of praise" reflected the characteristically medieval preoccupation with the human quest for honor and glory—a social obsession that endured for centuries.

By the seventeenth century, the ideals of honor and glory had at last started to lose their luster. Miguel de Cervantes (the Jon Stewart of his day) poignantly satirized medieval values in his masterwork, *Don Quixote*, in which the chivalric quest is retold as the story of a flawed, but deeply human, character—at once buffoon and hero—whose misadventures have entered the modern vernacular with the phrase "tilting at windmills."

Niccolò Machiavelli, Thomas Hobbes, and Benedict Spinoza, among other Renaissance and early Enlightenment philosophers, similarly insisted on considering human beings as they really are, and not as we would have them be. Where Saint Augustine endorsed coercive action by monarchs to keep in check the worst abuses of man (in this context, we really are talking mostly about men), Montesquieu and other Renaissance thinkers took the continued existence and potency of the passions as a given and focused their energies on the search for social arrangements that would repurpose the passions toward better ends—rational self-regulation, in a sense, rather than fanatical criminalization. Hirschman reminds us that it was Montesquieu who first formulated the idea of the "invisible hand"—a phrase later famously adopted by Adam Smith to describe the beneficial consequences of market exchange—to describe how the individual pursuit of glory constitutes "a force that makes men pursuing their private passions conspire unknowingly toward the public good." Vico, in *La scienza nuova* (*New Science*), wonderfully articulates this same principle:

> Out of ferocity, avarice, and ambition, the three vices which lead man astray, [society] makes national defense, commerce, and politics, and therefore causes the strength, the wealth, and the wisdom of the republics; out of these three great vices which would certainly destroy man on earth, society thus causes the civil happiness to emerge. This principle proves the existence of divine providence: through its intelligent laws the passions of men who are entirely occupied by the pursuit of their private utility are transformed into a civil order which permits men to live in human society.

In a book whose title, *The Fable of the Bees*, suggests interesting and mostly accurate parallels with my discussion in the previous chapter of swarm intelligence, Mandeville similarly discusses how "the Dextrous Management of the Skillful Politician" was required to convert "private vices" into "public benefits." In focusing on one particular vice—avarice—Mandeville set the stage for Smith, whose single-minded focus on economic interest as the rationalizing principle for society was to become synonymous with the invisible hand; the way to make people behave, according to Mandeville, was simply to ensure that it was in their economic interest to do so.

Redirecting the passions was not the only alternative to autocratic coercion considered by Renaissance thinkers. Another possibility was to array the primary passions against one another, the effect being to cancel out their most negative consequences. The notion of arraying passions against one another would later be reflected directly in the tripartite separation of powers set forth in the US Constitution, of which Alexander Hamilton wrote in the *Federalist Papers*, no. 51, "Ambition must be made to counteract ambition." It also inspired the provision that presidents should be permitted to seek reelection:

> An avaricious man, who might happen to fill the office, looking forward to a time when he must at all events yield up the emoluments he enjoyed, would feel a propensity, not easy to be resisted by such a man, to make the best use of the opportunity he enjoyed while it lasted, and might not scruple to have recourse to the most corrupt expedients to make the harvest as abundant as it was transitory. . . . His avarice might be a guard upon his avarice. . . . Add to this that the same man might be vain or ambitious, as well as avaricious. And if he could expect to prolong the honours by his good conduct, he might hesitate to sacrifice his appetite for them to his appetite for gain.

Hamilton conjectured that US presidents, if permitted to seek reelection, would be deterred from abusing their official power by their desire to avoid harming their reputations.

An essay on fanaticism by Luc de Clapiers, marquis de Vauvenargues, which dates from the same era, has a different take that is almost eerie in its contemporary resonance. Vauvenargues praises the "fanaticism of the patriot," because it alone can be deployed to counteract the fanaticism of the religious zealot. He writes, "Passions are opposed to passions and one can serve as a counterweight to another."

The ensuing decades have severely tested Enlightenment notions of self-regulation through an orchestrated balance among the passions. Two world wars and multiple incidents of genocide later, we hardly can claim as a success the Enlightenment project of designing societies to run like clockwork. Businessmen driven by lust for money, zealots driven by lust for power, and politicians driven by, well, all three medieval lusts, have, over the intervening centuries, proven fully capable of self-destruction— quite contrary to Enlightenment suppositions. In the United States, the tripartite balance of powers has appeared to settle into an intractable gridlock of incumbent political interests. Yet, underlying the undeniable turbulence of history and the epochal failures of human nature is a complex system that finds its true equilibrium in the balance between structure and search, order and adaptability.

As we have already seen, the genuine progress of society depends on the sustained courage of positive insurgents and the possibility for creative destruction that they represent. The project today is much the same as it was when Montesquieu first wrote about the invisible hand: repurposing the passions for the betterment of society. However, the means of doing this are now more apparent and the objective clearer. Human societies are not clocks needing to be tuned for endless repetition. They are, if anything, minds unto themselves. They—we—are learning.

Among the innovations that illustrate how the pursuit of private "interest" (in both relevant senses of the word) can and actually does move societies forward, perhaps none is more significant than the bill of exchange. To understand its role in the development of entrepreneurial capitalism, we need to go back further, to the seldom-considered historical era between the fall of the Roman Empire in the fifth century and the rise of Europe, which began in earnest in the twelfth century.

When the Roman Empire finally collapsed, at the end of a lengthy and tortuous process of degeneration, it took its institutions of money and credit with it. Centuries of economic depression, sharp deflation, and limited monetary circulation followed. In such conditions, even the simple channels of banking that had existed previously quickly atrophied. The credit that was available was offered on exploitative terms—what today we would term "loan-sharking." Unsurprisingly, given that the church controlled much of the capital during the Middle Ages, clerics were among the leaders in this trade. The practice of extortionate lending was curtailed, or at least made illicit, in 1049 when Pope Leo IX outlawed interest-bearing loans, declaring at the Council of Reims that "no cleric or layman should be a usurer." Only non-Christians were exempted, creating a social stigma around lending that carried forward to Elizabethan England, when the persona of the money-lending Jew was immortalized by Shakespeare in the character of Shylock.

The stranglehold on the availability of capital and the constraint on commerce which it represented began to ease at last when—not long after the declaration by Pope Leo IX—the first bills of exchange came into circulation. There is reason to believe that the two events were connected. The force of papal declaration reduced the role of the clergy in the provision of credit; in so doing, it created a space for entrepreneurial entry into this lucrative market.

What is a bill of exchange? Technically speaking, a bill of exchange is an order by one party (the drawer) to a second party (the drawee) to pay a third party (the payee). When the drawee is a bank, a bill of exchange is just a garden-variety check. The adoption of bills of exchange depended not only on the behavior of merchants, but also on the actions of medieval courts, which quickly came to uphold their validity in countries across Europe as well as in much of North Africa and the Middle East.

"What made the new banking different from the old," Robert Lopez, a pioneering scholar of medieval banking, has written, "was its shift from an agrarian to a commercial orientation and from an antagonistic to a collaborative attitude of borrowers and lenders." Bills of exchange were at the center of the new banking, not only because they enabled commerce to occur over long distances but also (and very importantly) because they created a loophole in the papal ban on interest-bearing loans. By careful design of their terms, bills of exchange were employed by the earliest merchant bankers as a way to extend short-term loans—fully legal despite the papal ban.

A division of labor in the banking industry ensued:

Three classes of credit agents were distinguishable: the pawnbrokers, the money changers and deposit banker, and the merchant bankers. The latter were the new elite of the profession, unprecedented in antiquity and in the early Middle Ages. Wealthy commercial and industrial entrepreneurs, uncrowned governors of their city-states, lenders to monarchs, relatives of popes, they were in no way embarrassed by canonical strictures. At the opposite level of the profession, the pawnbrokers were degraded successors of the early medieval usurers.

Today's investment bankers are not the only ones whose political reach seems above the law. According to Lopez, the roots of this seemingly very contemporary phenomenon reach centuries into the past.

The effect of bills of exchange went beyond the creation of a newly powerful commercial class. What mattered equally was that—in sharp contrast to the landed aristocracy—the nouveau-riche merchant bankers had the power to move their wealth from one place to another. The mobility of capital through trade and technology—via the use of bills of exchange—enforced new discipline on rulers, compelling them to account, for the interests of merchants as never before. In a chapter of *De l'esprit des lois* (*The Spirit of the Laws*) informatively titled "How Commerce Emerged in Europe from Barbarism," Montesquieu wrote revealingly of the impact the bill of exchange had on governance:

> Through [the bill of exchange,] commerce could elude violence, and maintain itself everywhere; for the richest trader had only invisible wealth which could be sent everywhere without leaving any trace. . . . In this manner we owe . . . to the avarice of rulers the establishment of a contrivance which somehow lifts commerce right out of their grip.

By allowing capital freedom of movement, even where physical freedom of movement remained constrained, bills of exchange permitted citizens to vote with their wealth if not with their feet. Invisible wealth activated the invisible hand—not the derivative Adam Smith version, but the original version articulated by Montesquieu—"a force that makes men pursuing their private passions conspire unknowingly toward the public good." Bills of exchange consequently represented the first step in a centuries-long, still-ongoing process by which the provision of trusted financial services devolved from family businesses to a global industry, and medieval trade routes developed into the globalized exchange economy of the twenty-first century.

A surprising reversal took place. Interest, which had been reviled in the deflationary Middle Ages, took on a decidedly positive meaning during the relative boom times of the Renaissance, into the Enlightenment period. To the moral philosophers observing these institutional developments as they occurred, the notion of interest was a conceptual innovation for a category of motivation that occupied a place between destructive passions and unreliable reason. In Hirschman's words, "Interest was seen to partake in effect of the better of each, as the passion of self-love upgraded and contained by reason, and as reason given direction and force by passion. The resulting hybrid form of human action was considered exempt from both the destructiveness of passion and the ineffectuality of reason."

Theories regarding the nature of capitalism from the late Renaissance and early Enlightenment envisioned that the pursuit of interest would have a supremely salutary effect on human behavior. In Montesquieu's words, which provide the title of Hirschman's book and the epigraph of this chapter, "It is fortunate for men to be in a situation in which, although their passions may prompt them to be wicked (*méchants*), they nevertheless have an interest in not being so."

The double meaning of interest provides an elegant hook for the connection between this early version of the notion of interest and its later articulations, which focus more narrowly on the beneficial impacts commerce can have on social functioning. Here Smith's famed invisible hand turns out to be only one articulation—and a relatively uninteresting one at that. Of much greater significance are the mechanisms by which trade and its partner, technology, enhance political freedom.

One of the reasons I focused most of chapter 4 on Afghanistan is that (to paraphrase a well-known song) if prosperity can make it there, it can make it anywhere. Afghanistan is not only poor and (these days) war-torn, but it is also mountainous and landlocked. When it comes to prospects for prosperity, that is as bad as it gets. Being born a citizen of a landlocked country has long been considered one of humanity's major misfortunes. This is because, until the arrival of the railroad, commerce almost invariably involved water. The world's oceans, seas, rivers, and canals were humanity's infrastructure of trade. Profit centered on ports, cities centered on profit, people centered on cities. People in mountainous, landlocked countries were disconnected, and disconnected people stay poor. Ergo, doom for Afghanistan, as for Rwanda, Nepal, and other such unfortunate nations.

Of course, to every rule there is an exception. For example, there is a mountainous, landlocked country in the middle of Europe that has done pretty well for itself—namely, Switzerland. By rights, Switzerland should be a sparsely populated and destitute place. Besides having no seaport, it has no natural resources of consequence. Its arable land is limited and mostly of poor quality. The Alps cover about three-fifths of the country. Trade routes through high mountain passes? Not if there's a better option. Although centrally situated on the European continent, Switzerland is an obvious crossroads only for ascetics and refugees.

And Switzerland was once poor, compared to its neighbors. It was a place noted for its goat herders and mercenaries, not its bankers and craftsmen. Yet the circumstances that made Switzerland poor also made it relatively free; the soil that was unfavorable to agriculture was also unfavorable to serfdom. In the fourteenth century, fellow Europeans viewed the freedom-loving Swiss with suspicion—if not outright fear, not unlike what we today reserve for the wily, mountain-dwelling Afghans. One folk song from the era warns of the dangerous example set by the Swiss cantons: "The peasants tried to learn /Evil tricks from the Swiss /And become their own lords."

So, how did the Swiss make the transition from a confederation of republics established by wild men to a bourgeois nation? The answer, you may not be surprised to learn, brings us back to clocks—or, more precisely, watches.

By the time the Swiss got into the watchmaking game, a small but rapidly growing industry centered in London and Paris was already established. The talent that made the Swiss watchmaking industry possible arrived there at the end of the sixteenth century, in the form of Huguenot craftsmen seeking refuge from religious persecution in France. Among them were master watchmakers who, following the model dominant else-where in Europe, established self-contained workshops in which all aspects of production took place. The puritanical Genevans in particular took to watchmaking with determination. As David Landes notes, "If Calvinists were not interested in time and its measurement, who was?"

Consumers elsewhere in Europe regarded the first Swiss watches much as Americans viewed Japanese cars in the 1970s—as products that were crude compared to those manufactured at the established production centers, but were also redemptively cheap and functional. Consequently, also like Japanese cars, the early Swiss watches found a market niche and sold well.

In Geneva, following the pattern prevalent in other industries, the successful watchmakers soon organized themselves into a guild. Their aim was to govern market entry and restrict competition among existing firms. As the city prospered further from the watch trade, incumbent producers successfully enacted laws that excluded both immigrants and women from employment in watchmaking and reserved work in the trade exclusively for *citoyens* (citizens) and bourgeois (burghers).

An interval of remarkable if concentrated prosperity for Geneva ensued. As the industry continued to develop, however, the city faced a challenge: with the watchmaking talent among the *citoyens* and bourgeois already fully employed, how could the watchmaking industry continue to grow without relaxing the restrictions on employment that had helped watchmakers earn their high incomes and elevated social standing? The solution, of course: outsource. (If you're starting to read "Geneva ca. 1650" as "USA ca. 1995," you're getting the subtext.) Rather than permit immigrants or women to be employed in the workshops of Geneva, the Swiss sent watchmaking work out to people living in the poor villages and towns in the Jura Mountains—inconsequential places, including one by the name of Neuchâtel. As Landes notes, "There [the work] found an extremely poor population squeezing a living from an infertile soil and compelled to rely more on livestock than cultivation."

The guilds held little sway in these mountain villages. Paying no mind to Genevan employment restrictions, therefore, producers in Neuchâtel and elsewhere in the Jura organized production around a model that suited their circumstances and predispositions. Rather than bringing workers together in a single workshop, they broke the work down into repetitive tasks, gaining production efficiencies that could best be attained by a division of labor.

Once the door of opportunity was opened to the shepherds of the Jura, they did not hesitate to rush through it. As Landes recounts,

> When watchmaking was introduced [in the Jura] in the early eighteenth century, it swept all else aside. It paid better than needlework, or than agriculture for that matter. It drew in all the members of the family except the very young and very old; and it called upon just those skills that centuries of isolation and self-reliance had fostered. . . . The subdivision of tasks made it possible for workers to acquire skill rapidly, while the familial character of this cottage industry meant that women and children were doing work that in Britain and France was reserved to highly trained journeymen.

Prosperity flowed uphill into this remote mountain region, turning snow-covered shacks in destitute villages into the chalets that are inextricably identified today with privilege.

The premise of this book is that we live in the most dynamic era in human history. The justification for this claim is that the benefits of four centuries of technological and organizational change are at last reaching a previously excluded global majority. My claim throughout the book is thus explicitly and unambiguously that (1) the technological and organizational changes that have taken place over the roughly four centuries covered by this chapter have been beneficial; and (2) the analogous changes happening elsewhere in the world will, in the next quarter century, have comparably beneficial effects.

In other words, on balance and in the long term, joining the global economy is a good thing.

There was in fact an era in the development of market-based democracies before the United Nations and the World Trade Organization, before Democrats and Republicans, before the US Constitution, and even before Adam Smith. Today that era is the daily reality in most of the world. One could say that most of the world is just now having its "Neuchâtel moment." Most of the world is just now having its battles of Lexington and Concord. Most of the world is just now getting in the game.

If you have any doubt how big a deal this is, think back to the Forbidden City. There, at the entrance to Tiananmen Square, Mao Zedong's portrait still hangs. But the Mao suits and other trappings of the Maoist era? They are nowhere to be found, having been swept aside by the global economy. And the emperors who presided over the Middle Kingdom for centuries from this palace among palaces: also gone. What remains? The gallery of clocks—an insurgency of delicately crafted Trojan horses—their work now done. Among them, Joseph Williamson's tireless automaton, who day-after-day crafts shape his ironic tribute to the Qing emperors: *wan shou wu jiang* (boundless longevity).

In a similar spirit, this chapter has been about how productive entrepreneurship shaped the institutions of democratic capitalism at their origin. The chapter that follows is about the end point of the same process: how the success of democratic capitalism, driven by productive entrepreneurship, might conceivably serve as its own epitaph.

9   WHAT'S GOOD FOR GM . . .

In a free enterprise, the community is not just another stakeholder in business, but is in fact the very purpose of its existence.

—JAMSETJI TATA

Chapter 1 of this book opened with a quote from Charles Erwin Wilson, a one time CEO of General Motors: "The price of progress is trouble, and I must be making a lot of progress." Originally, however, I had in mind starting with a different and much better-known quote attributed to Wilson: "What's good for GM is good for America."

On the surface, this quote seems to exemplify precisely the Industrial Age "old think" that I'm arguing has held back the United States and other free-market democracies as they have sought to make the leap into the twenty-first century. That's why I liked it. "What's good for GM is good for America" seems the ultimate expression of corporate arrogance—the belief that private fortunes are so inextricably tied to public ones that the difference between the two disappears. The interests of established incumbents come to define the national interest, which stymies entrepreneurship and stifles innovation.

All good so far. But, as I researched the context of Wilson's quote, I came across a curious fact: neither Wilson nor any other CEO of GM, for that matter, ever uttered the words, "What's good for GM is good for America."

What actually happened is this. In 1952, a newly elected President Dwight D. Eisenhower appointed Wilson (who was GM's CEO at the time) to the post of secretary of defense. During Wilson's confirmation hearings, senators questioned him pointedly about his holdings of GM stock. One senator asked Wilson directly if holding the stock did, or did not, constitute a conflict of interest. Referring to the senators as "you men," Wilson responded that he did not perceive any conflict of interest and offered the following elaboration: "For years I thought that what was good for our country was good for General Motors, and vice versa." (The senators were unconvinced: Wilson was ultimately compelled to sell his GM holdings before he assumed his new position, reportedly costing him $2.5 million—a high price to pay for doing public service.)

So, Wilson's famed quote is actually more about the reciprocity between private and national interests—along the lines of the statement above by Jamsetji Tata, founder of India's Tata Group—than it is about the primacy of incumbent advantage. Even more interestingly, Wilson himself was more of a loose cannon than a stuffed shirt. Here's a guy who, in the first seventeen weeks after his confirmation as defense secretary, fired forty thousand civilian employees. Over the three years he served as defense secretary, he cut the defense budget by $11 billion. In so doing, he may also have unwittingly contributed to the creation of Silicon Valley, since radio and electrical engineers in the Santa Clara Valley were suddenly compelled to look beyond defense department contracts for revenue and employment.

Wilson is not exactly the archetypical champion of bureaucratic interests that he is, by association, made out to be.

While Joseph Schumpeter keenly perceived the role of entrepreneurs in forcing the creative destruction of existing modes of economic activity, there is far more to his work than is conveyed by that single phrase; to sum up Schumpeter as the creative destruction guy is a bit like remembering Shakespeare as the "to be or not to be" dude. The localized phenomenon of creative destruction was, for Schumpeter, only one element of a much larger research program aimed at understanding how individual initiative generates global trends.

How did that larger research program turn out? On the surface, it was a bit of a bust. Schumpeter's attempts at grand theory never quite caught on with fellow economists. (There was not enough math in Schumpeter's theory, among other things.) What's more, the core prediction that followed from his most celebrated work—that capitalism, by its very success, would destroy its institutional framework and thereby invite the ascent of socialism—has, in a literal sense, turned out to be spectacularly wrong. Only with extreme historical myopia verging on outright ignorance can one characterize recent historical trends in developed economies—the focus of Schumpeter's analysis—as the triumph of socialism. Yet in the debris of Schumpeter's seemingly failed attempt at grand theory lie specific insights of enduring, if not increasing, relevance.

I already alluded, in chapter 7, to one of these: Schumpeter's description of how the very power of economies of scale that drove creative destruction through most of the twentieth century would allow successful firms first to gain monopolistic market advantage, and subsequently to repurpose their resources toward innovation. "Innovation itself is being reduced to routine," he observed with regret in *Capitalism, Socialism, and Democracy*. "Technological progress is increasingly becoming the business of teams of trained specialists who turn out what is required and make it work in predictable ways." The entrepreneurial process of creating new combinations that was, in his view, the heart of democratic capitalism was turning into just another corporate procedure. Instead of aspiring to build family dynasties (think Carnegie, Rockefeller, and Ford), rising entrepreneurs would henceforth have no higher objective than cashing their biweekly paychecks.

"In the end there is not so much difference as one might think between saying that the decay of capitalism is due to its success and saying that it is due to its failure," Schumpeter concluded. A process that begins with increasing prosperity terminates with the entrenchment of incumbents, the marginalization of entrepreneurs, and the end of innovation.

These dark predictions for the future of entrepreneurial capitalism are hardly implausible. According to a number of credible observers, they have in some form already come true.

In the spring of 2011, my George Mason University colleague Tyler Cowen published a widely read treatise titled *The Great Stagnation* arguing that the good ideas, that is to say, the best ideas, for moving human societies forward have already been discovered and put into practice. While the economic crisis, fiscal irresponsibility, and other transient factors may have contributed to the "Great Recession" in the United States, Cowen argues that the roots of America's economic slowdown are deeper: we have picked the "low-hanging fruit" of technological progress, and as a consequence, further economic advance will be slower and less dramatic than it was the past. If prosperity feeds at the banquet table of knowledge, then we're down to the leftovers. In Cowen's words,

> The American economy has enjoyed lots of low-hanging fruit since at least the seventeenth century, whether it be free land, lots of immigrant labor, or powerful new technologies. Yet during the last forty years, that low-hanging fruit started disappearing, and we started pretending it was still there. We have failed to recognize that we are at a technological plateau and the trees are more bare than we would like to think. That's it. That is what has gone wrong.

Cowen substantiates his claim with a carefully constructed fact-based argument, but his strongest points are still the intuitive ones. Think of a person born in the United States in 1891 or thereabouts (my paternal grandmother, for example) who looked out at the world on her sixtieth birthday, in 1951. The reality before her would have been almost wholly unimaginable at the time of her birth. Electric lights, the telephone, automobiles and airplanes, even flush toilets. All of these would have been either extremely rare or nonexistent in her childhood. But what of someone born in 1951 looking at the world today? Sure, we have cell phones and Facebook. The tools of medicine are quite a bit fancier. But, fundamentally, the architecture of modern life has not changed much. A US household today is only incrementally different from a US household sixty years ago. That, essentially, is the core point of *The Great Stagnation*.

Cowen goes on to note that most of the technologies that have defined the modern world—those that would have seemed marvelous to my grandmother on her sixtieth birthday—were first introduced at the end of the nineteenth century. Their impact on the economy peaked in the 1920s and 1930s. It was these technologies that drove the growth in both industry and government during the Industrial Age—the age of economies of scale that I described in chapter 1. The story of the social and economic changes wrought by these new technologies is, as I have argued, the economic subtext of the twentieth century.

Cowen is not alone in making this argument. Venture capitalist and entrepreneur Peter Thiel similarly received considerable attention for a fall 2011 piece in the *National Review* titled "The End of the Future." *New York Times* economics correspondent David Leonhardt echoed the themes in *The Great Stagnation* in an essay titled "The Depression: If Only Things Were That Good" that pointed to a surprising contrast between short-term and long-term trends at the time of the Great Depression:

> Underneath the misery of the Great Depression, the United States economy was quietly making enormous strides during the 1930s. Television and nylon stockings were invented. Refrigerators and washing machines turned into mass-market products. Railroads became faster and roads smoother and wider. As the economic historian Alexander J. Field has said, the 1930s constituted "the most technologically progressive decade of the century."
>
> Economists often distinguish between cyclical trends and secular trends—which is to say, between short-term fluctuations and long-term changes in the basic structure of the economy. No decade points to the difference quite like the 1930s: cyclically, the worst decade of the 20th century, and yet, secularly, one of the best.

All is well so far. But, haven't similar predictions of impending technological stagnation been made—and proved wrong—before? Yes, on a fairly regular basis. In fact, the last flurry of techno-pessimistic outpouring was in the in the 1920s and 1930s—exactly the time when, as Cowen and Leonhardt both accurately report, the great inventions responsible for past prosperity were peaking in terms of their aggregate impact. In chapter 1, I quoted John Maynard Keynes, who stated in 1928 that "it is common to hear people say that the epoch of enormous economic progress which characterized the nineteenth century is over; that the rapid improvement in the standard of living is now going to slow down." Similarly, here is Schumpeter himself, in a chapter titled "The Vanishing of Investment Opportunity," paraphrasing the view of his own techno-pessimistic contemporaries:

> Most of my fellow economists [feel that] we have been witnessing not merely a depression and a bad recovery, accentuated perhaps by anti-capitalist policies, but the symptoms of a permanent loss of vitality which must be expected to go on and to supply the dominating theme for the remaining movements of the capitalist

symphony; hence no inference as to the future can be drawn from the functioning of the capitalist engine and of its performance in the past.

This is about as succinct a summary as is possible of the arguments recently advanced by Cowen, Thiel, and Leonhardt.

Of course, the mere fact that arguments similar to those in *The Great Stagnation* have been advanced, and proven incorrect, in the past does not prove that contemporary versions are without merit. As I expect is evident both from my summary of Cowen's argument and my decision to feature it here, I am largely in agreement with at least one dimension of the core point he is making: that both scientific invention and market-based innovation are, in some sense, getting more difficult as time goes by.

Some years ago I organized a panel at a meeting held at the Kauffman Foundation in Kansas City (where I am currently affiliated) that focused on the relationship between technological complexity and the long-term future of innovation. Among the panelists who consented to participate was Ben Jones, a brilliant young economist recently graduated from the doctoral program at MIT. At the meeting, Jones summarized findings from two of his papers, "The Burden of Knowledge and the 'Death of the Renaissance Man': Is Innovation Getting Harder?" and "Age and Great Invention." These papers intrigued me because they offered a painstakingly argued validation of a conjecture I had been forming in my own mind at the time—that increases in the complexity of technology compelled scientists to specialize ever more narrowly in order to make significant advances, but at the same time they increased the returns to the difficult task of bridging disciplines to create fundamentally new economic combinations.

Jones found that the average age at which great inventors arrived at their breakthroughs was about six years later for inventors working at the end of the twentieth century than for those working at the beginning of the twentieth century. This finding supports the notion that the "low-hanging fruit" of scientific discovery has been harvested by earlier generations; as a consequence, for any given scientist, future advance will be increasingly challenging. Young scientists can compensate for this increasing "knowledge burden," as Jones terms it, by specializing ever more narrowly within a disciplinary area of study. But, such specialization comes at a well-known cost: an intellectual narrowing that, in the limit, results in knowing everything about nothing and nothing about everything. It is due to precisely this dynamic that the phrase "it's academic" has sadly come to be synonymous with "it's irrelevant."

Yet, despite evident costs to society as a whole, such long-term trends cannot be easily shifted, much less reversed. The reality today remains much as Jones found it to be a decade ago: without increased specialization, scientific discovery slows or ceases; without teamwork and collaboration across disciplinary boundaries, technological innovation slows or ceases. If technological complexity increases more rapidly than the average human life span, these two observations combine to suggest a sort of fundamental limit on the human potential to generate technological advance.

Will it someday be impossible to live long enough to acquire the knowledge needed to make advances on prior knowledge? Will new learning come to an end?

No. An end to technological evolution is no more likely than an end to biological evolution. The underlying reason is the same in both cases: the nearly unbounded power of combinatorial possibilities—the topic that was the focus of chapter 7.

If the current generations of techno-pessimists fail to see the creation of new combinations at work today, it's simply because they either can't glimpse them from where they sit, or they're just not looking hard enough. Granted, the technologies that drove past prosperity in the United States—electric lights, the telephone, automobiles and airplanes, flush toilets—are today improving only incrementally in comparison with the past. But those very same technologies are only now reaching the majority of the world's population. The resultant productivity gains are massive and reverberating in an epic fashion on a global scale. That process is just beginning.

What's more, the infrastructure technologies that will define the nature of both business and government in the coming century are just now coming into use. Where twentieth-century technologies reshaped the world around economies of scale, twenty-first century technologies will shape the world once again, this time around economies of collaboration. For a new generation of innovators, overcoming complexity is the paramount challenge. As Martin Weitzman has astutely observed, "The ultimate limits to growth may lie not as much in our ability to generate new ideas, so much as in our ability to process an abundance of potentially new seed ideas into usable forms." Contemporary tools are, unsurprisingly, particularly well suited to contemporary challenges: assessing the effectiveness of new combinations, rather than generating new building blocks.

As to whether that process—sorting the good ideas from the bad in a complex world—will itself ultimately get so difficult that human progress will terminate altogether in the twenty-third or twenty-fourth centuries, well, from a present-day standpoint, it's academic.

So much for the techno-pessimists. But what of Schumpeter's more specific concern: Will the natural advance of technology lead to the displacement of the entrepreneurial function? Even worse, is it possible that an oligopolistic economic system could beat entrepreneurial capitalism at its own game?

Again, the affirmative argument is, on the surface, actually somewhat persuasive. The hook? South Korea.

Why South Korea? While it is true, as I asserted at the outset, that China has achieved humanity's most massive economic turnaround, South Korea's is the most dramatic. Among the world's economies, none has progressed further or more quickly than Korea. Only Taiwan compares. Per capita income in China is fifteen times today what it was in 1950; in Singapore and Japan, per capita income has increased by a factor of twelve over the same time period; globally, income per capita is about four times what it was in the middle of the twentieth century. The comparable number for Korea? Twenty-two—per capita income in Korea today is twenty-two times what it was just before the outbreak of the Korean War.

To have seen in a single lifetime the same magnitude of economic advance as has been experienced by a sixty-five-year-old South Korean, an American would have had to be born in 1820; an Englishman, in 1700. That's a lot of change in a single lifetime.

What is more, nearly every other country that has achieved dramatic economic success—Japan, Turkey, India, Singapore, and Brazil among them, with Taiwan again being the only exception—had advantages of either history or resource wealth, none of which were possessed by the

South Koreans. Further, the South Koreans have developed their economy while locked in a sixty-year-old war with their countrymen to the north.

How did they manage this astounding feat? Did a broad-based culture of entrepreneurship suddenly spring up after the Korean War, gradually distributing economic power and increasing political freedoms in the manner I outlined in the last chapter? Not exactly.

South Korea is said to be representative of a so-called Asian model of development (a misleading moniker, given the vastness and diversity of the Asian continent) based on government support of incumbent business, not entrepreneurial challenges to them. The success of this Asian model ostensibly poses a challenge to entrepreneurial capitalism.

What appears to have worked in Korea was pretty much the opposite of the sort of Schumpeterian creative destruction that I have been celebrating throughout this book. Instead of a positive insurgency of new enterprise, government and private industry collaborated closely to groom key sectors of the economy for competitive success. The regime of President Park Chung-Hee, who assumed office in 1961 in a military coup, was as repressive politically as it was farsighted in economic matters. It developed and implemented South Korea's successful economic strategy based on export-led growth. An early milestone in this process occurred on November 18, 1964, when Park's regime selected for government support 167 companies operating export business in light industries such as textiles, hair goods, and knitwear. The government picked these industries not because they were ones in which Korea had previously been internationally competitive, but rather because they were ones that could readily absorb surplus labor.

So, is entrepreneurial capitalism under siege from the East? Does the success of South Korea in particular—but also those other centrally directed Asian economies that accommodate incumbent interests—evidence that Schumpeter was right after all, and socialism is on the ascent? No again.

Think about how political influence works. In one possible version of this story, government is the institution in society that is responsible for advancing public welfare, and the political process is a competition to run the government. Political parties win the right to run the government by persuading citizens that they understand the public interest best and have the most effective plan for governing. Political influence means persuading the government that the plan of action you have in mind is good for society. Simple.

That's one approach to telling the story of political influence.

A different approach is to think of government as a legalized protection racket. Citizens pay taxes to the government, and in return the government keeps away competing gangs (governments of foreign countries, of course, and also organized criminals of various types that would compete with the government). "Bad" governments just take from the people and give little or nothing in return. "Good" governments realize that citizens will support them more reliably if they are, in turn, taken care of, so good governments provide services to citizens and seek to ensure that the society functions smoothly. Political influence runs in the opposite direction, persuading citizens that the action of government is actually making them better off.

The appeal of the second way of understanding government is that it has nothing to do with altruism (which exists, but is fickle) and everything to do with the logic of criminality (which is ubiquitous and reliable). After all, as Mancur Olson has noted, "Other things being equal, a criminal is better off in a rich society than in a poor society: there is more to steal." A government that is a sort of stationary bandit can, by this logic, have at least the same incentive to improve social well-being as an altruistic government. Democracy—because it involves human beings and not saints—is not exempt from this calculus of legalized criminality. As Olson puts it, "Democratic leaders are just as self-interested [as autocrats] and seek to win by opportunistically obtaining majority support."

Here's how Olson's logic helps explain the success of South Korea. According to the foregoing, the more a ruling majority represents the interests of incumbent elites—which, for simplicity, I'll call the "rich"— the greater its incentive to increase taxes in order to invest in projects that increase the well-being of society as a whole. On the other hand, that same ruling majority representing the rich will, by virtue of its disproportionate wealth, also systematically prefer to keep tax rates low, because high tax rates constitute a redistribution of wealth out of their own pockets and to the society at large. The balance between these two incentives—to support public investments that increase national wealth but to oppose redistributions whose cost they disproportionately bear—creates the possibility for a best-of-all-possible-worlds outcome in which a ruling majority representing the rich will, as Olson puts it, "provide the same amount of public goods that they would have provided had they instead had a totally benevolent concern for the efficiency of the society." This favorable outcome is, arguably, exactly what Korea experienced in the 1960s and 1970s.

What made this balance possible was the highly egalitarian nature of Korean society during this time period—a circumstance attributable not to some mysterious societal virtue, but rather to the simple fact that the country was in a truly desperate situation following a calamitous half century that included the Japanese occupation and twenty years of war. The gap between the rich and everyone else was small because, for all practical purposes, there were no rich; the task of pushing back against incumbent economic interests was easy because there was no economy.

These dire circumstances were compounded by the South Korean people's location at the end of a peninsula, bounded to the north by a hostile enemy and to the east by a former occupying power. Unity of purpose was not simply a matter of shared ethnicity; it was a matter of survival. This was one factor vital to the economic success that followed; another was Korea's Confucian tradition of bureaucratic administration, which proved a significant asset. In an insightful paper published in 1995, Dani Rodrik, Gene Grossman, and Victor Norman summarized the conditions that were necessary for a favorable outcome in South Korea:

> What was required was a competent, honest and efficient bureaucracy to administer the interventions, and a clear-sighted political leadership that consistently placed high priority on economic performance [along with] an exceptionally high degree of equality in income and wealth—wealth distribution played an important role in shaping the political landscape in both countries. This is probably the single most important reason why extensive government intervention could be carried out effectively.

These are highly significant observations. Among them, the third may be the most important: because South Korea had an exceptionally high degree of equality in income and wealth (for reasons just described), its political leaders could expect that the near-term sacrifice needed to develop the country's future economic potential would be shared fairly broadly. The gains in an economy dominated by oligopolies? They would be likely to be relatively concentrated among an emerging elite. In this way, the narrow interests of leadership were aligned with long-term economic interests of the country as a whole.

This isn't to say that South Korea's bureaucratic administration was not more honest and efficient than that of other developing countries—as Rodrik and his coauthors assert. Nor it is to say that South Korea's leadership—political and business—may not have been driven by a notion of interests that went beyond economics. Both certainly may have been true. What matters for understanding is simply to place the interest-based horse before the behavioral cart.

That is not all. The above description of the conditions required for success in South Korea beg a further, important question: What of places where these conditions do not exist? What of places in which income and wealth are distributed unequally? What of places where bureaucracies are incompetent, dishonest, and/or inefficient? What of places with short-sighted political leadership that puts a high priority on perpetuating its own power?

Such places are not the exceptions. They are the regrettable rule.

In most of the world's persistently poor places, as a matter of fact, political leaders—autocratic or democratic, it doesn't matter which—have not actually needed citizens to pay taxes, or otherwise to participate in the functioning of government. That is, poor places are almost by definition places where wealth is not distributed among citizens. The country's wealth might be underground, in the form of gold, diamonds, oil, or natural gas. It might be in the fields, in the form of poppy grown for heroin production or other illicit commodities whose sale is only possible with the acquiescence of government. Or it might be in the form of international wire transfers—official development assistance sent from a government or international organization in a rich country to a government in a poor country. Whether the source of government revenue comes from extracting natural resources, trafficking in narcotics, or pleading for development aid, it has the same impact on governance: it undermines even a rudimentary incentive to invest in public goods. Once capital is mobile and the resources to govern come from external sources, citizens no longer matter. The rancher becomes a wolf and turns on his herd. "Instability is caused by the government and the Taliban," says the Afghan businessman I quoted in chapter 4. "They are the same."

The world's persistently poor places are likely to have remained poor because their governments are narrowly controlled by elites who systematically impede rather than facilitate development, and not because of inadequate policies to advance industrial development. The institutions of democracy, externally imposed, are not enough to guarantee escape from such a trap: the wealthy will game the system to avoid taxation, redistribution will trump investment, and the investments needed for future prosperity will not be made. Aid and the illusion of wealth created by the extraction of natural resources are not the solutions, either: whatever social value is created from the fraction of resources actually spent in the intended manner is likely to be outweighed by the inevitable distortions of governance that result from government access to external sources of revenue. Industrial policy is little better; in the absence of the particular conditions emphasized by Rodrik and his coauthors, the collusion of government and business will just enhance the power of incumbents and obstruct pathways to prosperity.

As my friend Iqbal Quadir has written with regard to the perverse impacts of aid (although his argument generalizes to resource- and narco-based distortions of governance),

> Aid empowers bureaucracies, promotes statism, and weakens government incentives to boost tax revenues through growth. Economic assets are often kept in the hands of the state, leading to monopolies, stagnation and extortion. All of this hurts entrepreneurs, who have the potential to create wealth and promote governmental accountability. The history of Western economic and political advancement illustrates that it is the economic strength of citizens—not governments—that gives rise to checks and balances.

There is a direct relationship between large-scale capital flight and the persistence of poverty, but it is not as simple as "money leaves poor places, and so they are poor." The fundamental issue concerns the relationship between the interests of ruling elites (political and economic) and the interests of society, considered broadly.

As for South Korea, the challenges of economic ascendency are gradually being replaced with those of economic maturity. The large conglomerates, known as *chaebols*, that have driven the country's success continue to prosper. Despite efforts at limiting their influence following the 1997 Asian economic crisis, the rule is still, "What's good for Hyundai (and Samsung, and Lotte, etc.) is good for Korea." But, as Schumpeter foresaw, the dominance of the *chaebols*—including their capacity for world-class innovation—has limited the scope for entrepreneurial initiative. Furthermore, a highly educated new generation is now looking to a future in which the availability of meaningful work may not be keeping pace with rising expectations. The very success of South Korea's past industrial policy thus implies that the country will, in time, face the same challenge of repurposing its capabilities that is the essence of the economic crisis in the United States today. It is no coincidence that the newest figure on South Korea's political scene is one who has taken a path to prominence outside of government ministries and the *chaebols*: Ahn Cheol-Soo, the entrepreneurial founder of the antivirus software company AhnLab.

Meanwhile, economic stagnation under the anachronistic and isolated communist regime that continues to hang on in North Korea has been almost as dramatic as progress in the globally connected South. The stark contrast between economic outcomes in North and South reinforces a point I have made throughout this book: that accounting of the coming prosperity must extend well beyond economics and encompass the manner in which the political order accommodates societal adaptability, or fails to do so.

As Mancur Olson accurately observed, "There is no way of explaining the extreme poverty of many nations without taking into account the extent to which they are misgoverned." In the long run, the neoclassical theory of growth is, to a point, correct: resources will flow to those places where unrealized productivity gains are greatest. But only if leaders do not act like bandits and refrain from impeding societal advance.

Leaving aside issues of historical authenticity, what then are we to make of the statement, "What's good for GM is good for America"? Is it justly pegged as the tagline for a lost era of American industrial dominance? Actually, this much-maligned phrase turns out to be a good slogan for America in the twenty-first century, but in a different way from what you might think. But before we get to the future, we need to spend a bit more time on the present—specifically, on what I mean exactly by "prosperity" and how entrepreneurship gets us there. That is what part 2 is about.

While entrepreneurship is usually identified with individual effort and rewards, prosperity is a team sport. And the players come from all over the place.

PARTICIPATORY PROSPERITY

The first and greatest error in thinking about entrepreneurship is that it is solely, even primarily, about economic profit. Rather, entrepreneurship is about creating value for other people. Similarly, authentic and enduring prosperity for societies is not about accumulating objects but rather about expanding opportunities for purposeful work and meaningful lives.

Whether for people, businesses, or countries, real prosperity is a participatory process of creating social value.

10 TIME TO BE WHAT MATTERS

It's kind of a recipe book for change.

—WIZARD FROM *WICKED* BY STEPHEN SCHWARTZ

In 1976 Dr. G. Venkataswamy (better known as Dr. V.), an ophthalmologist from the southern Indian city of Madurai, retired from his practice. He was young for retirement—only fifty-eight years old—but he didn't intend to stop working. He had a project in mind, and it had to do with cataracts.

Cataracts are deposits that build up on the lens of the eye and gradually impair vision. Globally, cataracts afflict people in wealthy places at about the same rate that they afflict people in poor places. The difference is that people in poor places generally don't have access to the half-day, outpatient surgical procedure universally available in wealthy countries that can remove cataracts when they become severe. As a consequence, for the majority of people on earth, the onset of cataracts leads to blindness.

Dr. V.'s ambition was to make high-quality cataract surgery available to all—not only the urban middle-class professionals who could afford to pay for the surgery, but also those with the smallest incomes living in the most isolated places. What's more, though he started out with an eleven-bed clinic in his house staffed by family and friends, he understood well the enormity of the challenge of eliminating needless blindness, and set out to come up with a system that would be its match. Having been to the United States, Dr. V. was inspired by the efficiency and standardization of American fast-food franchises. Was there a way to bring that model of efficiency and low-cost service provision to the cure of blindness? Could he create a McDonald's of cataract surgery?

Dr. V. set about to find the answer. Along the way he developed powerful partnerships with American organizations that understood, and had the capacities to support, his vision. These included the Lions Clubs International; the Seva Foundation, created by former Google.org executive director Larry Brilliant and his wife, Girija Brilliant; and, later, Project Impact, an organization founded by another MacArthur "genius grant" recipient, David Green. The result was a set of hospitals, clinics, and practices together known as the Aravind Eye Care System—an organization that, to date, has restored sight for more than three million people.

For a hardheaded analyst seeking to calculate the return on the investment in building the Aravind Eye Care System, how can we prove that Aravind is in fact the success story it pretends to be? Could not the resources spent on supporting Dr. V.'s venture have been better employed otherwise? To be sure, the Aravind Eye Care System has reached many people, but as a business it is uninspiring: after all, an average TGI Fridays restaurant in a US shopping mall may well do more business in dollar terms than an Aravind hospital. Aravind's direct contribution to the GDP of India is similarly paltry. Sure, it stands to reason that the three million Aravind patients who previously were blind, or headed toward blindness, and now can see are happier than they were in the past, but the analyst responsible for the impact assessment would be quick to point out that no reliable proof exists.

Yet the material fact remains: as the direct consequence of one man's retirement project, more than three million people who were blind, or would have been, can now see. To anyone whose own vision is not distorted, it is obvious that when human capabilities are enhanced in this way—when people attain capacities to function and possibilities for life that they did not previously possess—then no further measurement is required. The proof is in the people.

There's an inherent connection between the nature of prosperity and the discussion in chapter 8 regarding passions and interests. Not long after the Spanish conquistadors were famously sailing for "God, glory, and gold," European philosophers took up the question of how to limit the excess of monarchs driven by the three lusts (money, power, and sex). History amply illustrated that reason was a feeble weapon with which to oppose the lusts.

However, early social theorists conjectured that reason in the service of these three lusts—self-interest—might serve to stabilize rulers' behavior, and thus improve outcomes for the ruled.

Adam Smith's great innovation was to collapse the interests, representing the fundamental passions of man, onto the single dimension of economic interest. Notably, glory, which for centuries was exalted as the most elevated form of human ambition, was replaced with profit. The double meaning of the word "interest"—at once meaning both self-interest and income from an investment—underscored this shift. From the eighteenth century onward, the pecuniary motivations were imagined by political philosophers (and later, economists) as holding a place of primacy over other motivations. In the Middle Ages the accumulation of money was viewed as a base occupation, or at best a means to the end of glory, but by the nineteenth century it was accepted by social theorists as an end in itself. The mercantilist worldview follows directly from the elevation of economic interest. Trade is exalted because it represents the advancement of the interests of both parties involved—in contrast with banditry, which advances the interests only of the bandit, to the detriment of the victim.

By the eighteenth century, the central puzzle of political philosophy had shifted fully from that of controlling passions to that of assessing value. Of greatest concern was the difference between inherent value and market value. For example, why does water, which is essential for life, cost nothing, while diamonds, which are mere ornaments, are highly valued? The resolution to this problem turned out to be in the effects of scarcity: goods whose supply is low relative to demand will command a higher price than goods whose supply is abundant relative to demand.

Flash forward to the 1930s, in the midst of the Great Depression. Trade had collapsed, and along with it economic activity in every country in the world. Into the mayhem of the day emerged the larger-than-life figure of John Maynard Keynes—whose essay "Economic Possibilities for Our Grandchildren" I discussed in chapter 1—a uniquely gifted economic communicator who offered a compelling diagnosis of the ills of society, and with it an equally compelling prescription. Friend to poets and adviser to kings, Keynes identified a problem in the very absence of economic transactions. His solution, in a nutshell, was to create more transactions. If private parties weren't willing to create the transactions, then government should step in. The substance and composition of the transactions was less important than their aggregate magnitude. The concept of an economic stimulus was born.

In the process of quite literally writing the book on business cycles and how to escape from them, Keynes employed a then-novel approach to measuring economic growth at the level of a country that is dominant even today: the national income accounts. For the first time, economists could take the pulse of the economy—or, perhaps more aptly, its temperature. If the economy was overheating, Keynesian theories had a remedy; if it was cooling, they could use another more or less opposite remedy. Depending on technical specifics, the economy's temperature came to be known as the gross national product (GNP). The measures have been so powerful that over time they have become more famous than Keynes himself.

The GNP's dominance as a measure of societal advancement was accidental. Initially, it won almost by default. Other social scientists were a long way from developing the quantitative tools that might be required to assess economic outcomes. Only in the nascent field of macroeconomics was there, in the post–World War II world, the capacity and willingness to take on the challenge of keeping track of the health of an economy so policy makers could act accordingly. Its subsequent acceptance as the definite metric of national attainment reflected the almost universal belief in economic interest as a human motivator. By the 1950s, the glory days of the Middle Ages were long gone. National product was national purpose.

It wasn't until the 1960s that the shortcomings of GNP became evident. Echoing concerns that remain resonant even today, more than forty years later, Robert Kennedy in 1968 famously stated:

> Too much and for too long, we seemed to have surrendered personal excellence and community values in the mere accumulation of material things. Our Gross National Product, now, is over $800 billion dollars a year, but that Gross National Product—if we judge the United States of America by that—that Gross National Product counts air pollution and cigarette advertising, and ambulances to clear our highways of carnage. It counts special locks for our doors and the jails for the people who break them. It counts the destruction of the redwood and the loss of our natural wonder in chaotic sprawl.

It counts napalm and counts nuclear warheads and armored cars for the police to fight the riots in our cities. . . . Yet the Gross National Product does not allow for the health of our children, the quality of their education or the joy of their play. It does not include the beauty of our poetry or the strength of our marriages, the intelligence of our public debate or the integrity of our public officials. It measures neither our wit nor our courage, neither our wisdom nor our learning, neither our compassion nor our devotion to our country.

It measures everything in short, except that which makes life worthwhile. And it can tell us everything about America except why we are proud that we are Americans.

There was much more to Kennedy's remark than just rhetorical flourish. GNP—or, interchangeably in the context of my discussion here, the closely related alternative, gross domestic product (GDP)—is, in fact, a neutral statistic when it comes to the nature of economic exchange. A wedding adds to GDP, but so does a carton-per-week cigarette habit (and the treatment for lung cancer that will likely follow). The illegal harvest of old growth forest in a protected national forest counts in the same manner as expenditures on a reading and mathematics enrichment program.

In every one of these cases, transactions that take place between two parties on mutually agreed upon terms have impacts on third parties not directly involved. The third parties may be adversely impacted from the transaction in question (e.g., in the case of the sale of cigarettes, from secondhand smoke) or they may benefit (in the case of an educational enrichment program, which ultimately allows talent to be more affordable in the labor market). Economists refer to such effects, which are not explicitly priced in markets, as externalities, in reference to the fact that they create value external to the transaction. This is an important point, as much confusion arises from the term "externality." In no way are externalities understood to constitute effects outside of human society. Quite to the contrary: What is internal to the transaction is the interests of the parties directly involved; in contrast, the external effect *is* the social effect.

Now, to the extent that some transactions involve positive externalities, others involve negative externalities, and many involve none at all, one might rightly defend the use of GDP by arguing that these external effects cancel each other out. While GDP is not a good direct measure of human well-being, it might serve as a good proxy in many circumstances. That is the very argument that economists make in defense of the continued use of GDP: It's not perfect, but it's not bad.

In light of this fairly solid argument, the crux of the matter at the macroeconomic scale turns not on the inherent deficiencies of GDP as a measure of societal attainment (about which there is little disagreement) but rather on the availability of better alternatives. It was precisely the question of defining such improved alternatives—as well as an interest in complex systems to which I have already referred—that first drew me to the study of economics in the late 1980s. At that time, former World Bank chief economist Herman Daly was pioneering the creation of a new field of ecological economics, with a particular attention to the development of new measures of societal attainment that would better account for negative externalities. At about the same time, the United Nations Development Programme (UNDP) launched its Human Development Index (HDI), whose motivation I describe further below.

Today, alternatives to GDP—particularly the HDI—are widely consulted. The shortcomings of transactions-based measures of prosperity—most notably, GDP—have gone from being a narrow domain of academic research to a recurrent theme of popular discussion. In 2010, a blue-ribbon panel convened by French President Nicolas Sarkozy and led by Amartya Sen and fellow Nobel laureate Joseph Stiglitz issued a report that incisively examined the value and limits of GDP, and summarized alternative measures.

This further consideration of the difficult task of measuring societal attainment is important. But it is just the beginning of a much deeper and farther-reaching reexamination of the very concept of interest itself. As Keynes himself surmised, beyond a certain level of consumption, the allure of more begins to fade. Profit is no longer the same as purpose. Noneconomic interests begin to compete with economic return.

Glory makes a comeback.

Before we return to glory—particularly as it relates to entrepreneurial motivations—as well as the related concepts of social value and purpose that are integral to true prosperity, we first need to more precisely define the essence of private value derived directly from exchange.

Start with the most basic case in this category: Suppose I buy an ice cream cone at Ben & Jerry's for $3.50. As it happens, I was willing to pay up to $4.00 for the cone (I like ice cream); Ben & Jerry's spent only $3.00 to make the ice cream cone and bring it to market (including, of course, their time valued in terms of its next best economic use). I walk away with $0.50 of psychic benefit, forming the basis for what economists term "consumer surplus"; Ben & Jerry's walks away with $0.50 of profit, forming the basis for what economists term "producer surplus." The residual we each claim—the amount left over—is the lure that brings us to the market to exchange in the first place.

This is why markets exist: to create private value for both consumers and producers. Without it, markets quite simply have no reason to be. (Why should anyone take the trouble to trade if they don't get anything out of it?) The benefits derived from markets can be measured by adding up the producer and consumer surplus values. This is the reason why trade is considered to be socially valuable in the aggregate, and why transactions (a.k.a. GDP) are generally considered to be a plausible proxy for human well-being: The more exchange, the more value created.

To understand the meaning, and limitations, of this way of thinking about private value creation, let's return to story of the Aravind Eye Hospital with which I opened this chapter. Its product is the restoration of sight. Its customers are the blind, many of them desperately poor. With the benefit of an operation that is as universally available to inhabitants of the global North as it is inaccessible to inhabitants of the South, victims of cataract-induced blindness are made able to see. The challenge that faced Dr. V. was to reduce the cost of the procedure, and otherwise innovate to increase its availability. That Aravind offers its cataract-removal procedures to its poorest patients for free is only one side of the equation—and the less interesting one at that. Many goods are offered for little or nothing; most are worth not much more. What makes Aravind distinct is that the value to the patients of the service provided—the restoration of sight—is so great. What is of significance, in other words, is the difference between price and private valuation: the consumer surplus.

But there is a catch. Strictly speaking, consumer surplus is defined in terms of an individual's willingness to pay for a particular good. Yet, as is obvious, willingness to pay is a function of income. Someone making $1 per day, with few if any assets, can't pay more than the entirety of their income, plus whatever they are able to borrow with little or no collateral. From a human standpoint, we know that the ability to see is more valuable than an ice cream cone, even if they may be priced comparably. Is the field of economics so ethically bankrupt that it is unable to account for such an evident difference? Clearly, there is more to the story.

For most of the nineteenth century and part of the twentieth, economists saw themselves as moral philosophers, as qualified to comment on the equity of societal processes as their efficiency. That tradition came to an end rather abruptly in 1939, when J. R. Hicks published his classic *Value and Capital*, a work which, as the title suggests, took the creation of value as a starting point for fundamental theoretical synthesis.

Until the work of Hicks and his contemporaries (following on that of turn-of-the-century pioneers such as Alfred Marshall), economists explicitly or implicitly assumed that value for individuals—in the parlance of the discipline, "utility"—was as readily subject to quantitative measurement as height or weight. Economists from Jeremy Bentham onward had to that point taken as given that the objective of government was to increase the utility of all citizens, and that the utilities of different people could be directly, and objectively, compared. Without fear of ridicule, nineteenth-century economists could make the case that taking a dollar from a very wealthy man and giving it to a very poor one would likely lead to a net increase in social welfare, as the poor man would value the dollar more than the rich one had.

Hicks took exception to the passive consensus of a prior generation. At a time when ideological excesses were becoming the norm (fascism and communism being the limiting cases), Hicks and his colleagues at Cambridge were intent on reestablishing the field of economics upon firm scientific foundations, immune to whim or rhetoric. The project was a noble one which Hicks approached with seriousness of purpose. "We have now to undertake a purge," Hicks opened his masterwork, "rejecting all concepts which are tainted by quantitative utility, and replacing them, so far as they need to be replaced, with concepts which have no such implication." Hicks asserted forcefully that the field of economics should be based not upon the fantasy of objectively measurable happiness, but rather on subjective judgments of value as revealed through market transactions. The logic was, and is, impeccable: you can't see how someone feels, but you can see what they do. The change in the discipline of economics was profound and enduring. Since utility was immeasurable, interpersonal comparisons of well-being were out of bounds. The license previously given to economists to refer to themselves as moral philosophers was abruptly revoked.

Such was the state of the formal study of social welfare in economics until another of the great social scientists of the past century, Amartya Sen, set about to recover the metaphorical baby that Hicks and his colleagues had thrown out with the bathwater. While Sen's work is vast and nuanced, it is fair to say that one of his central contributions is establishing the theoretical basis for making interpersonal comparisons of well-being. The key was to focus not on commodities (and willingness to pay) as in the conventional model but rather on capabilities (and willingness to live).

For an economist (well, for this economist anyway), being in the presence of Amartya Sen is what meeting Vladimir Horowitz must have been for a pianist in a prior era—or perhaps most fittingly, for a Buddhist today to meet the Dalai Lama. A slight man with an erudite manner and an engaging smile, Sen in person projects a capacity for reasoning as deep as Lake Baikal. In 1998 Sen was awarded the Bank of Sweden Prize (a.k.a. Nobel) in economics for his work on social choice, a highly technical yet fundamentally significant field that can be summarized as the study of the decision-making processes by which societies are able to define shared purpose. In the course of a long career as a scholar and public intellectual, Sen has been a singular force whose efforts have done nothing less than to reintroduce empathy into the formal study of human societies.

At the center of Sen's work is the notion of capabilities (and its inverse, deprivation). Capabilities are just what they sound like—what people can do. Seeing. Walking. Talking. Thinking. Connecting. Capabilities are measurable. So is deprivation—the restriction of capabilities.

The basis of Sen's approach is to place the focus of prosperity on the capabilities and functionings of people, rather than on flows of goods and services disassociated from people (GDP) or on happiness disassociated from material circumstances (utility). The notion of capabilities broadens the scope of information on which determinations of social value can be based, suggesting potential metrics for value creation that go beyond dollar-denominated consumer surplus and producer surplus. To capture the fundamentals of human capabilities, and their relative attainment in different countries, Sen worked with the UNDP to construct the human development indicators. Now in their twenty-first year of publication, the HDI are perhaps the best-established, and most credible, alternative to GDP in assessing societal outcomes.

After a point, there is no making "cents" of enterprises that endeavor to restore eyesight, to end torture, or (as we'll see below) to cure neglected diseases. The restoration of sight is the restoration of a basic human capability in a way that the sale of an ice cream cone simply is not.

India's Tata Group is a $65-billion-a-year multinational corporation. It recently purchased the venerated British automaker Jaguar, but also produces the world's least expensive car (selling for approximately $2,500), dubbed the "one-lakh car." It is almost impossible to visit India and not to be aware of Tata Group's presence. It includes not only the industrial entities, but also a stunning array of public service institutions, including the Tata Cancer Hospitals, Tata Institute of Social Sciences, Tata Trusts, and the Indian Institute of Science in Bangalore. (Founded by Jamsetji Tata, the Indian Institute of Science is one of India's top technical universities. It was a major contributor to Bangalore's emergence as a global hub of information technology services, which in turn has been a significant factor in India's impressive economic resurgence over the past two decades.)

The founder of the Tata Group, Jamsetji Tata, was one of the world's first and most successful social entrepreneurs—an entrepreneur explicitly focused on creating social, as well as private, value. Nearly a century before anyone uttered the now-fashionable term "corporate social responsibility," Tata built a business empire that defined its mission as creating both profits and social value. I opened the last chapter with the following quote of Tata's: "In a free enterprise, the community is not just another stakeholder in business, but is in fact the very purpose of its existence." The contributions of the Tata Group to India's development were so evident even a century ago that they motivated Alfred Marshall, the great British economist to whom I referred in the previous chapter, to write in 1910 that "a score of Tatas might do more for India than any government, British or indigenous, can accomplish."

More than an illustration, the Tata story is an allegory. Entrepreneurial value creation and corporate value creation are not two different stories. They are, instead, distinct chapters of the same story: the social entrepreneur became a global purpose-built organization. The activities of the Tata Group and similar enterprises around the world (Cadbury and the Body Shop in the United Kingdom, and Ben & Jerry's and Patagonia in the United States, among many others) would not have been possible without the ability to provide the original paying customers with a desired service.

This brings us to the first and biggest error in conventional thinking about entrepreneurship: that entrepreneurship is solely, even primarily, about economic profit—in the Spanish triumvirate of motivations, gold. Spend time with any successful entrepreneur (we all know at least a few) and it quickly becomes evident that economic interest is only part of the equation. Many other motivations are also in play, not the least of which is the desire for recognition—in medieval parlance, glory.

Fundamentally, to be an entrepreneur is to be the person who walks away with, or (alternatively and importantly) is liable for, whatever is left over when the accounting is done—plus or minus. In economics, the person responsible for what is left over in a venture is known as the "residual claimant." This definition is key, because it helps to differentiate entrepreneurs from the many other people in society who create value in various ways. The mark of an entrepreneur is that he/she creates value by establishing a new venture, and that he/she receives whatever private benefit the venture generates that does not go to consumers, workers, or other suppliers.

However—and this is really the critical point, so often missed—to assert (correctly) that all entrepreneurship reduces to claiming the residual from a transaction does not in any way imply that all residuals are financial. In fact, the residual can take many other, nonfinancial forms. Among these, as noted above, reputation is perhaps the most important. For example, microlending pioneer Muhamad Yunus (recipient of the Nobel Peace Prize in 2006), may have been able to claim truthfully that he never received a dividend from Grameen Bank, which he founded in 1983. However, there is no doubt that he personally claimed a significant share of the reputational residual—glory—that the venture created. An institution of such a scale is not built by a single individual; yet it is a single individual, the entrepreneur, with whom the success or failure of the institution is most closely associated. In this regard Yunus is not different from John D. Rockefeller, Bill Gates, or Steve Jobs. Personal reputation—like a brand for a corporation—is a valuable privately held asset.

Another significant category of residual derives from a sense of meaning—a sense of ethical reward, or, for the conquistadors, God. The human desire for meaning, and the existence of an "ethical residual" in entrepreneurship it implies, is precisely what makes it possible for products that have a clear and persuasive value-based branding to be priced at a premium. Recognizing this, purpose-built organizations such as those listed above expend considerable resources to communicate to consumers their nonfinancial corporate goals. Similarly, the existence of such ethical residuals allows white-hat organizations such as the Sierra Club to pay less for legal talent than law firms whose client lists are dominated by tobacco or oil companies. Ethical residuals can also be tangible assets: charitable institutions such as the American Red Cross and Greenpeace have built sustainable business models based entirely upon the creation, and reinvestment, of the ethical residuals that motivate charitable giving, and that over time are capitalized in strong and enduring brands. Such price differentials are market reflections of human values. To note their existence is neither to affirm nor to place in question the values themselves; it is simply to recognize a fundamental and pervasive economic reality.

While it is possible to conceive of other categories, it is also fair to say that if an ostensibly entrepreneurial venture has no prospect of either earning a profit, building the entrepreneur's reputation, or creating meaning, it is in fact not much of an entrepreneurial venture.

It was the year 2000 and Victoria Hale was in an enviable position. At the age of forty she was a senior executive in a pharmaceutical company, earning a solid six-figure income helping to bring new drugs to market. Her path toward future career advancement was clear. That was until a simple exchange with a cabdriver prompted her to repurpose her abilities.

Making small talk as he drove Hale to one of the many industry conferences she attended, the cabdriver asked what business she was in. She answered that she worked for a pharmaceutical company. The driver laughed and shook his head. "You guys have all the money," he said finally.

Hale did not immediately know how to respond. Sure, the pharmaceutical industry was profitable, but were she and her colleagues not also on the forefront of an admirable effort to improve and extend the lives of people everywhere? The more she reflected, however, the more uneasy she became. For all the good that came from the efforts of Big Pharma, as the world's leading pharmaceutical companies have come to be known, Hale came to the conclusion that their beneficial impact was fundamentally limited by the industry's dominant business model. While the particulars of decision making in pharmaceutical industries are devilishly complicated, the basic equation is simple: no half-billion-dollar market, no product. Hale recognized that this simple decision rule meant that, to Big Pharma, the illnesses suffered by the majority of the world's population were, for all practical purposes, irrelevant.

So Victoria Hale quit her job. What she needed to do, she decided, was not just to create a new company on the same model. To realize the potential she glimpsed to create therapeutics for the many diseases neglected by Big Pharma, she would need to prototype an entirely new approach to developing drugs and bringing them to market in poor places.

Hale founded the Institute for OneWorld Health, a nonprofit pharmaceutical company—one without labs, and without the capacity to perform clinical trials. To make the institute work, Hale took advantage of a loophole of sorts in Big Pharma's business model. Because the bar to bring therapeutics to market is so high, many promising treatments don't make the cut. Others, formerly in production, are discontinued. These orphan drugs are treatments that have been proven to be both safe and effective, but that sit on the shelf in pharmaceutical companies because their market potential doesn't meet industry minimums. Among such orphan drugs, many have the potential to be effective treatments for neglected diseases.

The path for Hale was clear: match orphan drugs to neglected diseases and get effective treatments to people who need them most. Of course, taking her idea forward was not so easy. But with perseverance, good fortune, and the ability to create trust and build partnerships, the Institute for OneWorld Health succeeded in prototyping a new approach to developing therapeutics. Its first drug, a treatment for a deadly ailment known as ka-la-azar (black fever) that afflicts millions of the world's poorest in South

Asia, Sudan, and Brazil, was approved for use in 2006; it was later distributed by the Government of India and included on the World Health Organization's *Model List of Essential Medicines.*

Much has been made in recent years of the advent of the triple-bottom-line corporation: businesses commit, either formally or informally, to making decisions based not only on the traditional bottom line of economic profit but also the bottom line with regard to impacts of their actions on society and impacts on the environment. This is a real and significant trend. Among the factors that have driven corporations to think in terms of triple bottom lines is an increasing awareness—supported by analytics—that attention to external impacts and longer time frames can lead companies to adopt policies and procedures that actually enhance, rather than detract from, short-term operational effectiveness.

A parallel, but distinct, triple bottom line applies to entrepreneurial motivations. Once, risk takers undertook perilous voyages in the name of "God, glory, and gold." Today, entrepreneurs like Victoria Hale seek meaning, reputation, and profit. Methods have changed in addition to the words. In their role as modern-day conquistadors, entrepreneurs attack societal challenges, not other people. The contagion for which they are responsible is one of ideas and inspiration, not disease. If a form of intolerance motivates them, it is the universal intolerance of waste—waste of human talent, waste of resources, or simple waste of time—that has motivated innovators for millennia.

As I stated in the introduction, without purpose, there is no progress. It's time to be what matters.

The common thread is this: while the search for economic profit can be a tremendous motivator of beneficial social change, it is not the totality of human interest. In the world's wealthiest places as well as the poorest, some of the most remarkable entrepreneurs and innovators will always be those who think less of how they will benefit, and more about what they will change. The efforts of such individuals to push back against entrenched incumbent interests is an essential element of the coming prosperity.

As I'll discuss further toward the end of the book, the same principle holds for nations. Technique has no allegiance. However, as the story of the Tata Group illustrates, meaning does stick. In the twentieth century, growth was an adequate goal for national policy. No longer.

Along similar lines, the ties borne of national purpose are increasingly transcending national boundaries. In Shenzhen, China, which I mentioned in chapter 3, the government has built a twenty-story building to house "sea turtles"—emigrants seeking to renew their ties to their home country. Elsewhere the same trend is occurring: Where emigrants have for decades supported their families with financial remittances drawn from their income, in the next generation diasporic communities will increasingly contribute to the coming prosperity through knowledge remittances—the investment of ideas and energy to build the future. That trend is the subject of the next chapter.

For Americans and for Europeans, understanding this trend creates a powerful pathway for personal action. Every one of us—whether or not we are first- or second-generation immigrants with active personal ties to and affinities for our countries of origin—can connect with opportunities abundant elsewhere by making the most of our existing relationships and of the potential for new connections that is all around us. Your college professor—from Iran? Not just a teacher. The guy who paints your house—from Tibet? Not just a contractor. These and other members of the global diaspora that you know are your valued contacts. They may be your future partners.

When it comes to the coming prosperity, they are our collaborative advantage.

11 COLLABORATIVE ADVANTAGE

Our revolution is like Wikipedia, okay? Everyone is contributing content, [but] you don't know the names of the people contributing the content. This is exactly what happened. Revolution 2.0 in Egypt was exactly the same. Everyone contributing small pieces, bits and pieces. We drew this whole picture of a revolution. And no one is the hero in that picture.

—WAEL GHONIM

In 1975, at the invitation of a family friend, Ibrahim Abouleish took a trip to Egypt with his wife, Gudrun, and his two children, Helmy and Mona.

The Abouleish family had been to Egypt before, on multiple occasions, to visit family. Ibrahim Abouleish was born in Egypt in 1937. He left for Austria at age nineteen to study chemistry. Successful in his studies, he stayed on first to earn a PhD in pharmacology, and then settled permanently to take positions of responsibility in leading Austrian pharmaceutical companies.

This trip was different from previous ones the family had taken. Joined for the first time by a friend from Austria, the Abouleishes toured widely and saw the country through new eyes. The experience was a particularly unsettling one for Ibrahim:

I became aware of the changes that had befallen the country during my time in Austria, and saddened by the stark contrast between the depressed state of modern Egypt and the greatness, wisdom, and leadership the pharaohs showed thousands of years ago. I kept comparing what I saw with my memory of the country during my childhood and adolescence. The new should have been better than the old, but it was not.

The country's decline was particularly evident in agriculture, from which the people of Egypt had for millennia derived their sustenance and cultural identity. The practice of applying fertilizer, encouraged by the state to the point of compulsion, led to depleted soils and a dependency of farmers on chemical companies. Inheritance laws had resulted in an untenable fragmentation of agricultural plots. The environmentally disastrous practice of spraying cotton fields with pesticides only made matters worse.

On the flight home, Ibrahim reflected upon his good fortune: "I thanked Allah that I did not live in Egypt, but rather in beautiful and prosperous Austria, with my family and a successful career." However, as days passed, his sentiments changed. He could not shake the impressions from his visit.

After a time he devised a plan, which he conveyed in correspondence with friends in 1977:

> I have decided to leave Austria to start a farm in the desert in Egypt based on a holistic developmental impulse for country and people. . . . For my soul Austria was like a spiritual childhood garden. Now I hope that the souls of Egyptian people can be revitalized by a garden in the desert. After establishing a farm as a healthy physical basis for soul and spiritual development, I will set up a kindergarten, a school, a hospital, and various cultural institutions. My goal is the development of humans in a comprehensive sense— educating children and adults, teachers, doctors and farmers.

The vision was an inspiring one. However, a few obstacles existed to its potential realization. To begin with, Abouleish knew nothing about large-scale farming. Second, he was estranged from his country of origin. And third, there was the matter of his wife and children, all of whom were Austrian-born.

The last of these problems turned out to be the easiest to address:

> My wife Gudrun, an Austrian, loved Egypt. This strong inner motivation led her to want to join me. I told our children the story of a man who decided to move to the desert with his family and who

created a big garden there. Once I had painted the picture in great detail, I suddenly asked, "And what would happen if we were that family?" Spontaneous shouts of joy followed. Helmy was 16 at the time; my mother had already told him of the many things I had done at his age in Egypt that were not possible in Austria—like driving a motorbike in the desert. And my daughter Mona, then 14, was in love with horses. In the desert, she would be able to ride as long as she wanted. In this way everyone was inspired to undertake the journey.

So it was that the Abouleish family set out on their improbable adventure to create a garden in the desert in Egypt.

The history of humanity is the history of migration. Millions of years ago, *Homo sapiens* migrated out of Africa; ancient Siberians migrated across the Beringia land bridge into North America twenty thousand to forty thousand years ago, and at other times Indo-Aryans moved westward, and Celts eastward, back and forth across the earth's landmass.

From the earliest times in history to the present, people have migrated for one and only one reason: to search for a better life. In a prehistoric context, a better life meant a better chance for survival. The same was true much later—for the Jews who fled Spain at the end of the fifteenth century as well as the Huguenots who fled France (some to Geneva) and the Puritans who fled England in the sixteenth and seventeenth centuries (some to North America). By then, of course, the threats against survival originated not from the inhospitableness of the natural environment but from the intolerance of other people.

Ironically, the fact of persecution had the effect of systematically increasing the adaptability and resilience of persecuted groups, helping them to prosper in the long run. The historical advantage of Jews in trade and banking derives substantially from a combination of their exclusion from other trades and from the pogroms that tragically, but regularly, forced the relocation of Jewish populations. The consequence was that substantial Jewish communities existed for centuries literally all around the world—from Kaifeng in China, to Cochin in India, and of course from modern-day Iraq across the Mediterranean and into northern

Europe. Beyond reverence for learning and other celebrated qualities of Jewish culture, Jews were born with another advantage of great significance: a globally distributed network of trusted contacts.

In South Asia and along the east coast of Africa, Chinese traders were similarly discriminated against, and were prosperous. The strength of external ties more than compensated for the relative weakness of internal ones—even when the latter occasionally resulted in outbursts of antiforeign sentiment. Jewish and overseas Chinese communities developed an ability to migrate not only their skills and their capital, but, as needed, themselves. And they not only endured but prospered.

For merchants in general, the mobility of capital (enhanced by the invention of bills of exchange, as noted in chapter 8 above), as well as the potential mobility of people themselves, was a decisive component in the weakening of autocratic power. As Sir John Steuart wrote,

> The statesman looks about with amazement; he who was wont to consider himself as the first man in society in every respect, perceives himself eclipsed by the luster of private wealth, which avoids his grasp when he attempts to seize it. This makes his government more complex and more difficult to be carried on; he must now avail himself of art and address as well as of power and authority.

In the seventeenth century, as today, prohibition of emigration was the definitive trait of repressive governments.

When exit is prohibited and protest is banned, the only option left to citizens is loyalty. In many times and places, that third option has proven hugely unsatisfactory. After all, what was the point of the Berlin Wall? It was not to keep West Germans from entering East Germany, but just the inverse—it was a wall of containment, rather than exclusion. This makes perfect sense because, as Mancur Olson has so ably described, the only form of capital that was mobile in the Soviet system—the only lever for freedom—was the capital embodied in people. The power of the Soviet state was based on the implicit taxation of labor—low wages for high talent—and the prohibition of all other forms of private capital ownership. As a consequence, emigration was the equivalent of a bill of exchange. Chess champions and prima ballerinas escaped not only to be more free but also to realize the full value of the their talents. While democracies restrict entry, tyrants restrict exit. Emigration undermines the authority of the sovereign.

Émigrés from the Soviet Union were a numerically small, but otherwise significant, part of a new migration following World War II that developed into the most massive in human history. This was the migration of people everywhere from poor places to richer places. Much of this migration has been within national boundaries—former farmers moving to cities in a great, global process of urbanization. The remainder has been across national boundaries—with only the wealthiest, most fortunate, or most determined accomplishing the move from developing countries to developed ones.

For decades prior to this migration, the poor stayed put and the rich got passports. The consequence was the world of the globally wealthy and the locally poor to which I referred in the introduction. As a consequence, it is still the case that "where you are born, not how hard you work, is today the principal determinant of your material well-being," as Michael Clemens, an insightful analyst of migration policy at the Center for Global Development in Washington, DC, has observed. "A person born to a family living at the United States national poverty line enjoys ten times the living standard of the average person born in the Least Developed Countries defined by the United Nations."

Ibrahim Abouleish was among the fortunate group to get passports—a wave of talent that swept both from the global South to the North and from Asia across the Pacific to the United States. This great migration reinforced the advantages that industrialized countries held over places elsewhere. The most talented students, the most adept businesspeople, and the most tenacious entrepreneurs all sought to make their way to a few places: Cambridge (both UK and Massachusetts), Oxford, Palo Alto, Wall Street, or the Left Bank of Paris, where my own mother went to study in 1948. There, as a young woman from Tunis suddenly set loose at the Sorbonne, she did as I eventually took to doing as a student: studying in cafés. However, in her case, the locale of choice was the Café de Flore, at the corner of the Boulevard Saint-Germain and the Rue St. Benoit, a favorite haunt of Jean-Paul Sartre and Simone de Beauvoir. Talk about an education. Eventually she made it to Columbia University, where—waiting in line one day at the financial aid office—she met my father.

In addition to my mother, this generation of global migrants includes many who enabled the era of prosperity just past—superlative contributors to almost every domain of human activity. Amartya Sen, whose foundational contributions to economics I discussed in chapter 10, came to England from India in 1956 to study at Cambridge University. Daniel Chee Tsui, born in an farming village in Henan Province in 1939, came to the United States in 1958 to attend Augustana College in Rock Island, Illinois, where he ended up being the school's only student of Chinese descent; he continued his studies at the University of Chicago, ultimately making fundamental discoveries relating to semiconductors for which he was awarded the Nobel Prize in Physics in 1998. Vinod Khosla, famed entrepreneur and venture capitalist, came to the United States in 1975 at age twenty after failing at his first entrepreneurial venture—a soy-milk company whose intended market was the many people in India without a refrigerator. He went on to found Sun Microsystems and become a partner in the legendary venture capital firm Kleiner Perkins Caufield & Byers.

These are specific examples, but they are not isolated ones. As entrepreneur-turned-academic Vivek Wadhwa (himself an immigrant to the United States) has documented, 52 percent of the founders of Silicon Valley's start-ups were foreign-born.

Each of these immigrants, and many more like them (did I mention Albert Einstein?) came to the United States during the forty-year interval following World War II when educational and business opportunities in America exceeded those anywhere else in the world. The fact that every other major center of production and learning had either been obliterated or seriously damaged during World War II added to the allure of the US. But a relatively tolerant cultural environment, major investments in knowledge creation, and an open political system were significant factors in attracting people to the United States as well. This positive insurgency of talent was a key factor in building the global competitive advantage in invention, innovation, and entrepreneurship that the United States enjoys today.

That era is drawing rapidly to a close. This fact has little to do with the US, and a whole lot to do with everywhere else. China woke up first (chapter 3). Then India, South Africa, Brazil, Indonesia, and Turkey followed. As a revolution in mobile communications swept the globe, sub-Saharan Africa stirred. And then, in dramatic fashion, Tunisia, Egypt, and Libya shook off their postcolonial stasis and began the process of repurposing for the twenty-first century. The list will only grow. And every time the light of opportunity has started to shine anew somewhere in the world, the beacon drawing immigrants to the United States has shone, in relative terms, somewhat less brightly.

This inexorable trend toward increased prosperity and freedom is obviously good for previously poor and poorly governed places. But will the gains made elsewhere in the world come at the expense of the United States, Europe, and Japan?

The answer to that question is an emphatic *that depends*. If we ignore the reasons for, and sources of, the coming prosperity—or, if we go even further and cut ourselves off from the major trends driving global history in our lifetimes—then we citizens of currently rich countries will continue to feel ourselves becoming poorer and poorer. And we will, in fact, be poor. But the poverty we experience will be that of imagination, not that of circumstance.

There is another option, of course, and that is for us to celebrate the expanded opportunities being experienced by our fellow human beings. To rejoice in their freedom. And to join them in the creating a new future. For people in rich countries like the United States, the rule with regard to increasing prosperity elsewhere in the world is simple: since you can't beat it, join it.

Unsurprisingly, those most readily inclined to adopt this strategy are members of the diaspora themselves. These are people who know how to seek opportunity—that is what brought them to the United States and other wealthy countries to begin with. Now they are looking back in the other direction. Ibrahim Abouleish, with whose story I opened this chapter, is one example. My friend and colleague Iqbal Quadir is another.

Quadir came to the United States from Bangladesh. Eventually he ended up at Swarthmore, and then Wharton. The idea to start a mobile phone company in Bangladesh came to him during a subsequent stint as an investment banker as he looked out over lower Manhattan. The computer system had gone down, and he was waiting for it to come back up. Lack of connectivity meant time wasted. But as frustrating as it was to waste a few minutes, or an hour, waiting for connectivity, he thought, what about wasting half a day walking to a clinic, only to find that a needed medicine was not in stock? Such instances of time wasted due to lack of connectivity were, he knew, ubiquitous in Bangladesh. He turned that insight, based on experience in the country of his birth, into a company today worth half a billion dollars that is the major provider of communications services to the people of Bangladesh.

In the past decade and a half, the engagement of diasporic populations with their native lands has become so pronounced a phenomenon that the Chinese have even coined a term for former emigrants who return to seek opportunities at home: "sea turtles." Sea turtles globally are renewing connections with their native lands. In some cases members of the global diaspora actually move back to their native lands —consider Zhengrong Shi, who had an academic career in Australia and returned to China to found Suntech, the world's leading manufacturer of solar panels. In other cases, like those of Iqbal Quadir and Vinod Khosla, they reconnect through business relationships. In either case, they represent major assets to both countries to which they're connected. They carry with them the wisdom of two shores. They bring together the opportunities and the capabilities of two worlds.

In no place on earth are such potential ambassadors of prosperity found in greater abundance than in the United States. Viewed in terms of the particular opportunities of the next quarter century, this dispersed community of ambassadors embodies uniquely valuable social capital—a source of twenty-first-century collaborative advantage.

"Civilization becomes more complex and difficult in proportion as it advances," the remarkably prescient Spanish political theorist José Ortega y Gasset observed in 1933. "Of course, as problems become more complex, the means of solving them become more perfect. But each new generation must master these perfected means."

What does the challenge of complexity have to do with the global diaspora? A good way to answer that question is to return to Ibrahim Abouleish and his vision for a "garden in the desert" in Egypt.

When we last checked in, Abouleish had hauled his family from the comforts of Austria to pursue his vision of transforming his native land through organic agriculture.

Right away, some connection to complexity should be evident. If this was such a good idea, why had it not been done already, say, by an Egyptian already living in Egypt? And if it wasn't a good idea, why am I writing about it? The reality of the situation illustrates the resolution to this apparent paradox: Ibrahim Abouleish had a fundamentally accurate intuition, and a truly transformative vision. But turning that vision into a reality would not be easy. To the contrary, it would require a decade and a half of constant work and exceptional tenacity. The general principle is that easy problems are solved first. The problems that remain—those that endure—are complex ones. Overcoming complexity requires understanding. It requires adaptability. It requires perseverance.

What problems did Abouleish encounter? The first problem, of course, was to identify the particular piece of desert in which to sow the seeds for a renewal of Egyptian agriculture. This first, critical phase of Abouleish's project was complicated by the fact that no one he spoke with believed it was possible to do what he envisioned. On his third day in Egypt he happened across a plot of land near the Ismaili Canal. "The general opinion was that the land was not suitable," Abouleish recalls. The soil quality was poor and there was no direct road access. "When I look back I have to admit my immense naivete; I had not the faintest idea what it meant to cultivate and irrigate land in the desert." Advice the contrary notwithstanding, Abouleish purchased the land.

"As soon as I had signed the bill of sale the problems began." Even the simple task of identifying the boundaries of the land he had purchased proved a major obstacle; the state land surveyors could not be persuaded to drive the three hours from Cairo to the Ismaili Canal. And, of course, there was the problem of financing the ambitious and improbable venture, which Abouleish named Sekem, which means "sun." After he had prepared detailed plans he arranged a meeting with an Islamic bank recommended by a friend. "I assumed it worked according to Islamic principles. But it turned out the principles of this so-called Islamic bank were the same as any other financial institution." The bank insisted on a substantial equity stake in the new venture but subsequently disputed the valuation on which their investment had been based. A lengthy dispute followed, with an arbitrator ultimately called in to mediate. After some time, Abouleish's lawyer approached him with a proposal to resolve the dispute. "Listen, if you give the bank's lawyer 10,000 pounds then he will accept the estimated value." Abouleish wouldn't go for it. A deadlock ensued. "Once you have a dispute with one bank, all the other banks and the central bank know about it. This meant I was always rejected when I attempted to find a new investment partner for my project. The banks always told me to settle my disagreement with the Islamic bank before further negotiations with them would be possible."

After several more similar false starts—including an aborted investment by a wealthy Egyptian recently returned from Saudi Arabia—Abouleish played his last card and went to visit the director of the Egyptian National Bank. Understanding that any investment by the national bank would be covered by initial export contracts that Sekem had secured in the interim, the director agreed. The dispute with the Islamic bank and the other diaspora investor would take years more to resolve fully, at great cost to the new venture. But, with the loan from the national bank in hand, at last Sekem could begin its work in earnest.

Sekem began operations, built on its relationships with its original customer in the United States, the Elder Company in Ohio. Despite all the obstacles and resistance, the vision with which Abouleish had begun, of an oasis in the desert, slowly began to take shape. Different elements of the plan were working together.

Then one morning, as Abouleish was driving to the farm as usual, he was greeted by an astounding sight: army bulldozers pulling down hundreds of his trees. "I was met by soldiers with machine guns and suspicious expressions. I found out that a general had ordered our grounds to be made into a military area, even though it was only through our efforts that there was even a water supply on our land. They wanted me to leave without further negotiations. This felt like a declaration of war!"

Abouleish responded to this new challenge as he had to those that had preceded: by making use of all of his available contacts to fight back. "Anwar Sadat, the president of Egypt, was a good friend I had gotten to know during our adolescence, so I went to see him." He eventually met with the minister who directed the office of then-Deputy President Hosni

Mubarak. "I was so angry and upset that I made everyone's life miserable and repeatedly visited or phoned the minister to hurry up on the resolution. Still, it took weeks before all the military machinery was removed." While Sekem never received any compensation for the damage caused by the army's attempt to expropriate its property, the general responsible did ultimately send an apology.

As if these and other challenges Abouleish had faced in setting up Sekem were not enough, the most severe confrontation with the country's entrenched power interests happened later, when Abouleish undertook a campaign to end the universal practice of crop-dusting planes applying pesticides over the cotton fields.

Although Sekem did not grow cotton, the practices of the cotton industry became its concern when, at one point in its routine testing process, Sekem found that its own products—meticulously produced with biodynamic methods—were tainted with chemicals. How could this be? After carefully studying the problem, Abouleish and his team determined that the contamination resulted from pesticide spraying on an adjacent cotton farm. For Sekem's product to be truly organic, that spraying would have to stop. Like a true social entrepreneur, Abouleish concluded that the only way to stop the spraying of pesticides onto cotton crops next door was to stop the spraying of pesticides onto cotton crops throughout the country:

> I complained to the Minister of Agriculture. "We want to cultivate organic produce on our farms without using poisons," I said, "and you are destroying our efforts. We are powerless against crop dusting!"
>
> He looked at me with astonishment: "What do you want me to do? Is there an alternative?"
>
> "Stop spraying the pesticides!" I said.
>
> "Do you know what will happen if we do that?" he asked. Only then did I realize that this man was in a difficult position with the chemical companies.

After a lengthy and costly process of setting up test fields in the country and documenting the improved cotton yields that could be realized through organic methods, the minister of agriculture was ultimately persuaded that Abouleish was right. Three years after this process had begun, the minister canceled the country's remaining pesticide contracts with the chemical companies and committed the country to organic methods.

Predictably, the chemical companies did not sit still. Articles condemning organic methods as elitist and impractical began to appear in Cairo newspapers. "We were even accused of wanting to let people starve. Sekem was mentioned by name in many articles and I received anonymous threatening phone calls."

Sekem contended with these attacks over the period of weeks. Its sales appeared unaffected. The ministry of agriculture did not back down. Then the assault intensified:

> We were able to cope with all the attacks until one day an extensive article appeared in the local paper with the title "The Sun-Worshippers." A journalist had visited Sekem without our knowledge and had photographed us standing in a circle on a Thursday afternoon, at our end-of-week assembly. He asked what we were doing, and then answered it himself: we were worshipping the sun! He had photographed the Round House, and mentioned other round shapes in and in front of the company buildings. According to him they were all symbols of the sun!

This was serious. As Abouleish recalls, "For Muslims, worshipping the sun is like worshipping Satan for Europeans. People were indignant, in turmoil." Prayer leaders around mosques in the country started to preach against Sekem. "I began to fear that the chemical companies had won after all."

The head of the state secret police contacted Abouleish. "We know that not a word of the accusations against you is true. But I advise you to defend yourself and take legal action against these people." Abouleish did so, but with the fervor intensifying, he knew that legal action—which would take years, even if successful—was not enough.

So Abouleish decided to invite all of those mentioned as sources in the original article, as well as the mayor and influential sheiks in the area, to have a discussion about Sekem. On the day the group convened,

Abouleish began the proceedings by reading a brief passage from the Koran. Then the Sekem orchestra played a Mozart serenade. "Suddenly a man jumped up furiously, banged his fist on the back of the chair, and shouted, 'We will not listen to this work of the devil!' While the musicians bravely continued playing, I walked up to him and said, 'Calm down and listen.' After that episode all the visitors let these 'terrible' sounds wash over them."

For the remainder of the day, the participants debated with Abouleish the meaning of the Koran as it applied to the practices at Sekem. "I verified everything I said with verses from the Koran, quoting them by heart. Allah says, 'We are responsible for the earth, the plants, and the animals.'" As the day of discussion wore on, the tone of the exchange softened. A sense of fellowship took root among the participants. When the sheiks and political leaders departed, it was with embraces. "They gave us a plaque, written in beautiful calligraphy in golden letters: 'That the community of sheiks verifies that Sekem is an Islamic initiative.'"

The plaque that the sheiks presented to Ibrahim Abouleish now hangs in the entrance area of the school at the center of the Sekem campus—an oasis that occupies the same site Abouleish picked for his farm over thirty years ago. The Sekem Group today encompasses seven major companies— each a recognized brand with a global presence in different aspects of organic agriculture. Sekem not only offers primary and secondary school education to the children of its employees, but has established its own college, Heliopolis University, dedicated to the search for solutions to twenty-first century challenges. Helmy Abouleish, Ibahim's son, is now the group's vice chairman and managing director, and has been involved in representing Egyptian entrepreneurs in international fora.

"Garden in the desert" turns out to have been an understatement.

Egypt is, of course, not representative of the entire world. Furthermore, very few members of the global diaspora will seek to reconnect with their native lands by embarking on journeys as improbable as that of Ibrahim Abouleish and his family. Even among those that do, not all will be personal friends with the presidents of the countries to which they envision returning.

Nonetheless, I find the story of the founding of Sekem to be a compelling one: it illustrates the potential for positive change that diaspora entrepreneurs can realize. It also shows us why the social networks and cultural awareness of diaspora entrepreneurs are so vital to entrepreneurial success in ascending markets. The vision that Abouleish brought to Egypt was one he had created entirely as a consequence of relationships he developed in Austria. The techniques and approach he sought to bring to life in the Egyptian desert—not to mention the Mozart serenade—were foreign ones. To that extent, he returned to Egypt as an outsider. However, the fact of his heritage, and the personal connections he had developed by spending his entire youth in Egypt, proved invaluable as he sought to realize his dream of a garden in the desert.

I opened this chapter with a quote from another returned Egyptian émigré, Wael Ghonim, creator of the Facebook page that catalyzed the Egyptian revolution. Following his graduation from the American University of Cairo, Ghonim took a job with Google. He was soon promoted to head of marketing for the Middle East and North Africa, a position based in Dubai. When a young Egyptian Internet activist, Khalid Said, was beaten to death by police, Ghonim was moved to create, under the pseudonym "El Shaheed," a Facebook page titled "We Are All Khalid Said." That was the page used to announce the first of a sequence of large-scale protests that, as we all know, resulted in the end of the regime of Hosni Mubarak.

When Ghonim was released from detention and identified for the first time as El Shaheed, he repeatedly insisted that the revolution had been leaderless. "Our revolution is like Wikipedia, okay?" he said to one interviewer. And, of course, he was right. Ghonim was not the author of the change that occurred in Egypt. The protesters themselves, in all the cities in which they took to the streets, also did not alone create the historic transformation that captivated the world for seventeen days in the winter of 2011. That outsider incursion was complemented by insider acts of courage— from those still-unnamed soldiers and their commanders who, on the ground, advocated for restraint, to Mona El-Shazly, the correspondent for the independent Egyptian channel, Dream TV, who broadcast an interview with Wael Ghonim that was widely reported to have intensified opposition to the Mubarak regime at a critical point in the protests.

A general principle applies. When it comes to making change happen, outsiders are powerless. On the other hand, insiders are trapped. As a consequence, change happens as a consequence of outsider incursion and insider excursion. In this story, Abouleish is the outsider who was able to make a successful incursion. Various insiders—the director of the Bank of Egypt, the minister of agriculture, and, ultimately, the influential sheiks—possessed the cognitive adaptability to internalize the new vision that Abouleish was seeking to communicate, and the courage to act on that new understanding. Determined outsiders and courageous insiders are partners in real change.

When you are aware of, and open to, developing the relationships that define your environment, you are in a position to understand the possibilities of the present. This is a big deal. A brilliant sociologist by the name of Ron Burt has ably and persuasively documented that neither induced homogeneity nor rigid compartmentalization within institutional silos is a particularly good strategy for organizational success. Instead, the organizations that function best are those characterized by "integrated diversity"—clearly distinct areas of knowledge, experience, or understanding that are aware of, and communicate with, one another. Situational awareness and renewed diversity are preconditions for sustained learning and development. As I'll discuss in the next chapter, the most effective people within organizations harvest value by building bridges between different knowledge silos.

Similarly, resilient and prosperous societies are ones that create ample space for outsider insurgents and insider deviants. This social fringe—the boundary between what is and what cannot be—is the space occupied by entrepreneurs, inventors, and innovators. It is also a space naturally occupied by members of diasporic communities of all varieties.

As Wael Ghonim put it, it's a world of "everyone contributing small pieces, bits and pieces. . . . And no one is the hero in that picture."

Or, depending on how you look at it, everyone is a hero.

12 FROM PASSION TO PURPOSE

There is a saying that we should leave a better country to our children. But it's more important to leave better children to our country.

—CARLOS SLIM, *world's wealthiest man*

About a year ago a group of students at George Mason University, where I teach, asked me to moderate a panel at an event they were organizing featuring exceptional young social entrepreneurs in the Washington, DC, metropolitan area. I was glad to oblige, both because I wanted to support their efforts and because I'm always interested in hearing entrepreneurs tell their stories.

When it came time for the event, however, I was a bit concerned. The four panelists were there on time. But there were only about twice that many people in the audience, and half of them were organizers. A bit embarrassing.

Nonetheless, as the saying goes, the show must go on. We got started. A few more people trickled in. One after another, the panelists told their stories. There was Ben Lyon, a recent college grad leading an initiative to accelerate the uptake of mobile banking services in sub-Saharan Africa; Marga Fripp, a former journalist originally from Romania who founded Empowered Women International; and Fiona Macaulay, the founder and president of Making Cents International, a global organization dedicated to entrepreneurship education for youth. Each story was as compelling as the last. Something about the nearly empty room created a space conducive to sharing personal narratives.

Then Christopher Washington started to tell his story. I knew Christopher as the founder of SOLVE Coop, a platform for agricultural products sustainably sourced from sub-Saharan Africa. I had been impressed with his sharp mind and low-key, self-deprecating manner. But I wasn't sure about the concept for SOLVE Coop. The vision was great: entrepreneurial farmers everywhere vitally need opportunities to connect with customers who value the higher-quality products that they're prepared to bring to market. But the venture's reach seemed like it might exceed its grasp. It seemed unlikely that Washington would be able to execute without a focus on a particular country or market segment.

Washington fit the part of a charismatic young social entrepreneur very well, so I was a bit surprised to hear him start his story by describing how he had gotten himself kicked out of private school in southwest Michigan, where he grew up, for selling candy to fellow students "and making a lot of money doing that." The effect of Washington's business on the instructional environment at the school was almost as detrimental as the commerce itself: "The kids were so hyper that the teachers couldn't take it," he recalled with a mischievous glint in his eyes.

Getting kicked out of school wasn't enough to deter Washington's entrepreneurial initiative—no more than Harvard's famed disciplinary action against Facebook founder Mark Zuckerberg was enough to deter him. In both cases, young entrepreneurs saw potential possibilities that outweighed financial and reputational risks. Most of Washington's peers were from Benton Harbor, Michigan; with a median household income of about $18,000 per year, it is the second-poorest community in the state, next to Flint. "Not a lot of opportunity there," he commented with understatement. "So the way that people did things was to think of an idea and try to make it work. People didn't have a physical job, they had a hustle." Washington moved on from selling candy of a sweetened variety to candy of a narcotic variety. He dropped out of high school. "I figured—this is a way for me to develop myself and get a little bit of money."

In Benton Harbor, expectations weren't low; they were actually high— just in a negative direction. "Growing up as a young black male, just looking around, I was saying 'Everyone else is doing it, why not me?' I had been bombarded, bombarded, bombarded with that message." But along the way, Washington realized he wasn't going to be able to meet the expectations of his peers. "I wasn't good at what people were trying to tell me I should be doing. I wasn't the guy who'd say, 'Hey, gimme my money!'"

After four years out of school, he made a decision. He recalled a conversation with his father, who asked him simply, "So, what do you want to do?" Washington's response—sounding like a suddenly bankrupt hedge-fund manager—was to say, "You know what? I've spent all of this time not helping people. I kind of want to help people. I kind of want to help them do something better, something different."

With his father's support and assistance, Washington took the exam for a graduate equivalency diploma and gained acceptance to a private Catholic college. Washington was grateful for this opportunity at renewal, but he was also suddenly and dramatically out of his element: "My first semester I'm looking around, I'm looking around in every class. And I'm seeing that everybody, *everybody*, is white. I'm on my best behavior. But I don't get it. I really don't get it. You talk about culture shock. That is culture shock. I'm ready to drop out."

At that point, Sister Charlotte, a nun at the college, intervened. "You know Christopher," she said to him one day, "You don't have to stay here."

"What do you mean?" he responded.

"You don't have to stay *here* in order to go to school here. Have you ever thought about going abroad?"

Washington responded that he didn't have any money. Sister Charlotte answered, "I didn't ask you if you had any money. I asked you if you wanted to try studying abroad."

Specifically, Sister Charlotte proposed to Christopher that he continue his education in Italy.

At a convent.

At this point as I'm listening to Christopher's story and thinking to myself, yeah, right. What's the obvious way out for young black guy in shock from the transition from Benton Harbor to a nearby Catholic college? Well, a convent in Italy, of course! What could this nun have been thinking? Out of the frying pan, into the fire, for sure.

And that is exactly why prejudice and preconception are not, as it turns out, as valuable as empathy and understanding, because Sister Charlotte's suggestion wasn't an absurd one. "You know what?" Christopher answered, "I'm a go, because either that or I'm about to drop out of this thing and go back to my old life." He packed for Italy. And the experience changed his life.

"When I went over there, I started to notice things," he said of his arrival. "First off, the Italian nuns didn't know who I was. They were like, 'All right . . . and now we have a black guy!' It was kind of awkward. As soon as I walked in I remember this little nun coming up to me—she's like eighty years old—she comes up to me and says, 'My little chocolate baby!' Then she gives me this big hug and welcomes me to her home."

From the outset, the nuns did something that surprised Washington: they trusted him. They let him into their work. They even listened to his suggestions. "That experience in Italy had started—kick-started in me something that said, 'You know what? You can do something more.'"

After college, Christopher applied for, and was accepted to, the Peace Corps. He described to the handful of people scattered about the auditorium how he'd worked in Togo, in a village named Assahoun, as a small enterprise-development consultant to a microfinance bank organized for and by women. His role was to help the organization do their work more effectively. Eventually, he led an effort to increase re-payment rates by teaching clients how to come up with business ideas that would allow them to stand out in the marketplace: instead of giving a loan to a woman to grow and sell tomatoes, for example, the group encouraged the entrepreneur to experiment with creating a value-added product like tomato sauce. He further described how, when he returned home, he applied what he'd learned about agricul-tural supply chains in the Peace Corps to come up with the idea for SOLVE Coop.

His story done, Christopher turned back to me.

"We should have advertised this better," I thought to myself.

In 2010, Manpower Inc., a global employment services company with offices in eighty-two countries, released the results of a major survey of its clients worldwide. That study found that unemployment in industri-alized countries today is not caused by a lack of jobs. Rather, it is caused by a mismatch between the jobs that exist and the skills possessed by the unemployed: "Unemployment is persistently high in developed and even many developing countries, yet organizations worldwide report dif-ficulty filling key positions. There are not enough sufficiently skilled people in the right places at the right times." Similarly, in 2006, the American Society for Training and Development reported that as "the global, knowledge-based economy places an ever-growing premium on the talent, creativity, and efficiency of the workforce, business leaders talk of a widening gap between the skills their organizations need to grow and the current capabilities of their employees."

Precisely what talents are missing in the labor force? Why are they important, and why are they suddenly in short supply? Are employers looking for blue-collar workers? White-collar workers? Neither. They're looking for people like Christopher Washington. And Ben Lyon. And Marga Fripp. And Fiona Macaulay. And millions like them. Lacking any other term, I'm going to call them "black-collar" workers.

Who are black-collar workers? Black-collar workers are not seeking lifetime employment. They're seeking lifetime learning. They don't have secretaries; they don't have bosses. They just have teammates. They don't punch in at 9:00, and they don't time out at 5:00. They just connect, create, and contribute whenever and wherever it makes sense. They try to minimize their spending in order to maximize their flexibility.

Black-collar workers are everywhere and of all ages, but the exigencies of history have determined that they will eventually predominate among the young. The same Manpower Inc. study cited above described the differences among generations in the working world as follows: "Baby Boomers are more idealistic, loyal to their companies. Gen X are more pragmatic, loyal to their career. Gen Y are more spontaneous, loyal to their purpose."

Having taught in universities for the past twenty years, I find this characterization fairly accurate. The progressive shift in attitudes described by the Manpower report strikes me as particularly pronounced among the most recent college graduates—an incredulous cohort dubbed, in their own parlance, "Gen WTF." This generation indebted themselves as none before to earn their credentials only to find, too often, that the job market was looking for someone or something else.

Unlike those in my generation whose first step after college was, more often than not, onto a corporate conveyor belt, the students I see today are no more likely to be enthralled by the promise of a corner office than they are by a ride to the love-in on the Magic Bus. The *Bonfire of the Vanities* has thoroughly burned itself out; the memory of Woodstock has faded into self-parody. What remains? Nothing more or less glamorous than the determination to get something done.

Leila Janah was a junior in college when she was awarded a scholarship from the Lorillard Tobacco Company. Not satisfied to simply sign her scholarship check over to the bursar's office, she persuaded the granting committee at Lorillard to let her use the funds to spend a semester in West Africa. They agreed. (Leila is a persuasive person.) She found a position teaching middle and high school students at the Akropong School for the Blind in Akuapem, a town in eastern Ghana.

When she arrived at the school, she predictably found the students as eager as the resources were meager. The fact that she was charged with teaching sixty students yet supplied with only three books was not the deficiency that struck her the most. Rather, it was the lack of opportunity her students faced. "Here in the US it's easy to think that you live in a meritocracy, that there's some rhyme or reason to who makes it and who doesn't. But if you happen to be born in a small town in Ghana, good luck. You might be the next Einstein, but because you lost the birth lottery, you'll probably spend most of your life eking out a living."

Her initial impressions were intensified upon her return when she received one letter, then another, and then still more from former students requesting financial assistance in various amounts and for various purposes—even a request for a Nintendo Game Boy. While she had grown close to the students, their default mode for relating to her was as a potential source of charitable giving. Still, the requests for assistance stuck. She sought a way to address their spirit, without capitulating to the culture of dependency to which the students were, by default, connected.

The approach that Janah ultimately hit upon to address this issue was Samasource—a concatenation of *sama*, a Sanskrit word that means "equal," and the word "source." (Leila, who is of Indian origin but grew up in Los Angeles, has *sama* tattooed on her right wrist.) Samasource is a start-up company that provides digital work to people in remote places. Large tasks—say, removing stray characters and erroneous entries from a large data set—are broken down into microwork assignments that can be performed by someone with a simple computer or smartphone and a low-bandwidth Internet connection.

A UNESCO report that Janah likes to cite forecasts that more young people will receive a formal education in the next thirty years than have done so in all of human history to date. But, so far, greater numbers of youth are being educated than can be employed. "We work in communities where there's 70 percent unemployment coming out of the universities," Janah, a Vedic presence with penetrating brown eyes, remarks to a plenary audience at the Clinton Global Initiative in September 2010—more than holding her own alongside *New York Times* columnist Tom Friedman, White House senior adviser Valerie Jarrett, and the remarkable entrepreneurs Fadi Ghandour and Iqbal Quadir.

"We need to think of people as producers," she states flatly. Whether or not she has the definitive answers, she's asking the right questions.

Like nations, individuals have to find a functional balance between order (skills) and adaptability (creativity). An exclusive emphasis on either turns out to be a poor economic survival strategy. The United States in particular is no kinder to single-minded prodigies than it is to undisciplined dabblers; while a few among those with exceptional, but narrow, abilities will clear the bar of greatness, the majority will be compelled to respond with regularity to the painful question, "Yes, but what else can you do?"

Potential answers to that question are, of course, limitless. But, at the start of the twenty-first century, a few will stand out: "I know how to connect"; "I know how to create"; "I know how to contribute"; and "I know how to collaborate."

These are the abilities that create new work. They are the abilities that allow people to redirect their energies from passion to purpose. And they are the abilities that enable entire nations to loosen their respective grips on past glories and, instead, to reach out for what comes next.

That's the reason I started this chapter with Christopher Washington's story. Washington's story is still unfolding. The ventures in which he has been involved are still nascent, and his own career is unfolding. But his example nonetheless evidences one important dimension of what America does at its best: repurpose.

Washington's skill is the ability to find opportunity wherever it presents itself. It is on that skill—and not on myopic attempts at job creation, either by government directly or via subsidies to incumbent business interests—that the future of democratic capitalism depends.

The reason is simple: while democratic capitalism has, for centuries, been great at boosting average incomes in the long term, it has not been particularly good at ensuring employment security for particular groups in the short term. In *Capitalism, Socialism, and Democracy*, Joseph Schumpeter states the conclusion succinctly: "I do not think that unemployment is among those evils which, like poverty, capitalist evolution could ever eliminate of itself." He thought it also unlikely that capitalism would at some point in the future rid itself of boom and bust cycles; the book he considered his masterwork, published in 1939, is revealingly titled *Business Cycles: A Theoretical, Historical and Statistical Analysis of the Capitalist Process*. Capitalism without volatility was, to Schumpeter, like evolution without adaptability: impossible. As a consequence, capitalist economies were doomed to suffer episodes of relatively high unemployment, even in the face of increasing economic abundance. An increasingly comfortable public would, as a consequence, demand protections from capitalist vicissitudes.

Corporate encroachment into the economic domain of entrepreneurs—what Schumpeter termed "trustified capitalism," on which I focused in chapter 9—thus was not the only trend Schumpeter saw leading to the collapse of democratic capitalism. Another dynamic risk that concerned Schumpeter greatly was the increase in social discontent that—ironically but reliably—would accompany overall increases in well-being. In part the mechanism at work was the paradox of rising expectations—a variant on the paradoxes of prosperity I discussed in chapter 2—that was first noted by Alexis de Tocqueville nearly two centuries ago in his famed analysis of the French Revolution: individuals in prospering societies are more likely than those in stagnant ones to experience dissatisfaction with their circumstances. De Tocqueville described the phenomenon as follows:

> A paradox meets us at the threshold of the inquiry. The [French] Revolution was designed to abolish the remains of the institution of the Middle Ages: yet it did not break out in countries where those institutions were in full vitality and practically oppressive, but on the contrary, in a country where they were hardly felt at all; whence it would follow that their yoke was most intolerable where in fact it was the lightest.

The same phenomenon has been noted in the context of the popular uprisings in the Middle East and North Africa, which began in Tunisia, Egypt, and Algeria—relatively prosperous and free countries in relation to others in the region—and only afterward spread to less free and/or poorer places such as Libya, Syria, and Yemen.

Schumpeter does not merely restate Tocqueville, however; he updates him in a very specific way. In an emerging capitalist democracy such as that described by Tocqueville (France in 1789 or Egypt in 2011), the vestigial burden that becomes decreasingly tolerable with increasing prosperity is the tyranny of the state; as Tocqueville states with respect to France, "The destruction of a part of that system rendered the remainder a hundred-fold more odious than the whole had ever appeared." The prediction that follows is an irresistible tendency toward revolution.

In contrast, in mature, capitalist democracies such as those described by Schumpeter, the vestigial burden that becomes decreasingly tolerable with increasing prosperity is the persistence of individual economic insecurity. Schumpeter further foresaw a particular manifestation of the paradox of rising expectations that turns out to be relevant today not only to mature democracies, but elsewhere as well. As a society prospers, regardless of its starting point, its youth will adjust expectations to changing circumstances. In stagnant societies, talented students will aspire to leave the country for a prospering one (as my mother did, from Tunisia to the United States); in a trustified democracy, talented students will aspire to climb the ladder of corporate success. In either case, the pathway of aspiration will run through the same door: college. Governments will encourage this trend with loans and subsidies. University enrollments will swell. However, a good outcome is far from guaranteed: without suitable opportunities awaiting students at the conclusion of their journey through higher education, the lowest rung on the career ladder may remain elusive.

In this way Schumpeter foresaw the skills mismatch to which I referred above: "Inasmuch as higher education thus increases the supply of services in professional, quasi-professional, and in the end all 'whitecollar' lines beyond the point determined by cost-return considerations, it may create a particularly important case of sectional unemployment." How is it that, under conditions of 10 percent unemployment in an advanced economy such as that of the United States, businesses can credibly complain that they are unable to find qualified candidates?

Granted, the unemployment rate among college graduates in the US remains low, even now. Yet the employment opportunities that exist for Generation WTF often do not match the aspirations of recent graduates. Compounding this problem is the fact that the educational system continues to push students through career services offices around the country toward the same pathways followed by their parents, rather than encouraging students to map out new pathways that correspond to current realities. The consequence is frustration and disappointment on a large scale—not only among the economically marginalized, but even more so among the relatively advantaged.

A few months after his talk at George Mason, Washington was in a meeting with a program officer from a major foundation, seeking funding to move SOLVE Coop forward. The meeting wasn't going very well. The foundation in question just didn't have any funding to work on building global agricultural supply chains. However, the program officer was impressed with Washington's determination and vision. And they did have programs addressing nutritional deficits in the United States. Would Washington be willing to try out some of his ideas in the DC metropolitan area before taking them back to Togo?

It didn't take long for Washington to accept. SOLVE Coop merged with an existing organization to form Engaged Community Offshoots, or ECO for short. Like Ibrahim Abouleish, Washington imported skills he had obtained overseas to address structural flaws in the agricultural system of his native country. "When we relaunched as ECO we were really focused on the question: What is the food system problem in urban areas in the United States right now, and then what business—particularly for-profit business—could we launch to mitigate those problems? What we decided to do was to create a farm, in the city, that would launch new farms and train new farmers. So our farm is kind of a hub, a hub of activity for farmers."

What made the ECO model promising was the neglect of valuable human and physical resources in the markets they intended to serve— vacant lots, households without access to fresh vegetables, immigrants with farming skills, and young entrepreneurs seeking meaningful work. ECO was going to find ways to repurpose those assets productively.

By shadowing ECO's original founder, Margaret Morgan-Hubbard, Washington quickly developed a valuable skill of his own: the ability to talk with county officials, and specifically, the ability to persuade them to allow him to use empty plots of land for organic agriculture.

He also quickly developed an appreciation for the agricultural skill to be found among the region's substantial immigrant population—particularly the Central Americans, many of whom had been farmers before coming to the United States. "We train new immigrant farmers. They come in with a certain skill level. We just build upon those skills and show them how to do the work in an urban setting." As Shamoon Sultan found in the case of the Pakistani master weavers whose dormant skills he turned into the backbone of a successful textile business (see chapter 4), Washington and his partners found that immigrants with calloused hands were actually agricultural knowledge workers.

The ECO team worked tenaciously to build partnerships with area food retailers. In one case, they turned the decomposition of waste into a business. A major food retailer in the area "pays us to take their produce away," he explained, "then we turn it into compost, which becomes its own product. So it's a model where people are basically paying to have stuff taken away that they consider trash, we convert it into a product, and then we sell it back to them." It's not so much a value chain as a value circle.

ECO is a small-scale start-up, but in addition to being interesting in and of itself, it also serves as a metaphor for how decentralized systems—"many pieces, loosely joined," to use a favorite phrase of technology guru Tim O'Reilly—are poised to displace large-scale, centralized systems. "We don't look at agriculture as being thousands of acres in Iowa. That's not what we're doing. We're looking at agriculture as scatter plots, as a plot of land here, a plot of land there. But then the total could equal a thousand acres."

While urban agriculture is surging all over the United States, from New Orleans to Detroit, its promise is greatest in the rapid-growth cities in ascending markets elsewhere in the world. "Cities could actually feed themselves," Washington asserts. "Some major cities in China are working toward having 60 percent of the food they consume grown within a ten-kilometer radius of the city center, which is remarkable. Urban agriculture comes from their lifestyle. People are moving from urban areas into the city. They might not have money, so they start a garden in order to have vegetables like they're used to. This happens in Lagos. This happens in Nairobi. It happens all over the world. Except here."

To bring fresh vegetables to households and neighborhoods currently off the farmers' market circuit may only require one simple innovation: setting up operations to accept food stamps. "WIC, food stamps, those are going to communities with billions of dollars of spending power. No one is targeting them with services. That's an opportunity for us," Washington says. For the neighborhoods in the DC area where a lottery ticket can be had on any corner but the nearest head of lettuce is a mile away, ECO provides at least one attempt at an answer.

Passion alone can't pay the rent, much less "change the world." For passion to inform action—from simply earning a livelihood to launching a new venture—it must have a purpose.

As I have emphasized throughout this chapter, the imperatives that face individuals in the twenty-first century reflect those that face nations, and vice versa. Just as twenty-first-century workers must constantly redirect their skills to face new challenges and realize the potential of new opportunities, so must nations. That process repurposing at a national scale is the subject of part 4: the next America.

IV THE NEXT AMERICA

Since the first migrants from Asia crossed the Bering land bridge into present-day Alaska over twelve thousand years ago, America has been humanity's last stop. Over the intervening millennia the populations that sought America as a place have continually redefined America as an idea, in each era seeking new expression for humanity's greatest aspirations.

The future of America lies not in its preeminence as a place, but rather in its enduring appeal as an idea.

13 FEAR ITSELF

This is no cave.

—HAN SOLO, *The Empire Strikes Back*

One April weekend some years ago, when my older daughters were in preschool, I decided to make an attempt at converting the patch of dirt in front of our house into something that might qualify as a lawn. I'd built up a decent-sized landscaping business while I was in high school, but planting grass was a new challenge for me. The information available online wasn't particularly helpful, so I did the unthinkable: I went to the library to do some research.

With kids in the house, better living through chemicals wasn't an option. So I read up on the basics. What I learned was obvious, but no less helpful for that fact. It turns out that the key to making grass, or anything else, grow is not the grass seed, or the fertilizer. It's the soil. The authorities on the subject were unanimous: No air in the soil? Wrong pH balance? Poor prospects for the new lawn.

Armed with this information I did two things. The first was that I rented an automatic aerating machine—the sort that pulls up plugs of dirt and leaves them all over the lawn, making your yard look like a rest stop for geese on the go.

The other thing it turned out that I needed was powdered lime, to neutralize acidity in the soil. I drove over to our neighborhood hardware store—not a strip mall, or a big-box store, but a locally owned shop.

As soon as I walked in I knew I was in the right place. The displays were all about lawn care. Not knowing what a bag of lime looked like, I poked around for a bit before one of the hardware store graybeards approached me. "Need some help finding what you need?" I told him I was looking for a bag of lime. "In the back," he said. "How many bags do you want?" I bought three. They cost eight dollars apiece.

With the transaction complete I went home and set out preparing the soil for planting. In the midst of my labors, such as they were, I pondered the absence of lime in the front of the store. If all of the experts say that lime is what you need, why is the front of the store full of branded seed and fertilizer? In terms of "bang for the buck," those would seem to be pretty low on the list for any informed shopper.

Of course, no sooner had these thoughts crossed my mind than I was embarrassed at their innocence. Even at our trusted neighborhood hardware store, the front of the store was full of paid-for seed signage, as well as all manner of more or less extraneous but high-cost planting gear, because those are the items that make money. Generic lime at $8 per bag just doesn't clear the bar when it comes to allocating precious floor space at the front of the store. If customers want lime, they'll ask for it, just as I had done.

My experience with the lime turned out to be quite a bit more durable than the lawn I planted: after a promising late spring and early summer, it surrendered to the heat of August without much of a struggle. While I didn't see much green grass outside the kitchen window, I did start to see markets for lime pretty much wherever I turned. Not actual lime, of course, but the same dynamic played out again and again. How could I have been so foolish as to believe, even momentarily, that my local hardware store was not subject to the same market pressures that I already knew were routine in grocery and department stores? When physical space is scarce, it naturally goes to the products that yield the highest margins—in many cases, handsomely supplemented by the producer-paid green fees required to secure shelf space—and not to the ones that yield the greatest value to consumers. If consumers want low markup options, well, they can always ask.

In this story, the grass is prosperity, the soil is society, and entrepreneurship and innovation are the lime. Entrepreneurship and innovation are what works. They are what we add to the soil of society so that it maintains the necessary balance between order and flexibility.

There is nothing new about this claim. To the contrary, all I have done so far in this book is restate a consensus view argued previously—and far more eloquently—by a veritable roll call of great economists of the last century: Joseph Schumpeter, Albert O. Hirschman, Friedrich A. Hayek, Robert Solow, Karl Shell, Jane Jacobs, Mancur Olson, and Paul Romer, to name but a few.

Yet despite this overwhelming professional consensus, discussion of national priorities in our democracy has, for decades, strongly tended to keep entrepreneurship and innovation in the back room. Valued, of course, but a basis for US economic strategy? A functional principle underlying our engagement with people elsewhere in the world?

American democracy, like any other mature democracy, tends to be dominated over time by the big signs at the front of the store—the signs paid for by incumbent political and economic interests. Those signs may reflect what matters most for the long-term future of the country, but in all likelihood they will not. The more crowded the marketplace of ideas, the greater the incentive to scream to get attention. The bigger the lungs, the louder the screams. This is the dilemma of the demagogue that every democracy faces.

To be clear, there's no conspiracy at work here. The lime stays in the back room because it lacks an advocate at the front of the store. The same holds for entrepreneurs. As Schumpeter wrote in *Capitalism, Socialism, and Democracy*, "The capitalist process pushes into the background all those institutions . . . that expressed the needs and ways of the truly 'private' economic activity. . . . Dematerialized, defunctionalized, and absentee ownership does not impress and call forth moral allegiance." The signs at the front of the store advertise publicly held global brands. The scale of these large, incumbent corporations gives them the resources to situate themselves at the center of public debate. However, being owned through impersonal markets and administered by professional managers also creates, for a large corporation, an inherent distance between action and accountability that does not exist for a "truly 'private'" entrepreneurial venture. That same distance ultimately manifests itself as an ironic disconnect between nominally public corporate activities that are short-sighted and driven by narrow interest, and private entrepreneurial activities that are farsighted and create broad-based public benefit.

Part 1 of this book was about challenging dominant narratives of doom and highlighting what Keynes referred to as "the true interpretation of the trend of things": the coming prosperity on a global scale. In this chapter I return to that theme, but with a particular focus on the political narrative in the United States. With so many raising their sharply pitched voices to summon fear and alarm, I cannot address them all—and who would want to anyway? So the approach I take in this chapter is illustrative rather than encyclopedic. I focus on two particularly prominent narratives of domestic doom: one relates to external threats, the other to internal ones. In both cases, I will argue, exaggeration of threats has led to miscalibrated and ultimately self-destructive responses.

Among the items in the back of the hardware store, right next to the lime, is ammonium nitrate. Ammonium nitrate is good as fertilizer; it's also pretty good for making explosives. In fact, regular old agricultural fertilizer was the operative ingredient for the bomb used in the 4/19 attacks. Doesn't ring a bell? That was the bombing of the Alfred P. Murrah Federal Building on April 19, 1995. It killed 168 people. At the time it was the most severe terrorist attack on US soil.

Of course, the Oklahoma City bombing isn't forgotten. But it's not exactly remembered, either. Now, granted, the toll from the attack on the Murrah Building was about 5 percent of the toll from the destruction of the World Trade Center towers. And the Oklahoma City bombing wasn't broadcast live on TV, it didn't involve a pair of national landmarks (I'm including the Pentagon, which as you recall was also attacked on 9/11), and it didn't result in $30 billion in insured losses.

That said, would we remember the 4/19 attacks in the same way if they had been carried out by a posse of Koran-thumping extremists rather than a couple of homegrown ones? Let's be honest: despite (or perhaps due to) the fact that domestic groups have perpetrated the overwhelming majority of terrorist attacks in the US, head scarves make more of an impression than baseball caps on the cable news feed. At the end of the day, the story behind the Oklahoma City attacks just didn't sell—politically or otherwise. Terrorist attacks perpetrated by self-proclaimed ultrapatriots from the Midwest—well, they must be an aberration. The attackers? Dumbed-down Unabombers. No real information there. Just noise.

But how about this, from former Senator Rick Santorum in 2006: "In World War II we fought Nazism and Japanese imperialism. Today, we are fighting against Islamic fascism." Now that's more like it. From that eloquent starting point, security screamers can cut and paste the usual language of external menace. Our very way of life is at risk. The line is drawn. The struggle against terrorism is equivalent to World War III. And so forth.

What does any of this have to do with reality? Not much. Comparisons of Islamic fundamentalism to fascism in the 1930s or communism in the 1950s may have sounded good from the podium over the past decade, but they are almost entirely empty when considered from both economic and historical standpoints. Germany in 1930 was a country with demonstrated capacity as a global economic leader whose steady development had been halted at the start of the twentieth century only when the Treaty of Versailles brought a pointless war to its conclusion through a bankrupting peace. Even Japan, greatly underestimated in the West before it attacked Pearl Harbor, had steadily built its economic foundation and technical capabilities over a period of almost a century by patiently investing and strategically imitating Western techniques. Even in a worst-case scenario (much worse for the countries affected than for us) the countries that might conceivably be susceptible to the sway of Islamic fundamentalist ideologues today do not even have the economic capability of the Soviet Union in the 1950s; they do not compare at all with Germany or Japan of the 1930s.

Of course, innovation and technical change have also created new modes of attack that make small groups potentially threatening today in a way that only an entire nation could have been threatening in the past. But a historical perspective is valuable here, as well. Consider that, worldwide, over sixty million people lost their lives during World War II. Among armed combatants, the United States could count itself lucky in having lost only 290,000 of its sixteen million service members. Such losses are inconceivable today in the context of an attack by a terrorist adversary, touting Islamic fundamentalist ideology or not—even when we consider the truly nightmarish scenario of nuclear attack. Yet even eight decades ago, the democratic institutions, including the decentralized markets, had a remarkable capacity to adapt and respond following the World War II. For what reason might we believe that capitalism and democracy are any more fragile today than they were back then? By what measure can any present threat, posed by even the most malicious nonstate adversaries, compare with the combined industrial might demonstrated by the German, Japanese, and other Axis powers during World War II, or by the Soviet Bloc during the Cold War? Our respect for the capabilities of foes and our recognition of the reality of potential threats must be matched with an equally realistic appraisal of our society's resilience and capacity for recovery.

The simple reality is this: terrorists of various types exist, they are dangerous, and they will almost certainly be responsible for further deaths of innocents in the United States and elsewhere in the world in coming decades. But there is basically zero prospect that such attacks will alter the forward trajectory of global history—unless, of course, political leaders continue to increase their impacts dramatically through exaggerated responses.

In the United States, the proof is in the policies. The 9/11 attacks were serious and costly. But what of the response? What would follow were a pair of foreign wars whose cost will exceed a trillion dollars, the reversal of five decades of government prohibition against the use of torture, and unprecedented incursions into the civil liberties of US citizens.

In contrast, what was the reaction to 4/19? Did the federal government undertake to restrict the production and distribution of chemicals with potentially hazardous applications? No, not quite. In fact, at the very same time that American soldiers were risking, and losing, their lives in Iraq dismantling the famed WMD-program-that-wasn't, railcars filled with highly toxic ammonia were routinely transiting within half a mile of the United States Capitol—providing would-be attackers with a target of opportunity in the nation's capital that National Security Council's (NSC) former official Richard Falkenrath placed in the category of "the greatest risk."

So if the solution to national vulnerabilities isn't military action overseas, what is it? Don't we have to weed out terrorists—hunt them down wherever they might be hiding?

Ultimately not. The countries most experienced in confronting terrorism (Israel, Spain, and the United Kingdom among them) learned long ago that the way to deal with attacks that are going to happen no matter what you do is to respond effectively and recover rapidly.

Here's a story that makes the point. In the 1970s subway cars in New York City presented an unrestricted canvas for graffiti artists. As those who lived or visited the city at that time recall, and as the cinematic record readily attests, not a subway car in the city was out of reach for inventive vandals wishing to leave their mark. The graffiti was a public problem, however, in that it underscored a sense of lawlessness and deepened the malaise that affected the city at the time. Of course, fences were useless as a deterrent. Elected officials, sociologists, and columnists all weighed in on how to deal with the graffiti scourge. Some insisted on stiffer penalties for perpetrators (the War on Graffiti strategy), while others held that no progress would be made until someone addressed the cultural and economic root causes of the disaffection expressed by graffiti artists (the Hearts and Minds strategy).

But the folks at the New York Metropolitan Transit Authority had a better idea. Rather than try to prevent the vandalism that was, after all, inevitable, they would take aim at the satisfaction the vandals enjoyed from their work. How? Simple. They first undertook a massive rehabilitation of the cars in the system, so that more or less all were temporarily clear of graffiti. At the same time, they instituted a new policy: any car that came into the yard at night with graffiti on it would, without fail, be cleaned or painted before it went out again. They also tightened security in the yards themselves.

The outcome: the vandalism stopped not because it was prevented, but because it became pointless. Why go to all the trouble of painting a car if the graffiti was just going to be gone the next day? No return. So no graffiti.

Reduce the lasting impact of an attack, and the attack itself no longer conveys any information. It's just noise.

As suggested by my discussion in chapter 7 of the response to Hurricane Katrina, the actions required to respond effectively and to recover rapidly from extreme events—not just terrorist attacks but natural disasters, as well—are mostly taken at home, not abroad. They require not strident rhetoric but patient collaboration, forged over time in an atmosphere of trust, involving citizens, businesspeople, and the public officials who serve them both. Above all, such societal resilience requires an element that can't be purchased from a Department of Defense vendor and achieved through an international accord: it requires innovation and the same grassroots creative spirit that drives entrepreneurs.

Of course, in the United States at the start of the twenty-first century, foreigners don't have to plan terrorist attacks in order to be feared; sometimes all they have to do is show up to work or drop their kids off at day care. In this manner we arrive at the tale of America's leading anti-immigration activist, John Tanton.

In chapter 10 I told the story of Dr. G. Venkataswamy, the Indian ophthalmologist who in 1976 founded the Aravind Eye Hospitals. At about the same time that Dr. V. was opening his first clinic, John Tanton, an American ophthalmologist, was also expressing his passion and convictions through social action. Like Dr. V., Tanton had dedicated his professional life to preserving or restoring sight by performing cataract surgery, reportedly performing over four thousand surgeries during thirty-seven years of practice. Yet the touchstone of Tanton's social engagement related not to enhancing individual eyesight, but rather to conserving the natural environment.

Tanton's home in Petrosky, Michigan, lies just across Lake Michigan from Marinette, Wisconsin, the town where my own father spent his adolescence. (My paternal grandmother and Tanton's mother were also both descended from German Lutheran families that came to the United States in the same mid-nineteenth-century migration.) Having been born, raised, and so far lived his entire life in the same state, Tanton has developed a deep sense of connection to the varied ecologies and the wilderness of his native Michigan. Tanton's first foray into public advocacy was to provide support for a legal challenge, under the Michigan Environmental Protection Act, of construction of a proposed dam at Monroe Creek in Charlevoix County. In this as in subsequent leadership roles that Tanton assumed in the favor of environmental causes, Tanton saw himself as advocating for the long-term interests of conservation in opposition to the near-term pursuit of profit.

Another dimension of Tanton's concern for the environment—one shared with equal passion by his wife, Mary Lou—was population control. Like many of his generation, Tanton had from his twenties followed the public discussions regarding the threats to humanity posed by growing populations—threats that were the topic of Paul and Anne

Ehrlich's 1970 book, the *Population Bomb*, and the *Kissinger Report* of 1973, both which I discussed in chapter 2. In Tanton's view—one widely shared in the 1970s—the only way to address issues of resource scarcity highlighted by the Club of Rome's *Limits to Growth* report was to act assertively and immediately to control the growth of human population. As late as 1992—before demographers had documented the demographic transition in developing countries that has led to a dramatic slowing of population growth on a global scale—the presidents of the Royal Society of London and the US National Academy of Sciences issued a joint statement that included the following assertion: "If current predictions of population growth prove accurate and patterns of human activity on the planet remain unchanged, science and technology may not be able to prevent irreversible degradation of the environment or continued poverty for much of the world."

This statement from the pinnacle of the scientific establishment validated what Tanton was observing at eye level in northern Michigan: population pressures were slowly wearing down the natural environment. In time, Tanton worried, there would be nothing left for conservationists to conserve.

Tanton was a committed and successful organizer. He was the founder and, from 1965 to 1971, the president of northern Michigan's Planned Parenthood; served as chair of the Sierra Club's Population Committee from 1971 to 1974; and, from 1975 to 1977, was president of Zero Population Growth, a national organization dedicated to, well, pretty much what the name says. He and his wife found many kindred spirits among advocates for population control. But Tanton had another concern, beyond excessive fertility rates, that set him apart: immigration.

In 1975 Tanton authored an essay titled "International Migration as an Obstacle to Achieving World Stability," which earned him third place in the Mitchell Prize competition at the Limits to Growth Conference, which took place that year in The Woodlands, Texas. In that essay Tanton acknowledged that immigration was a controversial topic: "An aversion to discussing immigration is also understandable in light of the seamy history surrounding past efforts to limit immigration. These were marked by xenophobia and racism, and gave rise to the likes of the Know-nothing political party, and the Ku Klux Klan. Other-isms of past debates that we seldom hear today include jingoism and nativism. The subject was often highly emotional and divisive." Nonetheless, he argued, "it is time for environmentalists to deal with this important question."

Tanton became singularly committed to articulating the connection he saw between population growth, environmental impact, and migration. When a fellow Zero Population Growth board member evidenced unease with his insistence on extending standard conservation and population-control narratives to encompass the dangers posed by excessive migration, he founded a new organization to focus specifically on this topic: the Federation for American Immigration Reform (FAIR), serving as the chair from 1979 to 1987.

In 1994, at about the same time the presidents of the US National Academies and the British Royal Society were jointly issuing their population alarm, Tanton crystallized his vision in another essay titled "End of the Migration Epoch?," published in a journal he founded titled *The Social Contract*. In that essay Tanton argued for a shift from an "old paradigm" based on the illusion of abundance and the celebration of migration to a "new paradigm" recognizing the reality of scarcity and emphasizing the fixity of human populations:

> Each nation has a solemn responsibility to provide for the health, education, employment, and security of its own citizens. . . . No nation can expect to solve deficiencies in these areas by exporting its surplus people. . . . No nation should exceed what the biologists call its "carrying capacity." In setting its immigration policy, any nation must first look after the interests of its own citizens, including those at the bottom of the socioeconomic ladder.

The damage of migration to the poor countries from which emigration occurs is, Tanton stated, even greater than it is to the wealthier countries which immigrants choose as their destination: "Each nation should train its own technical and professional personnel, matching supply to demand. The developed countries in particular should not continue to encourage a brain drain from the less-developed countries, luring their talented people, and thus benefiting from the scarce capital that went into their education." His conclusion: "We are fast approaching the end of the Migration Epoch. Welcome inter-national migration—legal, and especially illegal—is no longer a practical option for almost all of the world's people. Rather, they will have to bloom where they are planted if they are to bloom at all."

Now, on the surface, Tanton might seem to be just the sort of insurgent, organizer, and builder that I have been celebrating in this book. From a modest base in the wilderness of northern Michigan, he has, over the span of thirty years, founded, funded, and otherwise supported the creation of half a dozen anti-immigration organizations that are today very active and influential in American politics. One, NumbersUSA, reportedly "doomed President George W. Bush's legalization plan four years ago by overwhelming Congress with protest calls"; another, FAIR, was involved in the drafting of the controversial law enacted in Arizona last year that gave the police new power to identify and detain illegal immigrants. Tanton has demonstrated an exceptional capacity to leverage the resources at his disposal to effect change on a large scale.

What's more, as I read about Tanton—particularly, via the hagiography written by his longtime friend and northern Michigan neighbor John Rohe—I was struck with how Tanton's path represented a sort of "road not taken" for my own father, and, by extension, myself. Where Tanton's destiny was to marry his college sweetheart and put down roots in his native Michigan, my father left his own home of Wisconsin immediately after college for New York City, and ended up marrying a graduate student from Tunisia, five years his senior. No surprise, in that sense, that I am predisposed to emphasize the benefits derived from immigration. The personal always anticipates the political. My case and Tanton's are no exceptions.

Viewed differently, however, Tanton's intellectual formation—in particular, his proximity to conservationist Garrett Hardin and the initial inspiration he drew from the writings of Paul and Anne Ehrlich—actually parallels my own. I myself chose graduate school in economics in part because I was interested in the then-emerging field of ecological economics, focused on exactly the domain of political, economic, and ecological interrelationships that have been at the core of Tanton's own writing. From the standpoint of ideas, therefore, I feel the sort vague affinity for Tanton you might have for a distant cousin or a teacher in high school who you liked but whose class you never took.

So why, in that case, do I highlight the anti-immigration initiatives of which Tanton has been a leader as a paradigmatic example of fear-based demagoguery? The reason is that I believe human societies go down the wrong road when they stop respecting the universal aspiration for freedom, connection to other people, and true prosperity—an aspiration to which the process of migration is deeply connected. What is more, Tanton and those who share his views are simply mistaken, both about historical facts pertaining to immigration and about its likely impacts in the future. Indeed, if anything will keep we Americans from realizing our potential in the twenty-first century, it will be misguided measures taken in the name of protecting our borders that will serve only to attenuate our connection to the coming prosperity.

With regard to immigration in particular, the retrospective story is clear. Indeed, we don't need to go back to Ellis Island or to recall the role of Chinese laborers in building to the transcontinental railroad to tell a powerful story about the contributions of immigrants to America's prosperity past. Serious scholarship on the more recent impact of immigration on the US economy indicates that immigrant labor (both skilled and unskilled) has been largely complementary to, not competitive with, that of native-born citizens. For example, a carefully done study by Gianmarco Ottaviano and Giovanni Peri published in 2004 found that "US-born citizens living in metropolitan areas where the share of foreign-born increased between 1970 and 1990, experienced a significant increase in their wage and in the rental price of their housing."

Furthermore, we know that immigrants have played a disproportionate role in driving technological innovation in the United States—not only in their positions in university research labs but also as the founders of new companies. One-quarter of all new firms started in the United States from 1995 to 2005 had at least one immigrant founder. Among Silicon Valley's technology and engineering companies, 52 percent launched during the same time period were founded by immigrants. In the year 2005 alone, immigrant-founded tech companies generated $52 billion in revenue and employed 450,000 workers. So we know that the United States was not only built, to a significant extent, by immigrants; it continues to be enriched by them.

And while the historical benefits of migration to recipient countries have been dramatic—particularly in the case of the United States—comparable or even greater benefits have accrued to emigrants' countries of origin. As Michael Clemens (quoted in chapter 11) has noted, the ubiquity of home-country returns from out-migration has been obscured by enduring analytic biases summed up in the term "brain drain":

> The departure of some people—such as the skilled or talented—from a poor country might reduce the productivity of others in that country. Such an effect would tend to offset the gains from emigration. Externalities like these are often assumed to be so pervasive that the literature refers to skilled migration with a pejorative catchphrase— "brain drain"—embodying the assumption. (To see why economists should avoid this term, picture reading a journal article on female labor force participation that calls it the "family abandonment rate.")

As Clemens and researchers at the Migration Policy Institute in Washington, DC, among others, have documented exhaustively, countries that send emigrants forth into the world—emigrants like Ibrahim Abouleish, whose story I told in chapter 11—benefit tremendously via the monetary and knowledge remittances that the same emigrants subsequently send home. These positive impacts on human well-being are massive, and could be even greater. Surveying the existing literature, Clemens estimates the overall gains from elimination of barriers to migration to be an astounding 50 percent of global GDP. Compared with, for example, the much-discussed topic of trade restrictions, migration is arguably the killer app of global development: "A degree of increased labor movement from poor to rich countries of just 5%," Clemens notes, "would bring more economic gains than the total elimination of every tariff, quota, and barrier to capital movement in the world."

Having said all of this, I grant that the demonstrable falsity of most retrospective analyses ostensibly supporting a hard line against immigration is almost beside the point. What matters more to current immigration policy in the United States is the relevance of such analyses to the future. Here the verdict is even clearer: xenophobic fears are on the wrong side of history. Though events have overtaken the story of demographic doom, the storytellers have not caught up. The greatest risk for the United States in the twenty-first century is that it may end up as John Donne's proverbial "island unto itself"—disconnected and decreasingly relevant.

To avoid this fate the United States needs to build more bridges, not erect new barriers. As author and law professor Amy Chua has noted,

> At any given historical moment, the most valuable human capital the world has to offer—whether in the form of intelligence, physical strength, skill, knowledge, creativity, networks, commercial innovation or technological invention—is never to be found in any one locale or within any one ethnic or religious group. To pull away from its rivals on a global scale, a society must pull into itself and motivate the world's best and brightest, regardless of ethnicity, religion or background.

Or, as Sun Microsystems' cofounder Bill Joy famously quipped, "No matter who you are, most of the smartest people work for someone else."

As the Swiss watchmaking story that I related in chapter 8 illustrates, openness to global talent can create substantial and enduring competitive advantages. Difference is information, and information is essential to organic growth. Success lies in the alignment of diverse interests for collaborative success. The high walls at our borders that industrial-era lawmakers constructed to keep wealth within the United States are increasingly serving to keep opportunity out.

Fear is a wonderfully unifying force. It cuts across lines of economic status and ideology. By what tortuously constructed pathway did an abiding love for the white birch stands of northern Michigan evolve into the rationale for the detention of people in Arizona suspected by police to be in the US illegally? (Put differently, by what process of toxic fermentation did the wine of ecological thinking decompose into a vinegary sludge of fear-based politicking?)

Tanton's tale turns out to be a humbling parable of the limitations—even dangers—of analysis disconnected from empathy. We are all immigrants in our own way, in our own time.

"The only thing we have to fear . . . is fear itself." These famous words, delivered by Franklin Delano Roosevelt in 1933 in his first inaugural address, are an enduring legacy. Americans arguably have greater reason to be fearful today than at any point in the past of fear itself, and of fear-mongers.

I started this chapter by observing that the intense competition in the marketplace of ideas that is characteristic of a democratic society creates incentives for both exaggeration and simplification. As the always insightful James Fallows has observed, "Football coaches roar and storm in their locker-room speeches at halftime to fire up the team, and American politicians, editorialists, and activists of various sorts have roared and stormed precisely because they have known this is the way the nation is roused to action." When that tendency combines with both the natural inclination of entrenched interests to defend their current advantages and the appeal to fear, you end up with the worst but most predictable product of democracy—the demagogue.

The demagogue's voice is loud. The demagogue's organization is well funded. And the demagogue's message is simple: be more afraid.

Demagogues are the more or less precise equivalent of the weed killer at the front of the hardware store. The enemy is clearly defined: the intruder, the insurgent, the newcomer. The strategy for dealing with the enemy is correspondingly straightforward. Attack. Exterminate. Eradicate.

The pragmatic problem with fear-based narratives is that they lead to waste. Waste of people. Waste of time. Waste of resources.

The reason is that fear-based responses are superficial. Enraged by the dandelions in your yard? Running around frantically to pull them out will, as we all know, serve only to send their seeds flying. Poisoning them will appear to make a difference. But they'll be back. And in the interim you'll have polluted your own environment, and other environments to which you are connected.

But let's get back to the lawn problem, because I brought it up to begin with to make a serious point.

If a lawn—a top-down, disciplined approach to ordering your immediate environment—isn't working, what alternative do you have? Maybe the whole project needs a rethink.

One seemingly appealing option to the challenges of growing and maintaining a lawn is to turn your yard into a meadow. Forget the fertilizer! Return your yard to nature.

This is the landscaping equivalent of a "free-market" approach to economics. In politics it is known as anarchy. And it certainly has an appeal. (More on that in the next chapter.) The problem with just letting your yard go is that the outcomes are usually ugly. Visibly, verifiably ugly. Kudzu Korner. Destructive entrepreneurship and "unnovation" run amok. In urban planning, the outcome of such a laissez-faire philosophy has a name: Houston. It ain't Paris.

So what you want is a middle ground between a perfectly manicured lawn—with all the resource intensity and waste that requires—and Crabgrass Corner. You might ideally want to restore your property to its original beauty. You might want to create a meadow. As the *New York Times* reported a couple of years ago, "With the growing interest in sustainable gardening and the widespread dissatisfaction with the time, expense and chemical fertilizers required for traditional lawn care, meadows are becoming increasingly popular." But it turns out that creating a meadow where one doesn't already exist is not as easy as it seems: "As random and natural as a meadow looks, there is nothing haphazard about creating one. Planting a meadow . . . is as rule-bound and time-consuming as planting any perennial border."

For the privileged few who would like to look out of their bay windows to a meadow in their front yard, the cost is between $3,000 and $10,000 per acre. For those who want to create a meadow on their own, landscape designer Larry Weaner has the following advice: take some time to learn about the complicated processes that govern plant growth. Beneath the meadow's surface are "intricate interactions working together to foster the plants in the meadow and suppress invasive weeds."

Pretty much exactly the same advice holds when it comes to entrepreneurial ecosystems. Absolute laissez-faire is not a way to create vibrant, self-sustaining communities in poor places or rich ones. It's a way to create vacant lots full of weeds.

But the opposite approach—heavy-handed intervention—doesn't work any better. More seed. More fertilizer. Don't worry if anything is taking root. Just let loose with the spending. Elaborate packages constructed for this policy don't change the nature of its content: reactive, short-sighted, and, ultimately futile.

There has to be a better way.

14 LEFT, RIGHT . . . FORWARD

Meanwhile, the youth group wants to burn down the church and build something more energy efficient.

—CELL PHONE CONVERSATION OVERHEARD IN
WASHINGTON, DC (may 2009)

Charlie McCormick was the son of a missionary. He was born in Morelia, Mexico, on June 9, 1896. Thereafter, he lived in Puerto Rico, France, and in various places across the United States before his family settled in Baltimore in 1912. He spent his summers through high school working in the spice company that his uncle Willoughby had founded.

Willoughby McCormick was a determined, old-school entrepreneur. He had an exacting motto: "Make the best. Someone will buy it." When his factory burned down in the Baltimore fire of 1904, he rebuilt. As the country grew in the early part of the twentieth century, before the Great Depression, so did McCormick & Company of Baltimore.

Where Willoughby McCormick did not excel was as a manager. As the company's longtime plant superintendent recalled in an interview many years later, "Willoughby was a good church member, gave money to charity and all that, but he had no feeling at all for the human relations in his business." On occasion his nephew would make suggestions about how the business might be run. Willoughby was not interested. "This is my business, and I'll do the thinking for it," he would tell Charlie. "You are not paid to think; you are paid to work." The atmosphere in the factory was oppositional: "The workers thought management was out to beat them down and get as much out of them as they could, at just as little pay," the superintendent recounted. "The management thought that the workers were out to loaf around and take it easy and had to be watched all the time. There was no trust." Attuned to Willoughby's routine of exiting his office at regular intervals during the day to walk through the factory, McCormick & Company workers developed an elaborate system of signals to warn one another that the boss was on the move. "Boy, we had to work so hard to make him think we looked good when he made those visits through the plant that we just had to let him down the rest of the day."

In the aftermath of the crash of 1929, the company's fortunes took a turn for the worse. Profits turned to losses. In 1932, at the height of the Depression, Willoughby McCormick died. The board of McCormick & Company elected Charlie McCormick—or C. P. as he known by then—as president.

C. P. McCormick was in a tough position. The company over which he was suddenly presiding was on the verge of failure. The economy wasn't the only problem. Years of autocratic management had also taken their toll. Productivity at the company's plant was on a downward trajectory. Morale among employees—never high—sank further as rumors of wage cuts circulated.

The younger McCormick's response to the company's predicament was a non sequitur. Rather than cut wages, he increased them across the board by ten cents an hour—a significant sum at that time. At the same time, he cut working hours from fifty-six to forty-five per week and created new structures within the company to make decision making more inclusive. "A lot of people around Baltimore then thought Charlie was just plain crazy," the plant superintendent recounted.

The concept? "I realized that while I was thirty-six years old, nearly all the members of the Board of Directors were over forty-five and several had passed sixty," McCormick later wrote. "They had acquired the habit of automatically yessing my uncle's judgment." McCormick created a new board, which he called the "junior board," comprised of assistant managers within the company who had demonstrated initiative. "I had taken stock of myself and had arrived at the conviction that I possessed neither the ability not the inclination to be a one-man manager of a multimillion-dollar business."

Long before William Deming developed the theories of inclusive management widely credited with driving Japan's remarkable post–World War

II economic recovery, C. P. McCormick was putting very similar ideas to work in Baltimore. In addition to the junior board, McCormick later created a system of faculty boards designed to solicit—actively, formally, and regularly—the insights of production workers regarding potential process improvements. The objective was to capture and apply the tacit knowledge distributed throughout the company:

> The [Multiple Management] board system not only throws together men of diverse talents, but in operation it causes them to recognize their interdependence. . . . Our supervisors are not practicing clever psychology when they look to their people for help and suggestions. They have come to realize that we can all learn something from each other—and the man on the job is often the man best fitted to give advice about it.

Along very similar lines, picking up on the systems theory developed by Norbert Wiener (as introduced in chapter 1), Deming would later state, "A system is a network of interdependent components that work together to accomplish the aim of the system. A system must have an aim. Without aim, there is no system. The aim of the system must be clear to everyone in the system." Furthermore, "the most important figures that one needs for management are unknown or unknowable." These two statements together suggested the need for just the sort of approach to management that C. P. McCormick had pioneered in Baltimore: an active system to engage workers at all levels in an active and ongoing discussion about the company's work, and its purpose. As Umair Haque, the insightful author of *The New Capitalist Manifesto* and *Betterness*, tweeted a little while back, "The Boss drives group members. The Leader coaches them. The Builder learns from them." In this story, Willoughby was the quintessential boss, and C. P. the prototypical builder.

The perceived opposition between blue-collar and white-collar work defined the political divisions of the twentieth century and perpetuates its tired legacy even today: labor in opposition to management, and unions in opposition to corporate interests. As the famed John Kenneth Galbraith wrote in 1952, "Power on one side of the market creates both the need for, and the prospect of reward to, the exercise of countervailing power. . . . This means that, as a common rule, we can rely on countervailing power to appear as a curb to economic power." According to Galbraith, the mid-twentieth-century dominance of large corporations in the economy—a direct consequence of the overwhelming power of economies of scale that I described in chapter 1—induces an inevitable response from workers and consumers, tempering the corporate influence. The balance of economic powers between big business, labor, and government—what many have termed the "Iron Triangle"—reflected in economic life the balance among interests that defined the American political system. The role of Government, in turn, was presumably act both to balance interests in markets and to moderate the adverse impacts of business cycles. Keynes redux.

Yet today, the wages paid to American workers are determined not by cigar-chomping oligopolists meeting in New York or Detroit boardrooms but by labor markets that extend globally from Adelaide to Zurich. In such a world, the vestiges of large corporate dominance have, in recent years, sought to join forces with the vestiges of traditional organized labor to preserve the tattered remnants of a social contract rendered obsolete by nothing other than the inexorable forward movement of history. The futility and moral dubiousness of the desire to restore a world where well-paid workers in the United States produced goods for relatively impoverished foreigners has little do with whether the 1950s—the era understood and appreciated by John Kenneth Galbraith—were, in total, better or worse than today. The issue is simply that 2012 is not 1952. The way forward is not the way backward.

Recall how, in November 2008, the Big Three autos executives first flew (in private jets, at taxpayer expense), then drove, and ultimately were nearly compelled to walk from Detroit to Washington to plead their case for government support to avert bankruptcy. At their side during these hearings sat representatives from the United Auto Workers and other organized labor organizations, whose "countervailing power," as John Kenneth Galbraith so astutely noted, turned out to depend—as much in the present as sixty years ago—on the "original power" of the corporate behemoths against which they were supposedly arrayed.

Bankruptcy would be an unmitigated disaster, the Big Three executives argued. "We believe that retail sales will plummet dramatically," Chrysler CEO Robert Nardelli stated flatly. "Given our common supplier base, the bankruptcy of any one automotive manufacturer, we believe, threatens the viability of all automakers."

Now flash forward—from November 2008 to November 2010. An auto bailout did go through—but not the sort of no-strings-attached deal that the automakers were looking for. Instead, each of the Big Three followed its own path. Ford went without government assistance entirely. GM ended up 60 percent owned by the US taxpayers, but was also liberated from the debt and health-care obligations it had accumulated during the decades that workers and executives had colluded to put off their collective day of reckoning. In Chrysler's case, labor faced a difficult choice: buy the factory or buy the farm. They chose the latter; in a stark affirmation of the de facto alliance between union and management interests, Chrysler went into bankruptcy, according to a plan by which the United Auto Workers assumed majority control of the company.

Labor? Management? . . . Left? Right?

Getting back to the discussion in chapter 9, what has recently been good for GM—a day of reckoning that compelled long-deferred changes— is in fact what would be good for America. Susan Docherty, GM's director of US sales (not the world's lowest-stress job) said this in 2009: "You know that there's not much good that comes out of bankruptcy. But it is a force that helps you change a culture." As suggested by the quote with which I opened this chapter, we occasionally need to burn the church down and build something more energy efficient.

When cultural change is inclusive and infused with a sense of purpose, it can enable enduring value to sprout, even among the ashes of past failures. The same applies to nations. Sure, national bankruptcy is not a commonly experienced phenomenon, since governments don't (usually) default on their debt. But that's not the point. The analogy in terms of cultural change and renewal hinges on bankruptcy not as a technical outcome but as a behavioral process. In Detroit, the recipe was to keep moving cars out the door at all costs. If that meant cheap lease deals based on unrealistic resale forecasts, then fine. If it meant relentless price cuts to clear lots, then fine. As long as money kept coming in to pay workers and keep the lights on—and as long as the financial markets were willing to cover any shortfall—the strategy made sense. After all, what was the alternative? Cut production. Close plants. Fire workers. Neither management nor unions was happy with that strategy. So the short-term thinking continued. For decades.

And, until very recently, what was the US government's strategy to advance the nation's growth? Deficit spending? Check. Low interest rates? Check. Assertive action to increase the money supply and devalue domestic currency? Check. But reduce oil and farm subsidies? Push back against entitled unions and all manner of crony capitalists? Invest heavily to rebuild the nation's infrastructure? The will wasn't there. So short-term thinking continued. For decades.

The United States in particular is not immune to Mancur Olson's logic regarding the relationship between politics and government. The vitality of democracy itself depends on the fluidity of economic interests. Without such fluidity, rich countries can start to look very much like poor ones: the wealthy game the system to avoid taxation, political patronage trumps genuine development, and investments required for future prosperity are not made. Democracy needs entrepreneurship, it turns out, at least as much as entrepreneurship needs democracy.

Would such an alternative strategy of aggressive pushback against entrenched interests—a positive insurgency on a national scale of the type I've been proposing—have spelled trouble? Sure. But, as Charles Erwin Wilson said long ago, that's the price of progress.

Now—let me be clear—I am talking about economics here. I understand that words have meaning if people believe they have meaning. So, from that standpoint, the very fact that the terms "Left" and "Right" continue to be used suggests that they have some meaning to someone. My point is simply that, from the standpoint of economic fundamentals, the dichotomy is an illusion—useful for political marketing, but not much else.

Take, for example, the idea of the free market. Presumably a political conservative (someone from the Right) believes in the power of the free market to achieve efficient outcomes, where a liberal (someone from the Left) believes that there are limits to what the market can accomplish, and consequently is in favor of a significant role for government as a guarantor of the public interest. Furthermore, since this book is about entrepreneurship, I must really be advocating in favor of "free-market" approach, since entrepreneurs are, well, not part of the government.

Therefore, not Left, but Right.

Right? No. Incorrect.

For starters—nineteenth-century fantasies to the contrary notwithstanding—there is in fact no such thing as a purely "free" market. None ever has existed; none ever will exist. Government (or, in a state of anarchy, the localized power to coerce) sets the context for economic activity—and not just by guaranteeing property rights and raising an army to protect borders. Furthermore, private business creates the context for public action—and not just by paying taxes to government. Furthermore, as I discussed at length in chapter 9, government and established private interests are, in any actual human society, inextricably linked, for better or worse.

Perhaps more to the point, even in an idealized world in which nothing but the flimsiest shadow of a government or other coercive authority was present, there would be absolutely no reason to believe—based on economic fundamentals—that market-based outcomes would turn out to be efficient (much less, equitable). Even in the total absence of any government intervention, substantial inefficiencies in market outcomes would be expected whenever participants in markets don't share the same information (competitive advantage is possible), the practices of firms differ (management consultants are possible), the environment is characterized by significant uncertainties (insurance is possible), and transaction costs are not zero (lawyers are possible)—not to mention circumstances where market prices don't account for social costs and benefits (pollution and invention are possible). Because such "market failures" are ubiquitous, free-market nirvana will fail to materialize everywhere and always. As a consequence, those who seek naïvely to equate free markets with economic efficiency are engaged in horse-and-buggy reasoning that has no place in any serious, twenty-first-century discussion of economic challenges and their solutions. Period.

Here's the clincher: these very market failures—the ones that drive a wedge between predicted market outcomes and economic efficiency—are exactly the ones that create the context for entrepreneurship. No private information? No transaction costs? No uncertainty? Then you will also have no productive entrepreneurship. Zero. Under conditions of rigorously defined perfect competition, Schumpeterian business opportunities simply do not exist.

These aren't opinions. They are Econ 101 definitions. Ask your favorite economist (one with a degree). Economic theory establishes that perfect competition will result in socially efficient outcomes. But perfect competition is a theoretical idealization. It has nothing to do with the concept of the free market as it is colloquially understood—that is to say, markets in which a government role is limited to the narrowest of functions described above.

What does all of this mean for the role of public policy in bringing about the most favorable possible version of the coming prosperity? To quote Nobel laureate Ronald Coase,

> It is possible to conceive of better worlds than the one in which we live. But the problem is to devise practical arrangements which correct defects in one part of the system without causing more serious harm in other parts.
>
> Whatever we may have in mind as our ideal world, it is clear that we have not yet discovered how to get to it from where we are. A better approach would seem be to start our analysis with a situation approximating that which actually exists, to examine the effects of a proposed policy change and to attempt to decide whether the new situation would be, in total, better or worse than the original one.

The situation that exists in any real-world market is one rife with market failures. Those market failures are the source of opportunities for entrepreneurs. From such a starting point, a change in the market environment created by government may move the market either toward, or away from, efficiency; and toward, or away from, greater opportunity for entrepreneurs.

Entrepreneurial initiative can complement government action, or substitute for it. As the example in chapter 7 of the Coast Guard's actions following Hurricane Katrina indicates, it is not impossible for agencies of government to act nimbly and responsively. It just turns out to be difficult.

The world is moving rapidly in the right direction. But careful action by governments can smooth the transition from the Industrial Age to the age of entrepreneurship. It certainly is possible to conceive of worlds in which market failures were less dominant. But the problem is to devise practical arrangements which correct defects in one part of the system without causing more serious harm in other parts.

If my emphasis on entrepreneurship cannot be legitimately associated with an economic agenda of the Left or the Right—which I maintain it cannot—then perhaps the very bullishness of my narrative betrays a political leaning. Yes, those in the top 1 percent of income and wealth distribution are prospering. But what about the remaining 99 percent of the population? Where is the discussion in this book of inequality? Or of the fact that, for the vast majority of Americans, real wages have not increased in a generation? I made passing reference at the outset to this dimension of economic reality in the United States and other mature economies. But it has not come back since.

Wage stagnation—if not decline—for the majority of workers in the United States is a real and significant phenomenon. Its fundamental causes—technological change and increases in the global labor pool— have been recurrent themes in this book. As Michael Spence has recently highlighted, the only professions that have experienced wage growth in the past two decades are those in the economy's nontradable sectors, notably health and education. As I have noted, even these professions may be soon subject to wage pressures driven not by overseas competitors, but rather by digital disrupters—insurgent businesses offering services comparable in quality to the current standard but at far lower cost.

These complex, global phenomena transcend the tiny labels that political marketing campaigns in the US seek to affix to them. Likewise for allegedly ideological divisions about the economy that are not entirely manufactured by political consultants—both the Tea Party and Occupy Wall Street movements are, fundamentally, about deep-seated and broadbased frustration at the power of entrenched incumbents to obstruct needed change. That they respectively direct their ire at different coalitions of interests is almost beside the point. Like ostensibly competing mills on opposite sides of a deep river, they derive their populist energy from the same historical currents; whether they choose to color their flour red or blue does not change the essence of the river's flow. To prosper in the twenty-first century, people in the United States will have to connect, create, contribute, and collaborate as never before. It's as simple as that.

Now, to be clear, there is a bias in my argument. But it is one not in favor of the Right over the Left, or vice versa; rather, it is one in favor of the long term over the short term.

Recall what life was like for average Americans in the 1930s. It may not come as much of a surprise that in 1934, fewer than 15 percent of households possessed a telephone or an automobile. But it is also a fact that in 1934, 31 percent of US households had no running water, 39 percent had no shower or bathtub, and 32 percent had no indoor plumbing. Yes, one-third of Americans had no toilet.

Of course, if we were to make everyday life today comparable to that in the 1930s, we would also have to do away with antibiotics and all the rest of medicine. I didn't say "modern medicine," because medicine in the 1930s was closer to the days of Hippocrates than it is to medicine today; as a consequence, life expectancy in the United States in 1930 was fifty-nine years—about what it is today in Ghana.

If it was 1930 we would also have no social security, no Federal Deposit Insurance, no unemployment benefits. We would have no Gmail, iPads, or, (don't freak out here guys) any other pads for that matter.

So, from the standpoint of lived experience, human experience, our current economic woes do not compare with those in the past.

What do these facts have to do with the value of long-term thinking? They illustrate the overwhelming trend of progress over the past sixty years. Instead of enduring another Great Depression—as even commentators who should know better have, since 2008, occasionally suggested is the case—the average American has continued to enjoy a life much closer, in quantitative, historical terms, to *The Great Gatsby* than to *Little Orphan Annie*. These trends have affected every member of society. The very poor in the US today are much better off, in absolute terms, than their counterparts in 1930; those in the middle of the income distribution are also much better off, in absolute terms, than their Depression-era counterparts.

Now, of course, those who have drawn lines between the Great Recession and the Great Depression have not intended to say that the United States has been transported back seventy-five years, when a toilet was a luxury. That would be absurd. But therein lies the essence of the miscomprehension, the key fact omitted. The entire point of this book is that levels of human well-being—the sort of statistics offered above—actually do matter. In fact, they matter quite a bit more than the relative statistics—unemployment rates, growth rates, and trends in global trade flows—that are the usual point of reference in comparisons made between the two eras.

Why? As I have insisted throughout this book, the poor unfortunates previously confined to the developing world have suddenly turned out to be the people whose increased productivity is going to be driving global growth for the next fifty years. Those people—people who matter a lot both to America's future and to its recent past—aren't taking their toilets for granted. As James Fallows observed in an important essay titled "How America Can Rise Again" that he authored for *The Altantic* upon his return to the United States after three years living in China, "One look at the comforts and abundance of American life—even during a recession, even with all the people who are suffering or left out—can make it seem silly to ask about anything but the secrets of the country's success. . . . If this is a 'decline' it is from a level that most of the world still envies."

Yes, it is true that even in terms of conventional measures to which I referred above, the current downturn—with unemployment seemingly stuck near 10 percent, as compared with 25 percent at the height of the Great Depression—is not in the same ballpark as the Great Depression. But that is not the main point. Even these comparisons between the Great Depression and the Great Recession in terms of shifts in GDP, employment, and international trade miss the most important trend of all: the trend of history that connects the two eras—which is to say, they miss the toilets.

How did C. P. McCormick's management experiment turn out? Well, take a look in your kitchen cabinet, which (if you live in the US or many other parts of the world) most likely contains a bottle of McCormick or Schilling spices. (Schilling is a West Coast brand that McCormick acquired in 1947.) McCormick & Company grew rapidly during the thirty-seven years that C. P. McCormick led the company, ultimately establishing successful operations on every continent and becoming a global leader in its industry.

Beyond his work building McCormick & Company, C. P. McCormick also represented the United States to the International Labor Organization, in the process developing a network of contacts with business leaders around the world, including India's Naval Tata. (Naval Tata was the grandson of Tata group founder Jamsetji Tata, whose pathbreaking insights into corporate purpose I discussed in chapter 10). Naval had inherited his grandfather's farsighted vision, and shared with McCormick the view that there was more to business success than the search for profits: "More and more businessmen are becoming aware that fulfillment of societal goals is not generosity but an obligation," he said in 1972. "They realize that they have to change, or change will be forced on them." McCormick was similarly conscious of the need for business either to lead societal change, or to be its victim: "When any segment of society offends the essential human dignity of the people who make their living in a business enterprise, when power becomes so great that the rights of individuals are subordinated to dictatorial authority, then the will of the people asserts itself and there is a change." Compare this statement with one from Che Guevara: "I am not a liberator. Liberators do not exist. The people liberate themselves."

So, now, having read C. P. McCormick's story, would you say that he was a liberal, or a conservative? Was he prolabor or promanagement? Left or Right?

I have been considering C. P. McCormick's story for twenty-five years now, since I first came across his book *Power of People* during a year's leave of absence in college. (I was working for a business historian charged with organizing the McCormick & Company archives.) C. P. McCormick's story lurked in the back of my mind as I first read Joseph Schumpeter in a course on comparative political systems. His focus on the search for incremental improvements to shop-floor operations came back to me during graduate school as I worked with Stuart Kauffman and Karl Shell on production-recipe models of organizational learning. And it returned to me once again in my capacity as the editor of the *Innovations* journal as I followed the recent surge of interest in corporate social responsibility and social entrepreneurship.

These years of reflection on C. P. McCormick's story have given me an appreciation for how—not long after Henry Ford was building the monstrous River Rouge plant on the banks of the Dearborn River and long before management theorists came up with concepts like quality circles and triple bottom lines—C. P. McCormick understood deeply and intuitively that "the great working force of any business is a collection of individual human beings, all with individual rights and individual problems worthy of consideration by management and government." Collaborative advantage.

He understood that "the destiny of man lies in being of service to others." No progress without purpose.

He believed that "we were placed here to improve that society in which we live and that should be the goal of business and professional leaders today, tomorrow, and forever." Left? Right? No. Forward.

15 YOU AIN'T SEEN NOTHIN' YET

My Dear Parents,
Through the goodness and tender mercies of God, we are at length at the place which we expect will be our home for life.

—ASA BOWEN SMITH

Before Silicon Valley and Wall Street, before Ellis Island and the River Rouge, before Jamestown and Tenochtitlán, before the first migrations across the Bering land bridge—there was the wilderness of the Americas.

Vast and teeming with life, the Americas were the last among the continents to be inhabited by humans. For the earliest Siberian migrants just as for seventeenth-century colonists and for twentieth-century immigrants, the Americas have, for millennia, represented humanity's final terrestrial frontier. (Hold the *Star Trek* overdub here, please.)

But the prehistoric migrants to the Americas, and their descendants, differed fundamentally from the later arrivals from Europe in their outlook. To those who, in time, became the native people of the Americas, dependency on the wilderness was a given. Conquest of nature was not on the agenda. The highest human aspiration was to live in harmony with the environment. And really, what other option did they have?

The European settlers arrived with a different outlook. While the Bibles and bacteria they brought with them wreaked havoc on native peoples, their most disruptive import was secular and nonmicrobial: progress.

For the native peoples of the Americas, history generally pointed backward in time, toward tribal ancestors. Time itself was demarcated by the natural cycles of birth, life, and death. To the new arrivals from Europe, the arrow of history pointed in the opposite direction—forward, from the primitive to the civilized.

Progress meant overcoming savagery and conquering the wilderness. The account of the "New Found Land of Virginia," written in 1588 by Thomas Harriot following a visit to the ill-fated Roanoke colony, typifies this European vision:

> And by how much they upon due consideration shall find our manner of knowledge and craft to exceed theirs in perfection . . . by so much the more is it probable that they should desire our friendship and love, and have the greater respect for pleasing and obeying us. Whereby may be hoped if means of good government be used, that they may in short time be brought to civility, and the embracing of true religion.

To this line of reasoning a Cherokee named Kai-yah-teh-hee (a.k.a. Corn Tassel) offered the following rebuttal in a speech delivered to US treaty commissioners in 1777:

> You say: "Why do not the Indians till the ground and live as we do?" May we not, with equal justice, ask "Why do the white people not hunt and live as we do?" You pretend to think it no injustice to warn us not to kill our deer and other game from the mere love of waste. But it is very criminal in our young men if they kill a cow or a hog for food when they happen to be in your lands. . . .
>
> The great God of Nature has placed us in different situations. It is true that he has endowed you with many super advantages. But he had not created us to be your slaves. We are a separate people!

Corn Tassel's objections may have been fundamentally consistent with Americans' avowed commitment to the rights of man, but they conflicted entirely with the new nation's vision of progress. No principle was strong enough to restrain the recent arrivals' compulsion toward westward expansion.

In the middle of the nineteenth century, the determination to civilize native peoples and lands took on the stature of US national policy. The term "manifest destiny," specifically coined by John O'Sullivan in an 1845 essay, was intended to signify a singular connection between the evolution of the United States as a nation and the larger phenomenon of European migration across the North American continent—a westward expansion that created new possibilities for millions of people in the mid-nineteenth century, including Asa Bowen Smith, whom I quoted at the start of this chapter, and my own ancestors on my father's side.

In an earlier essay, O'Sullivan had advanced the idea that the United States was destined to be the "great nation of futurity" as a consequence of its unique qualities and origin:

> The American people having derived their origin from many other na-
> tions, and the Declaration of National Independence being entirely
> based on the great principle of human equality, these facts demonstrate
> at once our disconnected position as regards any other nation. . . . We
> are the nation of human progress, and who will, what can, set limits to
> our onward march?

When the dream of westward expansion was fulfilled and the frontier closed, the energies of venturesome Americans turned to extending to other nations the reach of its values, institutions, and, of course, economic influence. The internationalist vision famously championed by Woodrow Wilson received a very substantial boost on December 7, 1941, when the Imperial Japanese Navy undertook its exceptionally ill-considered attack on Pearl Harbor. America's engagement in the world was institutionalized following World War II when—with every other major global center of production either destroyed or severely damaged—the United States took leadership of the global reconstruction effort among countries outside the Soviet sphere of influence.

In the decades that followed, the somewhat accidental fact of American postwar dominance renewed Americans' sense of manifest destiny—though this time on a global scale. The historical and institutional excep-tionalism to which O'Sullivan referred became inextricably linked to, and tested by, the competition with the Soviets. By 2007, author and foreign policy analyst William Pfaff would correctly assert, "It is something like a national heresy to suggest that the United States does not have a unique moral status and role to play in the history of nations, and therefore in the affairs of the contemporary world." Exceptionalism had turned out to be as convenient a concept in its modern articulation as it was in the Renais-sance version summarized in 1588 by Thomas Harriot: it has served as a justification for exporting the values and institutions of the United States, at the same time that it has provided a built-in excuse for failure to do just that. Why do we seek to fit other places to our mold? Because we are exceptional. Why do other places subsequently fail to conform? Because, of course, they are not exceptional. The Cherokee, it turns out, are not the only "separate people" in the world.

The narrative of American exceptionalism has had a good run. In different forms over a century and a half it has been championed with equal vigor by Democrats (James Polk and Woodrow Wilson) and Republicans (Ronald Reagan and George W. Bush). It would not have endured the way it has if it didn't have significant elements of truth. But it is finished. The United States is no more uniquely responsible for the coming prosperity than China or Switzerland. What's coming is bigger than all of that.

This reality neither disproves nor validates the concept of American exceptionalism as viewed in the rearview mirror. What it reflects is simply that American exceptionalism has ceased to be an interesting idea. What is interesting, and what matters for the future, is the truly universal human aspiration for freedom, connection to other people, and prosperity. That's what the future is about.

Does that mean that America, and Americans, no longer have a particular purpose in the world? What is America without a frontier?

Not to worry. The frontier is still there. But it does not lie across a continent. It does not lie on the other side of the world. The next American frontier isn't external at all, as a matter of fact.

Somewhat uncomfortably, the next frontier—the next America—is staring us in the mirror.

Now, before you get too alarmed by that last sentence, let me be very clear right now: I do recognize that my training as an economist does not qualify me to conclude this book with a rousing call to introspective change. As I indicated at the outset, that's just not my comparative advantage, value added, or whatever you want to call it. Leave the motivational speaking to Tony Robbins, and the one-word wisdom to Malcolm Gladwell. They have the hair for it.

My actual job, of course, is teaching at a school of public policy. So what I should be doing, to conclude this extended epistle on the possibilities of the present, is to present you, the patient reader, with a list of recommendations, or takeaways, or action items, or any sort of list that provides clear guidance and instructions.

Now I don't want to disappoint entirely on this topic. I'm going to get to a list. But, for now, I just want to indicate my generic suspicion of any list (including one of my own) that pretends to enumerate the myriad pathways to the coming prosperity or provide bullet-pointed instructions about how to find them.

Why? At this point, the reason has most likely become fairly obvious. I do not possess the recipe for the coming prosperity. I don't feel too bad about that, since anyone who says they do possess such a recipe is making it up. That is the real point of this book. That is the real reason why I have emphasized entrepreneurial narratives and sought to describe how entrepreneurship drives societal change—because new recipes are coming together all the time. We don't know which ones will work. We only know that they'll be created.

Make no mistake about this point: Entrepreneurship itself is not the recipe for the coming prosperity. It is our name for the process by which the new recipes are created and tested out. It is our name for the method by which individuals and teams realize their capabilities, create new combinations, and challenge existing practices.

Entrepreneurship is a method that very naturally starts from the position of ignorance, which I assert is our common condition: "We don't know what we're doing," we confess to one another as a team. "We have to pay attention to the world around us." (Connect.) But it also starts from a position of commitment: "Despite that fact, we're going to try to get something done. We're going to get started." (Create.) If it is genuine entrepreneurship—productive entrepreneurship—it also starts with a purpose: "We have a vision. We have a goal." (Contribute.) And finally, if it has any chance of succeeding today, entrepreneurship ultimately involves trust: "We have a partner." (Collaborate.)

Now, being a policy wonk—guilty—I am of course aware that, in terms of the conventional statistics whose significance I sought to challenge in chapter 10, entrepreneurship is inarguably the future of American economic renewal. For example, does it mean something that all net job creation in the United States for the past twenty years has come from new and growing businesses? Of course it does. It means a lot. But it is also not surprising. The companies of the twentieth century are in retreat, because the core competitive strategy of the twentieth century—being big—no longer creates decisive twenty-first-century competitive advantage.

Does it matter, as I have also noted above, that more than one-quarter of all new firms started in the United States from 1995 to 2005 had at least one immigrant founder? Yes, of course it does. More generally, as Anne-Marie Slaughter, former dean of Princeton's Woodrow Wilson School and director of the State Department's Office of Policy Planning, has noted,

> The United States . . . has long attracted the world's most entrepreneurial, creative, and determined individuals. A vast mixing of cultures has created an atmosphere for a fruitful cross-fertilization and innovation. . . . The key to succeeding in a networked economy is being able to harvest the best ideas and innovations from the widest array of sources. In this regard, the United States is plugged into all corners of the global brain.

As I emphasized above, a deep bench of skilled immigrant talent is an essential element of our twenty-first-century collaborative advantage.

Does it matter that new technologies are distributing economic power as never before? Yes, of course it does. While I have emphasized the disruptive, and constructive, potential of mobile phones, other technologies are on the horizon with comparable potential to redefine economic fundamentals. What types of new "black-collar" jobs will be created when 3-D printing technology reaches maturity? (Three-dimensional printing is just like regular printing, except that its output is an object, not a sheet of paper. It is truly amazing.) Will every home be its own factory? The term "cottage industry" will require a reinvention.

Does it matter that the connections enabled through twenty-first-century technology are enabling entrepreneurial new combinations at a greater rate than at any prior time in human history? As I noted in chapter 9, getting to the frontier of knowledge requires ever greater effort and specialization; at the same time, creating new technologies requires ever more intensive collaboration across disciplinary and institutional boundaries. Our collective ability to fully realize the potential for the coming prosperity will depend vitally on our capacity to build and sustain the civic infrastructure necessary to catalyze and quickly test these new combinations.

The real growth industry for the United States in the twenty-first century isn't nanotechnology. It's not algae-based fuels. It's not even 3-D printing or the development of mobile applications. If any of these technological innovations will have a part in the coming prosperity, it is because they help to expand the capabilities of people, or to realize the patterns that connect human beings.

Umair Haque puts it like this: "Tomorrow's products and services have to be designed not just for mere consumption, but 'designed for meaning.' They must yield lasting, shared, meaningful economic gains—or else. . . . That's the big picture that tomorrow's radical innovators must redraw." So-called innovations yielding only short-term gains—what Haque terms "unnovations"—are a path toward irrelevance and ultimate bankruptcy, not prosperity.

The only reason that exploitative strategies appeared to work in the past was that, in generations gone by, the short term was long enough to yield substantial return on investment. While the short term remains the default time frame for thinking in business as well as government, in our volatile world it keeps getting shorter. As a consequence, short-term returns just aren't what they used to be. Just ask the former employees of Lehman Brothers: pursuit of exploitative strategies can rapidly turn the venerable into the vulnerable.

For that reason, if the United States is to grow sustainably, it must do so from its entrepreneurial core rather than its exploitative edge. And entrepreneurial success will have more to do with meaning margins than profit margins.

As I have emphasized throughout this book, the present also differs from the recent past in terms of the structure of production. The economic fundamentals of the twentieth century worked against the humanization of exchange. Large-scale mechanized manufacturing was, to understate the matter, not wholly compatible with individual inventiveness and distributed initiative. What's more, as a matter of historical record, the balance of economic returns in the twentieth century was skewed in favor of the owners of capital, rather than the providers of labor. Structural imbalances and expanding inequality were the consequence— within rich countries, just as between rich and poor countries.

That is changing. Now. Powerfully distributed technologies at a human scale are democratizing personal productivity as never before. Previously closed networks of production and knowledge are now open and accessible to creative and determined people nearly everywhere. In combination, these trends are, as I asserted at the outset and have sought to demonstrate since, creating opportunities as never before for individuals and collaborative teams to create value for themselves and for the communities of which they are a part.

These trends are global. But, at the same time, they are of singular importance to the United States. Why? The reason is that, whatever our manifest shortcomings, uncorrected errors, and irredeemable sins, we Americans have a very strong—though I'll refrain from saying exceptional—record of creating shared value and authentic prosperity. The Declaration of Independence and the Constitution were a good start. The Underground Railroad, the campaign for women's suffrage, and the civil rights movement renewed Americans' founding covenants of freedom. Such fundamental assertions of human dignity and rights—both in writing and in deed—are at the core of the American character. As John O'Sullivan wrote over 150 years ago, "American patriotism is not of soil; we are not aborigines, nor of ancestry, for we are of all nations; but it is essentially personal enfranchisement, for 'where liberty dwells,' said Franklin, the sage of the Revolution, 'there is my country.'"

Yet it is also true that episodes of political violence are abundant in American history; the persistence of xenophobic fear suggests they could recur. Furthermore, examples of courage and determination abound in every part of the world. For this reason, for all the importance of America's democratic legacy, our nation's greatest distinction ultimately may lie in our history of creating shared economic, rather than political, value. Those among America's inventors, entrepreneurs, and innovators whose work has helped set into motion the trends just described have had a disproportionate role in creating the unparalleled possibilities of the present. As President Obama stated in his inaugural address, "It has been the risk-takers, the doers, the makers of things—some celebrated but more often men and women obscure in their labor, who have carried us up the long, rugged path towards prosperity and freedom." There could be no more fundamental statement than this of America's collaborative advantage, past as well as future.

Now I'm a person who's spent twenty-four of the last twenty-seven years in one or another university. Universities are not exactly the most rapidly adapting institutions in society. So I know something firsthand about resistance to change. Universities aren't alone, of course. Indeed, nearly all of us are part of one or another entrenched interest group— which is another way of saying that nearly all us are part of a community ready for change.

To renew will not be enough. To thrive in the twenty-first century, America needs to repurpose. The efforts of entrepreneurs are a vital element of repurposing, but they are not the totality of the process. So here is the list I promised.

We need to repurpose the capabilities of government, liberating resources spent on programs in order to create platforms for innovation. (What was the most significant single action taken in the Clinton administration? It may prove to have been Executive Order 12906, which opened up the government's geospatial information systems to public and commercial use, creating a platform for innovation that may end up being as significant as the Internet. This is a model for the future.)

We need to repurpose our cities so that they fully realize their creative potential and the possibilities of the resources they contain. (Recall the large-scale urban gardening project in which Christopher Washington was involved that I described in chapter 12? That project is significant in itself, but also contains a metaphor. Cities are, and have always been, the centers of societal development. We can't afford to have any of them lie fallow.)

We need to repurpose the assets locked in our large-scale institutions— corporations, universities, and large nonprofit organizations—so that they can more rapidly and openly be reconfigured to create new products, services, and opportunities for meaningful work. (A massive, technologically driven disruption is coming to higher education—comparable to that which hit the newspaper industry in the last decade. This disruption can be a disaster for existing colleges and universities or an opportunity for genuine reinvention. Many institutions of higher education will not make it through the transition to come, but those that do have potential to be truly astounding places to connect, create, contribute, and collaborate. We have to make sure that happens.)

We need to repurpose the capabilities and connections of immigrants, the children of immigrants, and all others with strong ties to places outside the United States—valuing them actively not only for their labor and intellectual capacity, but just as importantly for the particular insights and relationships that they have to offer. (Nations around the world are seeking to reconnect with their diaspora communities. The United States is home to more international migrants than any other country. These facts together add up to a path forward for the US: realize the potential of our global collaborative advantage by capitalizing on other countries' strategies of diaspora engagement.)

And perhaps above all, we need to repurpose the energy and abilities of our youth, so that they are not wasted in vain search for yesterday's jobs, but instead are engaged in creating the work of the future. (Maker Faire, Youth Venture, Lemelson-MIT InvenTeams, FIRST Robotics, the Network for Teaching Entrepreneurship, AshokaU—these are some of the organizations and initiatives that are today providing young people in the US, like my three daughters, with the opportunities they need to be twenty-first-century creators and change leaders. We need to multiply these initiatives a thousandfold, toward the aim of creating what Ashoka founder Bill Drayton has memorably termed "an everyone a changemaker world.")

There is not a single institution more than a decade old in the United States that is not ready to be repurposed. This book has described the global historical trends with which any twenty-first-century effort at repurposing must contend. How repurposing happens in specific organizations and where it can lead is a topic big enough for another book unto itself.

On January 20, 2009, I huddled on a hill in the shadow of the Washington Monument with my wife and my three daughters. Before us was a frigid and unforgettable spectacle: a crowd of well over a million people massed on the National Mall to witness the inauguration of Barack Obama as president of the United States.

An air of historical import hung heavily over that day. Even among the partisan participants, the desire to celebrate was tempered not only by the cold but also by the stark and somber mood of the moment. For those few hours in the dead of winter, time seemed to have stopped. Even the Potomac River was frozen. Away from the Mall the streets were empty—as if the nation's capital had been evacuated to spare itself from celebration.

At the time, the mood seemed a natural one to me. The new president faced enormous challenges, seemingly unprecedented in recent memory. The election that brought him into office had only aggravated the already deep rifts within the electorate.

The president's inaugural address, tuned as it was to notes of cautious optimism, could not help but also to underscore the funereal tone of the day. As Barack Obama proclaimed that a new America was on its way in, there could be little doubt that an old America—six decades of global greatness—was on its way out. Sure, on that January day we could believe that better times might lie ahead. But the best of times? Gone.

Contrast this vision of the future of the United States of America with the one articulated by Warren Buffett in his 2010 letter to Berkshire Hathaway shareholders:

> Throughout my lifetime, politicians and pundits have constantly moaned about terrifying problems facing America. Yet our citizens now live an astonishing six times better than when I was born. The prophets of doom have overlooked the all-important factor that is certain: Human potential is far from exhausted, and the American system for unleashing that potential—a system that has worked wonders for over two centuries despite frequent interruptions for recessions and even a Civil War—remains alive and effective.
>
> We are not natively smarter than we were when our country was founded, nor do we work harder. But look around you and see a world beyond the dreams of any colonial citizen. Now, as in 1776, 1861, 1932 and 1941, America's best days lie ahead.

I think it's worth paying attention to what Warren Buffet has to say here, and not only because he is famous and a billionaire. It's also because Warren Buffett—the Ben Franklin of our day—is hardly a man prone to hyperbole or irrational exuberance. To the contrary, he is a man who has built a large fortune for himself and small fortunes for thousands of others on a philosophy of identifying, and investing in, value. And his tip on an undervalued investment prospect for today: the United States of America.

But if you don't like Warren Buffett's angle on the future of the United States, then take it from the Sex Pistols. (The Clash isn't the only British punk band with enduring insights of value to Americans today.) The one and only album recorded by the Sex Pistols contains this lyric, definitional for a generation:

You've got a problem, the problem is you!

Problems—what you gonna do?

Problems—the problem is you!

Now what does this 1978 lyric have to do with the possibilities of the present in the United States—or, for that matter, any country? Everything. Because what this youthful rant is about is taking a look in the mirror.

Resource scarcity is a problem. Climate change is a problem. Denial of human rights is a problem. The lack of opportunity for youth—one key source of the Sex Pistols' frustration with Britain of the 1970s—is a problem.

But globalization has the word "global" in it for a reason. It means that everyone's in. We've got a problem? The problem is us. We're all part of the traffic.

That's the bad news. The good news? So is the solution. The exceptionalism that matters for the twenty-first century is an exceptionalism of possibility: the particularly collaborative possibilities each of us brings to solve problems of which we're a part. "Problems—what you gonna do?"

That's what opportunity in the age of entrepreneurship is about. And that's why it's the key to the coming prosperity. Entrepreneurship doesn't just mean building new companies. Entrepreneurship means connecting to a problem, and by so doing, connecting to a solution.

If America is truly exceptional, it is because America is not a place. It is an idea. It is an idea that changes, adapts, and evolves. At its man-on-the-moon best, the last America was magnificent. But it had its problems. And, in any event, it's gone. The less time each of us spends building levies against inexorable tides of change, the better off we will all be.

Appreciating the nature of the coming prosperity may not, in itself, constitute a plan for the future. But it may be enough to suggest to us a next idea. A next promise. A next possibility.

A next America.

ACKNOWLEDGMENTS

This book has been in the works for a long time. I started to shape it about two years ago. But the ideas and experiences I relate here started to shape me long before that.

Reading Gregory Bateson's *Mind and Nature: A Necessary Unity,* a gift from my uncle to me when I was nineteen years old, provided significant initial impetus along the path that led to the ideas and convictions expressed in these pages. I was pushed further by a year of travel made possible by a small contract with McCormick & Company of Baltimore to research its international operations. That trip, covering nine countries in Asia, included many memorable experiences, notably (in the context of this book) an opportunity to meet the famed Indian industrialist Naval Tata, whom I quote in chapter 14. In the midst of those travels I spent three months working at the Foreign Languages Press (Waiwenju) in Beijing—an experience I describe in chapter 3, made possible by a family friend, Mrs. Jane Shaw.

In the years that followed I had the chance to explore questions related to the organization of human society, prompted by the formative experiences just described, under the guidance of some truly remarkable mentors: the sociologist Juan Linz, who was my academic adviser in college; the economist Karl Shell, who, though not formally on my dissertation committee, offered hugely valuable guidance to me at an early stage in my career; the evolutionary biologist Stuart Kauffman, whose work significantly influenced my own contributions to the theory of entrepreneurship and innovation; and the physicist turned innovation-policy pioneer Lewis Branscomb, who has been a close friend and collaborator for over a decade. To each of them I owe a lifelong debt.

To list other colleagues who have influenced me in developing the ideas in this book is a dangerous matter. I inevitably will recognize later that I made regrettable omissions. However, in roughly chronological order dating from the time of our first acquaintance, I must thank, David

Audretsch, Richard Florida, Iqbal Quadir, Maryann Feldman, Don Kash, Christopher Hill, Zoltan Acs, Pamela Hartigan, Martin Fisher, Deborah van Opstal, and Nadeem Haque.

Fast-forwarding to the matter immediately at hand—writing and publishing this book—my first thanks have to go to the Kauffman Foundation, which, through two separate grants, contributed substantially both to the initiation of this project and to its successful conclusion. Among my colleagues at the Kauffman Foundation, where I am currently a Senior Fellow (on leave from my faculty position at George Mason University), I owe specific thanks to Carl Schramm, who personally encouraged me in this undertaking from the outset, and to Bob Litan, Lesa Mitchell, and Dane Stangler, who have offered both general insights on themes integral to this book and specific comments on the book itself.

In the earliest stages of developing a proposal and finding a publisher, my agent at Dystel & Goderich, Jessica Papin, was enormously helpful. Her initial feedback on my proposal is significantly reflected in the final product. Similarly, I similarly thank Ben Rudnick for his insightful early feedback; I also thank Tyler Cowen, John Berger, Gardiner Harris, and Mark Chait for valuable counsel in the early stages of this project.

The editors with whom I have worked at Oxford University Press, Terry Vaughn and Joe Jackson, connected immediately with the core themes of the book and have remained actively engaged throughout the production process. I thank both of them, and the rest of the creative team at Oxford University Press, for having taken on the book to begin with, and for supporting it so steadfastly.

Numerous friends and colleagues offered detailed comments on the draft at different stages. Among them, I must specifically acknowledge Adam Hasler, Sandra Maxey, Peter Davis, and Erin Krampetz, who each read, and even reread, the entire draft and whose thoughtful feedback has been of great value. I am similarly grateful to Helen Snively, Dody Riggs, Peter Boettke, Gregory Lee, Christina Sass, Jeehye Lee, and Jinee Lee for their very helpful comments on various parts of the manuscript.

In this age of social networking, I would be remiss not to acknowledge the loosely bounded community to which I am connected via Twitter—the people who know me simply as @auerswald. Through the process of writing this book I have been alerted to many valuable research resources, and otherwise have learned a good deal, from many people to whom my connections are only virtual.

In a related category, I must acknowledge Javier Rivas, the founder and owner of the Modern Times Coffeehouse at Politics & Prose bookstore in Washington, DC, as well as Mark and Stephen Fedorchak, founders and owners of Northside Social in Arlington, Virginia; their establishments are reliable homes-away-from-home for many authors, entrepreneurs, and generally office-averse types (including me).

Authors customarily conclude their acknowledgments by thanking their families. Now that I've completed my first full-length, single-authored book, I understand why. It is not possible to complete a book—at least, it was not for me—without substantially disrupting domestic routines. My wife, Katje, and my daughters, Isabel, Helena, and Cecelia, consequently were destined to support me in this project whether they liked it or not. However, my family did much more than to tolerate my absences and my perpetual state of distractedness during the many months I worked on this book. They also gave me the energy every day to keep pushing forward.

Finally, I thank my mother, Huguette, who will read this book, and my father, Paul, who regrettably did not live long enough so that doing so would be an option. In addition to bringing me into the world, offering their unconditional love, and supporting me in all my endeavors, my parents also imparted to me their own joy in discovering and sharing ideas. I know I would have had many lively conversations about the content of this book with my father, were he still alive. He was the first to advise me to take note of the fact that the tide of history was shifting away from the political ideology of the Cold War and toward large-scale economic integration. He understood globalization before it acquired that name. As I hope this book evidences, I was listening.

NOTES

pg. 7, "creating today's unprecedented era of prosperity"—Three notable exceptions are David Audretsch, *The Entrepreneurial Society* (New York: Oxford University Press, 2007); William Baumol, Robert Litan, and Carl Schramm, *Good Capitalism, Bad Capitalism, and the Economics of Growth and Prosperity* (New Haven, CT: Yale University Press, 2008); and Richard Florida, *The Great Reset: How New Ways of Living and Working Drive Post-Crash Prosperity* (New York: Harper, 2010).

pg. 9, "I have chosen to feature in *Innovations*"—In the fall of 2008 *Innovations* published a special issue, with an introduction written by John Holdren, titled "Time for Change: Creating Energy and Climate Solutions," that was released at a daylong event at the National Academy of Sciences. Subsequently we published an edition dedicated entirely to the topic of water, titled "Clear Necessity: Addressing Global Water and Sanitation Challenges." See http://mitpress.mit.edu/innovations.

CHAPTER 1

pg. 14, "Norbert Wiener was to the information age"—The analogy to Einstein also holds with regard to Wiener's conscience as a scientist. Like Einstein but in sharp contrast to many of his scientific contemporaries—notably John von Neumann, cofounder of game theory and allegedly an inspiration for the character of Dr. Strangelove in Stanley Kubrick's classic film of the same title—Wiener was deeply concerned about the potentially adverse societal impacts of his work. He was under no illusion that a future full of intelligent machines would be an unambiguous boon to humanity. In 1948, Wiener wrote of the nascent field of robotics that he had been instrumental in developing: "Long before Nagasaki and the public awareness of the atomic bomb, it had occurred to me that we were in the presence of another social potentiality of unheard-of importance for good and for evil." While robotic slave labor might liberate people from menial tasks, it could also be placed in direct competition with human labor, resulting in widespread unemployment and a sharp deterioration in the living standards of the many to the benefit of the few.

pg. 14, "his PhD from Harvard in mathematical philosophy"—Shortly thereafter, as World War I raged on the Continent, Wiener joined the army's research facility in Aberdeen, Maryland, to work on methods to improve the accuracy of artillery fire. It was at Aberdeen that he began the work that would develop into cybernetics. Flo Conway and Jim Siegelman, *Dark Hero of the Information Age: In Search Of Norbert Wiener—Father of Cybernetics* (New York: Basic Books, 2004).

pg. 14, "one contemporary's description"—See http://www-history.mcs.st-and.ac.uk/Biographies/Wiener_Norbert.html.

pg. 14, "two decades before the creation of the first web page"—Conway and Siegelman, *Dark Hero of the Information Age.*

pg. 15, "likely could not be suppressed"—Letter from Norbert Wiener to Walther Reuther, in the *Papers of Norbert Wiener*, MC.0022, folder 102 (Cambridge, MA: Institute Archives, Massachusetts Institute of Technology, August 13, 1949).

pg. 15, "The idea never came to fruition."—Telegram from Walther Reuther to Norbert Wiener, in the *Papers of Norbert Wiener*, MC.0022, folder 103 (Cambridge, MA: Institute Archives, Massachusetts Institute of Technology, August 22, 1949).

pg. 16, "increased efficiency and lower cost"—Industrial-organization economists continue to engage in active study of the fundamental factors that determine the distribution of firm size as it evolves over time. John Sutton of the London School of Economics is among the leading contirbutors to this area of research. He proposes an alternative, though potentially complementary, explanation to that which I offer here. Sutton presents evidence dating back to the early 1960s that firm size is not driven directly by economies of scale in production, but rather by firms' need to average R&D and advertising expenditures—significant fixed costs of production—over large scales. For this observation to be valid also for firms at the start of the twentieth century, the discontinuity in the distribution of firm sizes experienced at that time would need to be explainable by a surge in R&D expenditures—that is, an unprecedented intensity of the use of organizational techniques requiring cumulative learning and of technologies requiring cumulative investment. (Thanks to Peter Davis for this insight.)

pg. 19, "good choices would be followed by bliss"—This was precisely the outcome predicted by the earliest model of economic growth which was developed, reportedly at the suggestion of Keynes, by another brilliant young Cambridge economist, Frank Ramsey.

pg. 20, "a factor of 1,400 in a quarter century"—Bank for International Settlements, "Financial Globalisation and Emerging Market Capital Flows," *BIS Papers* 44 (December 2008). Net capital flows were over $400 billion.

pg. 20, "accounts for 40 percent of the total"—Of 1,012 billionaires in the 2010 Forbes count, 395 resided in the United States and 247 in advanced industrialized countries (e.g., members of the Organisation for Economic Co-operation and Development) other than the United States. In contrast, 277 resided in developing countries, excluding countries of the former Soviet Union, whose economic trajectories have been based on a resource-based growth dynamic different from that described here. See http://www.forbes.com/2010/03/10/worlds-richest-people-slim-gates-buffett-billionaires-2010_land.html.

pg. 21, "They lost fifteen million."—Daniel Ikenson, "Manufacturing Discord Growing Tensions Threaten the U.S.-China Economic Relationship," Cato Institute Center for Trade Policy Studies, Working Paper no. 29, May 4, 2010. Thanks to Brink Lindsey for bringing these facts to my attention.

pg. 22, "Keynes identified decades ago"—For an interesting recent articulation, see W. Brian Arthur, "The Second Economy," *McKinsey Quarterly* 4 (2011): 91–99.

pg. 22, "endless ways to create and produce and distribute"—Anya Kamenetz, "Occupy-WallStreet Organizer's Ideas for a New 'Human Economy,'" *FastCompany.com*, October 5, 2011.

pg. 23, "General Motors drove itself to ruin"—Alex Taylor III, "GM and Me," *Fortune*, December 8, 2008, 92–100.

CHAPTER 2

pg. 24, "John D. Rockefeller III"—Phyllis Tilson Piotrow, *World Population Crisis: The United States Response* (New York: Praeger, 1973), 49.

pg. 25, "should exhaust the mines"—Quoted in Arthur Herman, "The Pessimist Persuasion," *Wilson Quarterly* (Spring 2009): 60. Vol. 33, No. 2.

pg. 25, "one and a half times that rate"—Angus Maddison, "Statistics on World Population, GDP and Per Capita GDP, 1–2008 AD," (2010). Unpublished data resource. See http://www.ggdc.net/MADDISON/Historical_Statistics/vertical-file_02-2010. xls. See also *The World Economy: A Millennial Perspective* (Paris: Organisation for Economic Co-operation and Development [OECD], 2001), table B-18.

pg. 25, "to justify truly horrific acts"—Regarding the latter, see Edwin Black, *War on the Weak: Eugenics and America's Campaign to Create a Master Race* (New York: Thunder's Mouth Press, 2004).

pg. 26, "produce subsistence for man"—Thomas Malthus, *An Essay on the Principle of Population* (Oxford: Oxford University Press, 2008), 13.

pg. 27, "distance from the wished for goal"—Ibid., 9.

pg. 27, "one million BC to the present—no mean feat"—Michael Kremer, "Population Growth and Technical Change, One Million B.C. to 1990," *Quarterly Journal of Economics* 108, no. 3 (August 1993): 681–716.

pg. 29, "a likelihood of more great ideas"—Maddison, "Statistics on World Population." Gregory Clark, an economic historian at UC–Davis, takes an even bleaker view of the advance of human society prior to the Industrial Revolution: "The average person in the world of 1800 was no better off than the average person of 100,000 BC. Indeed in 1800 the bulk of the world's population was poorer than their remote ancestors. The lucky denizens of wealthy societies such as eighteenth-century England or the Netherlands managed a material lifestyle equivalent to that of the Stone Age. But the vast swath of humanity in East and South Asia, particularly in China and Japan, eked out a living under conditions probably significantly poorer than those of cavemen." Clark, *A Farewell to Alms* (Princeton, NJ: Princeton University Press, 2007), 1.

pg. 30, "number of people on the planet"—For a further development of this concept, see Duncan Foley, "Stabilization of Human Population through Economic Increasing Returns," *Economic Letters* 68 (2000): 309–17.

pg. 30, "Call it the 'population boon.'"—Foley, "Stabilization of Human Population," fig. 3. Data from Angus Maddison, *Monitoring the World Economy 1820–1992* (Paris: OECD Development Center, 1995).

pg. 30, *"Implications of Worldwide Population Growth of US Security and Overseas Interest"*—National Security Study Memorandum (NSSM 200), "Implications of Worldwide Population Growth for U.S. Security and Overseas Interests," December 10, 1974. Full text accessible at http://pdf.usaid.gov/pdf_docs/PCAAB500.pdf.

pg. 32, "to our humanitarian values"—National Security Council, National Security Study Memorandum 200, April 24, 1974, par. 19.

pg. 32, "the gap between rich and poor"—Ibid., par. 15.

pg. 33, "second half of the twentieth century"—See "Go Forth and Multiply a Lot Less," *Economist*, October 31, 2010, 29–32. Data from the UN Population Division. Wonderful data visualization tools illustrating these points are available at http://www.gapminder.org.

pg. 34, "tend to increase with income"—Partha Dasgupta, "The Population Problem: Theory and Evidence," *Journal of Economic Literature* 33 (December 1995): 1879–1902. That fertility shifts have occurred mostly for economic reasons is evidenced by the fact that the only part of the People's Republic of China in which the ratio of women to children is 1:1 is Hong Kong, which is also the only part of the People's Republic of China where the Chinese government's one-child policy does not apply. (Thanks to Gapminder.org for that observation.)

pg. 35, "crash programs embarked upon now"—Paul R. Ehrlich and Anne H. Ehrlich, "The Population Bomb Revisited," *Electronic Journal of Sustainable Development* (2009).

pg. 35, "global agricultural production"—These technological and organizational innovations, referred to as the "Green Revolution," were responsible for a doubling in the output of cereals in developing countries between the early 1960s and the mid-1980s. The term "Green Revolution" itself was coined by William Gaud, then administrator of the U.S. Agency for International Development, in 1968—about the same time the Ehrlichs were writing *The Population Bomb*. See William S. Gaud, "The Green Revolution: Accomplishments and Apprehensions," remarks to the Society for International Development, March 8, 1968. http://www.agbioworld.org/biotech-info/topics/borlaug/borlaug-green.html.

pg. 36, "if you're curious"—For a clear description of the economic fundamentals, see Jonathan E. Hughes, Christopher R. Knittel, and Daniel Sperling, "Evidence of a Shift in the Short-Run Price Elasticity of Gasoline Demand," *Energy Journal* 29, no. 1 (2008): 93–113.

pg. 36, "agro-industrial complexes has proven entirely correct"—Ehrlich and Ehrlich, "Population Bomb Revisited," 100–105.

pg. 38, "because they have remained abundant"—While oil and gas companies are today cast (mostly rightly) as pariahs in the battle to address adverse impacts from climate change, it is worth pointing out that oil barons were the alternative-energy pioneers of their day. If there are any whales around today for Greenpeace to save, it is arguably due to the efforts of John D. Rockefeller (whose grandson I quote at the top of this chapter) and others of his ilk who brought to market a substitute for whale oil that was cheaper and more effective.

pg. 38, "What is of interest is the long-term trend."—As financier George Soros stated in the midst of the bubble, "You have a generalized commodity bubble due to commodities having become an asset class that institutions use to an increasing extent. On top of that you have specific factors that create the relative shortage of oil and, now, also food." Saijel Kishan and John Rega, "Soros Says Commodity 'Bubble' Still in 'Growth Phase' (Update3)," Bloomberg.com, April 17, 2008.

pg. 39, "goal of an economy-wide carbon tax"—If legislation requiring carbon pricing were to be enacted and the price of carbon was to reach equilibrium at, say, twenty dollars per ton—a high estimate—it would cause consumers in the United States to pay twenty cents per gallon more at the pump. That's only one-tenth of the two-dollar increase in the price of gasoline over the past six years, which is attributable to pressures in global oil markets.

It is true, however, that oil price increases do induce exploration for new sources of oil. That effect serves to offset the beneficial impacts of oil price increases, with regard to a reduction in carbon dependency. The argument I am making here presumes that the supply elasticity of oil—that is, the extent to which oil-price increases motivate producers to discover new oil sources—is lower than the demand elasticity—that is, the extent to which oil-price increases motivate consumers to seek alternatives to oil. In this instance, a carbon tax is different from a price increase, since it drives a wedge in the price received by producers for oil and the price faced by consumers; consumers may substitute away from carbon-based fuels as a consequence of the carbon tax, but producers will not have an increased incentive to seek new sources of carbon-based fuels.

pg. 40, "No historical process that is understood is inevitable."—Mancur Olson, *Power and Prosperity: Outgrowing Communist and Capitalist Dictatorship* (New York: Basic Books, 2000), 198.

pg. 40, "solitary, poor, nasty, brutish, and short"—Thomas Hobbes, *Leviathan* (London: Andrew Crooke, 1651), chap. 13, par. 9.

pg. 41, "with the cognitive freedom that entails"—Amartya Sen, *Development as Freedom* (New York: Anchor, 2000).

pg. 42, "than at any other time in human history"—Cambridge University's Partha Dasgupta has been a leader in documenting the complex ecological interaction between locally increasing population, persistent poverty, and environmental damage. The evidence is strong that positive feedback among these factors can create enduring poverty traps. There is a notable silver lining in this analysis, however: if some factor enters into the environment to disrupt this downward spiral (potentially, the introduction of a new productivity enhancing technology like the mobile phone, or a reduction in the local population due to migration to cities), what was a negative feedback loop can turn into a positive one. Reduced poverty can lead to lower birthrates, which in turn can lead to less local pressure on the environment. This is the trajectory of change that will be experienced with increasing frequency in poor, rural places around the world. Dasgupta, "The Population Problem," 1879–1902.

CHAPTER 3

pg. 43, "good cat so long as it catches mice"—Remarks at Guangzhou conference, spring 1961.

pg. 45, "We need a steadier vision."—US Department of State, "Future Foreign Policy Challenges for the U.S.," Fortieth Anniversary Celebration of the Establishment of the Policy Planning Staff, Washington, DC, May 11, 1987 (unpublished).

pg. 48, "codified the return of family-based farming"—Yasheng Huang, *Capitalism with Chinese Characteristics: Entrepreneurship and the State* (New York: Cambridge University Press, 2008); and Kate Xiao Zhou, *China's Long March to Freedom: Grassroots Modernization* (New Brunswick, NJ: Transaction Publishers, 2009). I thank Iqbal Quadir for having shared with me his insights on this topic.

pg. 48, "turning point in human history"—Huang, *Capitalism with Chinese Characteristics.*

pg. 51, "caused by greed at ExxonMobil"—For more on the root causes of the recession as it relates to Asia's (particularly, China's) savings, see Ravi Jagannathan, Mudit Kapoor, and Ernst Schaumburg, "Why Are We in a Recession? The Financial Crisis Is the Symptom, Not the Disease!" National Bureau of Economic Research Working Paper 15404 (Cambridge, MA: National Bureau of Economic Research, 2009), http://www.nber.org/papers/w15404.

pg. 51, "lining the aisles in stores around the world"—Nicholas Kristof, "Pirates and Sanctions," *New York Times*, May 24, 2007.

pg. 52, "in the ballpark of its norm in centuries past"—Maddison, "Statistics on World Population." See also *World Economy.*

pg. 53, "today's debate over China and trade"—William Earl Weeks, *John Quincy Adams and American Global Empire* (Lexington: University Press of Kentucky, 2002), 20. For more on Adams's views on trade, see David W. McFadden, "John Quincy Adams, American Commercial Diplomacy, and Russia, 1809–1825," *New England Quarterly* 66, no. 4 (December 1993): 613–29.

pg. 54, "wages have risen"—Harold L. Sirkin, Michael Zinser, and Douglas Hohner, "Made in America, Again: Why Manufacturing Will Return to the U.S.," Boston Consulting Group, August 2011.

pg. 55, "some sort of turning point has already been reached"—Even for those who have been successful, the ride is uneven. The last time I reached Zhang Runbo, in spring 2011 via a Chinese-speaking assistant, he reported that he has left Chun Hing and does not hold any ownership stake in the business.

pg. 55, "pick up where government leaves off"—Observations here on the central role of philanthropy in the dynamics of entrepreneurial capitalism originate with Zoltan Acs. For more see Philip E. Auerswald and Zoltan J. Acs, "Defining Prosperity," *American Interest* (Summer 2009): 4–13.

CHAPTER 4

pg. 59, "high-quality jobs throughout the country"—Numbers current as of spring 2010. Quotes from Karim Khoja and information on Roshan have been drawn from two talks given by Khoja at MIT's Legatum Center for Development and Entrepreneurship, from the case narrative for the *Innovations* journal authored by Khoja, and from personal correspondence. Legatum Conference, "Progress through Innovation," October 31, 2008: Panel of Entrepreneurs from Afghanistan, India and Kenya, http://legatum.mit.edu/content-167. Karim Khoja, Legatum Lecture, MIT, March 6, 2009, http://techtv.mit.edu/genres/20-entrepreneurship/videos/3560-legatum-lectures-karim-khoja-ceo-roshan-afghanistan. Karim Khoja, "Connecting a Nation: Roshan Brings Communications Services to Afghanistan," *Innovations: Technology, Governance, Globalization* 4, no. 1: 33–50, http://www.mit-pressjournals.org/doi/abs/10.1162/itgg.2009.4.1.33.

pg. 62, "Col. Marty Leppert of the National Guard's Agribusiness Development Team"—The National Guard's description of this initiative is available at http://www.ng.mil/features/ADT/default.aspx.

pg. 63, "even in the absence of a stable, formal government"—See BBC News, "Telecoms Thriving in Lawless Somalia," November 19, 2004, http://news.bbc.co.uk/2/hi/africa/4020259.stm; see also *The Guardian*, "In Somaliland, less money has brought more democracy," August 26, 20011, http://www.guardian.co.uk/global-development/poverty-matters/2011/aug/26/somaliland-less-money-more-democracy.

pg. 64, "lay in bouquets of roses"—The document itself was confidential. The essence of the approach, developing supply chains, is a sound one. Compared with disjointed projects, an integrated supply-chain development strategy is definitely preferable. However, for a large and complex country like Pakistan, an export-led strategy narrowly pursued for a few markets is a bit like performing cosmetic surgery on a patient in the intensive care ward. In the absence of other interventions occurring in parallel the patient may look better for a while—but not for long.

pg. 65, "consequence of terrorist attacks since 2006"—See http://travel.state.gov/travel/cis_pa_tw/tw/tw_930.html.

pg. 66, "the family access to their own market"—Four manufacturers of automotive products have dominated the Pakistani market for the past thirty years. See Competition Commission of Pakistan, "State of Competition in Pakistan" (Islamabad, Pakistan: Competition Commission of Pakistan, 2009). Accessible at http://www.cc.gov.pk/.

pg. 66, "his son now goes to a super college"—Interview with Shamoon Sultan, Karachi, October 2010.

pg. 67, "he says matter of factly"—Interview with Monis Rahman in Lahore, October 2010.

pg. 68, "recalls of the launch with a laugh"—Interview with Seema Aziz in Lahore, October 2010.

pg. 71, "absent from the conversation at the CFR"—Jake Cusack and Erik Malmstrom, *Bactrian Gold: Challenges and Hope for Private-Sector Development in Afghanistan*, Kauffman Foundation Research Series: Expeditionary Economics (Kansas City, MO: Kauffman Foundation, 2011).

pg. 71, "They are the same."—Erik Malmstrom and Jake Cusack, "Afghanistan's Willing Entrepreneurs: Supporting Private-Sector Growth in the Afghan Economy" (Washington, DC: Center for a New American Security, 2010). Full text available at http://www.cnas.org/node/5346. Audio of remarks at the Center for Strategic and International Studies on November 18, 2010, available at http://csis.org/multimedia/snapshot-challenges-and-hope-private-sector-development-afghanistan.

CHAPTER 5

pg. 75, "James Fisk, crooked financier?"—For a similarly themed reference to the Panic of 1857, see Paul Kedrosky, "Introduction: The Next Frontier," *Washington Monthly*, May/June 2009. Full text available at http://www.washingtonmonthly.com/features/2009/0905.kedrosky.html.

pg. 77, "half the people on earth had mobile phones"—Data drawn from a report I prepared for the Gates Foundation titled *Profiles in Development Progress: Using Mobile Phones to Extend the Reach of Financial Services*, draft December 12, 2009.

pg. 77, "And before that? Fire."—The observation about radios is widely made. I thank Joel Selanikio, the founder of DataDyne, for the particular point about fire having been the only technology before radio to make it to the village level on a global scale.

pg. 78, "double every eighteen months"—Gordon E. Moore, "Cramming More Components onto Integrated Circuits," *Electronics* 38, no. 8 (April 19, 1965): 114–17.

pg. 79, "porcelain over the span of generations"—As a glance to prehistory affirms, economic systems have long tended to start out closed and to exhibit little initial division of labor. In the words of Gideon Sjobert, "Other facets of the pre-industrial city are associated with its particular system of production. There is little fragmentation or specialization of work. The handicraftsman participates in nearly every phase of the manufacturing of an article, often carrying out the work in his own home or in a small shop nearby and, within the limits of certain guild and community regulations, maintaining direct control over conditions of work and production." "The Preindustrial City," *American Journal of Sociology* 60 (April 1955): 438–45.

pg. 82, "prospect of elected resident government"—"Better than Freedom? Why Iraqis Cherish Their Mobile Phones," *Economist*, November 12, 2009, http://www.economist.com/world/middleeast-africa/displaystory.cfm?story_id=14870118.

pg. 83, "banking and money-transfer channels"—World Bank, *Migration and Remittances Factbook 2008* (Washington, DC: World Bank).

pg. 84, "that is the coming prosperity"—Total official development assistance from rich countries to poor ones in 2010 was just over $150 billion. Flows of illicit capital in the opposite direction—out of poor countries to rich ones—are estimated to total over $500 billion. Raymond Baker and Eva Joly, "Illicit Money: Can It Be Stopped?" *New York Review of Books*, December 3, 2009, http://www.nybooks.com/articles/archives/2009/dec/03/illicit-money-can-it-be-stopped/. The relative size of these two numbers says something about the magnitude of potential returns to society from improved governance in comparison with returns from increased aid effectiveness.

Both flows are situated within a $60 trillion global economy in which spending by middle-class consumers outside of North America and Europe accounts for over $7.5 trillion. Homi Kharas, "The Emerging Middle Class in Developing Countries," OECD Development Centre Working Paper No. 28, January 2010, http://www.oecd.org/dataoecd/12/52/44457738.pdf).

pg. 84, "the more likely you are to get hit again"—Remarks at Tech@State Mobile Money conference, Department of State, Washington, DC, August 2, 2010.

pg. 84, "Kenya's adult population"—Fiona Graham, "M-PESA: Kenya's Mobile Wallet Revolution," BBC News, November 22, 2010. Accessible at http://www.bbc.co.uk/news/business-11793290.

pg. 85, "in seventeen countries in sub-Saharan Africa"—Data compiled in the report I prepared for the Gates Foundation titled *Profiles in Development Progress*. Background and data are available in the "Mobilizing Markets" special issue of the *Innovations* journal and on the Mobile Active blog, http://www.mitpressjournals.org/toc/itgg/4/1. http://mobileactive.org/.

pg. 85, "exporting their model to other countries"—See http://www.txteagle.com.

pg. 86, "literally put in Filipino hands"—Reuters, "Cellphone Text Revolution Helps People Power Revolt," Indian Express Newspapers (Bombay) Ltd., January 24, 2001, http://www.expressindia.com/news/ie/daily/20010124/iin24003.html.

pg. 86, "demonstrators who were in the field"—Interview at the 2011 annual meeting of the World Economic Forum, Davos, Switzerland, http://www.youtube.com/watch_popup?v=z7DxNjPz7zM&vq=medium. For a more complete description of the role that social media are playing in the Tunisian and Egyptian revolutions, see Jeffrey Ghannam, *Social Media in the Arab World: Leading Up to the Uprisings of 2011* (Washington, DC: Center for International Media Assistance, 2011).

pg. 86, "We are given freedom of initiative."—Interview at the 2011 annual meeting of the World Economic Forum, Davos, Switzerland. Accessible at http://t.co/E5DLUOz.

pg. 87, "known as the human voice"—Malcolm Gladwell, "Does Egypt Need Twitter," *New Yorker* online (blog post), February 2, 2011. Accessible at http://www.newyorker.com/online/does-egypt-need-twitter.html.

pg. 87, "a force that is often irresistible"—Sir John Millar, cited in Albert O. Hirschman, *The Passions and the Interests: Political Arguments for Capitalism Before Its Triumph* (Princeton, NJ: Princeton University Press, [1977] 1997), 93.

CHAPTER 6

pg. 90, "narrower than it was a few generations back"—For example, in the United States, Holstein cows now make up more than 90 percent of dairy cattle, and white Leghorn chickens produce almost all of the country's white eggs. Daniel Hillel and Cynthia Rosenzweig, "Biodiversity and Food Production," in *Sustaining Life: How Human Health Depends on Biodiversity*, ed. Eric Chivian and Aaron Bernstein (New York: Oxford University Press, 2008), 360. This shift has also had a substantial and irreversible effect on biodiversity. More than 90 percent of crop varieties have been lost from farmers' fields in the past hundred years, and 690 livestock breeds have become extinct. In one startling example of the decline in biodiversity, of the 7,100 types of apples that were grown in America in the nineteenth century, 6,800 are now extinct. Other plant species reflect a similar trend. Tom Standage, *An Edible History of Humanity* (New York: Walker, 2009); SARD, Policy Brief 16, 2007. Accessible at ftp://ftp.fao.org/sd/sda/sdar/sard/biodiversity-india.pdf, 9/30/2010, p. 241.

pg. 90, "earliest evidence of writing itself"—The oldest known written recipe is one for beer, etched into stone about four thousand years ago. See http://www.beer-institute.org/tier.asp?bid=139.

pg. 92, "circumvented scarcity problems in the past"—Martin Weitzman, remarks at the "Between Invention and Innovation" workshop, Kennedy School of Government, Harvard University, May 2, 2001.

pg. 93, "big business, not entrepreneurship"—See, for example, Richard Nelson, ed., *The Rate and Direction of Inventive Activity: Economic and Social Factors* (Cambridge, MA: National Bureau of Economic Research, 1962).

pg. 96, "some question, however small"—Joseph Schumpeter, *The Theory of Economic Development: An Inquiry into Profits, Capital, Credit, Interest, and the Business Cycle* (New Brunswick, NJ, Transaction Publishers: 2005), 20; originally published as *Theorie der witschaftlichen Entwicklung*. (Leipzig: Duncker & Humblot, 1912); English translation by Redvers Opie, *The Theory of Economic Development* (Oxford: Oxford University Press, 1934).

pg. 97, "not just the inputs and the outputs"—See Philip Auerswald, Stuart Kauffman, José Lobo, and Karl Shell, "The Production Recipes Approach to Modeling Technological Innovation: An Application to Learning-By-Doing," *Journal of Economic Dynamics and Control* 24, no. 3 (2000): 389–450; Philip Auerswald, "Entrepreneurship in the Theory of the Firm," *Small Business Economics* 30, no. 2 (2008): 111–26; Philip Auerswald "Entry and Schumpeterian Profits: How Technological Complexity Affects Industry Evolution," *Journal of Evolutionary Economics* 20, no. 4 (2010): 553–82.

CHAPTER 7

pg. 98, "buses around to get them out"—Eric Lipton et al., "Breakdowns Marked Path From Hurricane to Anarchy," *New York Times*, September 11, 2005.

pg. 98, "sentences of up to 175 years"—CNN, "Nursing Home Owners Face Charges," CNN.com, September 13, 2005.

pg. 99, "what they were being charged with"—Bob Warren, "Manganos Not Guilty in St. Rita's Nursing Home Case," *Times-Picayune*, September 9, 2007.

pg. 101, "better shape today, in my judgment"—Risk consultant Marc Groz writes, "The old adage 'garbage in, garbage out' certainly applies. When you realize that VaR is using tame historical data to model a wildly different environment, the total losses of Bear Stearns's hedge funds become easier to understand. It's like the historic data only has rainstorms and then a tornado hits." Joe Nocera, "Risk Management," *New York Times Magazine*, January 4, 2009. And John Maynard Keynes writes, "A sound banker, alas, is not one who foresees danger and avoids it, but one who, when he is ruined, is ruined in a conventional and orthodox way with his fellows, so that no-one can really blame him." John Maynard Keynes, "The Consequences to the Banks of the Collapse of Money Values," *Essays in Persuasion* (New York: W. W. Norton & Co., [1931] 1963), 176–77.

pg. 101, "lingered into its twenty-first century"—Auerswald and Acs, "Defining Prosperity."

pg. 102, "to secure future growth"—Martin Weitzman, "Soviet Postwar Economic Growth and Capital-Labor Substitution," *American Economic Review* 60, no. 4 (1970): 686.

pg. 103, "been around for over five hundred million years"—See http://www.livescience.com/animals/050207_extremophiles.html.

pg. 104, "he had the wrong species"—Edward O. Wilson, "Karl Marx Was Right, Socialism Works," unpublished interview by Frans Roes, Harvard University, March 27, 1997. Full text accessible at http://www.froes.dds.nl/WILSON.htm.

pg. 104, "extreme contractual arrangements"—Ibid.

pg. 105, "Ants, like humans, succeed because they talk so well."—Bert Hölldobler and E. O. Wilson, *Journey to the Ants* (Cambridge, MA: Harvard University Press, 1994), ix.

pg. 105, "the variation was wholly artificial"—James Kennedy and Russell Eberhart, "Particle Swarm Optimization," in *Proceedings of IEEE International Conference on Neural Networks* (Piscataway, NJ: IEEE Press, 1995), 1942–43.

pg. 106, "will destroy any cooperative behavior"—Mark M. Millonas, "Swarm, Phase Transitions, and Collective Intelligence," in *Artificial Life II*, ed. C. G. Langton (Reading, MA: Addison Wesley, 1994).

pg. 107, "departments may churn chaotically"—Stuart Kauffman, "Technology and Evolution: Escaping the Red Queen Effect," *McKinsey Quarterly* (February 1995): 128.

pg. 109, "to call it Socialism or not"—Joseph A. Schumpeter, "The Instability of Capitalism," *Economic Journal* 38, no. 151 (September 1928): 385–86.

pg. 109, "it also ousts the entrepreneur"—Joseph A. Schumpeter, *Capitalism, Socialism, and Democracy* (New York: Routledge, [1942] 2010), 119.

pg. 110, "government of the United States failed"—See http://www.newt.org/newt-direct/newt-gingrich-senate-commerce-subcommittee-technology-innovation-and-competitiveness.

pg. 110, "Walmart's response to the disaster"—See http://www.washingtonpost.com/wp-dyn/content/article/2005/09/05/AR2005090501598.html. See also Steven Horwitz, "Best Responders: Post-Katrina Innovation and Improvisation by Wal-Mart and the U.S. Coast Guard," *Innovations: Technology, Governance, Globalization* 4, no. 2 (Spring 2009) 93–99.

pg. 110, "above all, do the right thing"—Kennedy School of Government Case Program C16-07-1876.0, "Wal-Mart's Response to Hurricane Katrina: Striving for a Public-Private Partnership," 5.

pg. 110, "a full week after the storm"—Amanda Ripley, "How the Coast Guard Gets It Right," *Time*, October 23, 2005. See also Stephen Barr, "Coast Guard's Response to Katrina a Silver Lining in the Storm," *Washington Post*, September 6, 2005, B02.

pg. 111, "use local knowledge effectively"—Horwitz, "Best Responders," 98.

pg. 111, "responsive to local information"—Ibid.

CHAPTER 8

pg. 115, "being in harmony with nature"—The situation in Europe was comparable to that in China, in that the pope reigned supreme. One illustration of the extent of the Church's power at its height is that in 1582 Pope Gregory XIII removed ten days from the calendar by edict. Randy Alfred, "October 8, 1582: Nothing Happens . . . in Catholic Lands," *Wired*, October 10, 2010. Available at http://www.wired.com/thisdayintech/2010/10/1008gregorian-calendar-skips-days/.

pg. 115, "what we would today call public policy"—On July 28, 1976, an earthquake took place in Tangshan, killing over a quarter of a million people—the second deadliest earthquake in recorded history. That event was widely seen in China as portending the end of the Maoist era. Mao Zedong died less than two months later. I have a glancing connection to this event, as I was among a group of foreign experts invited to participate in the ceremonial reopening of the city in the summer of 1986, ten years after the calamity.

pg. 116, "When they died, the secret died with them."—David Landes, *Revolution in Time: Clocks and the Making of the Modern World* (Cambridge, MA: Belknap Press, 1983), 15–16.

pg. 116, "began as automated bells"—Ibid., 68.

pg. 116, "and then in villages and town"—Ibid.

pg. 116, "limited opportunities for abuse"—Ibid., 75.

pg. 116, "palace on the Île de la Cité"—Ibid.

pg. 117, "an end to imperial power itself"—Ibid.

pg. 117, *"The Passions and the Interests: Political Arguments for Capitalism before Its Triumph"*—Hirschman, *Passions and the Interests*.

pg. 118, "and now are distributed globally"—Classics on this topic include David Landes, *The Unbound Prometheus: Technological Change and Industrial Development in Western Europe from 1750 to the Present* (Cambridge: Cambridge University Press, 1969); Douglas North and Robert Thomas, *The Rise of the Western World: A New Economic History* (Cambridge: Cambridge University Press, 1973); and Nathan Rosenberg and L. E. Birdzell, *How the West Grew Rich: The Economic Transformation of the Industrial World* (New York: Basic Books, 1986). Recently published and also of interest is Gregory Clark, *A Farewell to Alms: A Brief Economic History of the World* (Princeton, NJ: Princeton University Press, 2007).

pg. 118, "mainly, the love of praise"—Hirschman, *Passions and the Interests*, 10.

pg. 119, "not as we would have them be"—The anti-idealistic rhetoric of this bygone era reminds one rather strikingly of modern-day critiques of such undertakings as the United Nations Millennium Village project, promoted and led by Columbia University economist Jeffrey Sachs.

pg. 119, "conspire unknowingly toward the public good"—Hirschman, *Passions and the Interests*, 10.

pg. 119, "which permits men to live in human society"—Ibid., 17.

pg. 120, "convert 'private vices' into 'public benefits'"—Ibid., 18.

pg. 120, "in their economic interest to do so"—Ibid., 17.

pg. 120, "set forth in the US Constitution"—Ibid., 28, including footnote 34.

pg. 120, "to his appetite for gain"—Ibid., 30.

pg. 121, "serve as a counterweight to another"—Ibid., 27.

pg. 122, "no cleric or layman should be a usurer"—Robert S. Lopez, *The Dawn of Modern Banking* (New Haven, CT: Yale University Press, 1979), 3–4.

pg. 122, "entry into this lucrative market"—In the late Middle Ages, banks were rare, which meant that, until the advent of bills of exchange, commerce was disproportionately a family affair. For similar reasons, family firms also dominate today in developing countries. Bills of exchange consequently represented the first step in a centuries-long, still-ongoing process by which the provision of trusted financial services devolved from family businesses to a global industry, and medieval trade routes developed into the globalized exchange economy of the twenty-first century. Avner Greif, "The Study of Organizations and Evolving Organizational Forms through History: Reflections from the Late Medieval Family Firm," *Industrial and Corporate Change* 5, no. 2 (1996): 473–502; Raymond de Roover, *Money, Banking and Credit in Mediaeval Bruges* (Cambridge, MA: Medieval Academy of America, 1948).

pg. 122, "of borrowers and lenders"—Lopez, *Dawn of Modern Banking*, 8.

pg. 123, "successors of the early medieval users"—Ibid., 6–7.

pg. 123, "lifts commerce right out of their grip"—Hirschman, *Passions and the Interests*, 72.

pg. 124, "unknowingly toward the public good"—Ibid., 10.

pg. 124, "and the ineffectuality of reason"—Ibid., 43.

pg. 124, "an interest in not being so"—Ibid., 73.

pg. 125, "one of humanity's major misfortunes"—For a fairly recent summary, see John Luke Gallup, Jeffrey D. Sachs, and Andrew Mellinger, "Geography and Economic Development," *CID Working Papers*, no. 1 (Cambridge, MA: Center for International Development at Harvard University, 2009).

pg. 125, "And become their own lords"—Paul H. Freedman, *Images of the Medieval Peasant* (Stanford, CA: Stanford University Press, 1999), 195.

pg. 126, "rely more on livestock than cultivation"—Landes, *Revolution in Time*, 242.

pg. 127, "reserved to highly trained journeymen"—Ibid., 258–59.

CHAPTER 9

pg. 129, "Jamsetji Tata"—Undated quote from the website of the Tata Group, http://www.tata.com/0_about_us/history/pioneers/quotable.htm.

pg. 130, "for doing public service"—See http://www.time.com/time/magazine/article/0,9171,827790,00.html.

pg. 130, "he is, by association, made out to be"—From 1951 to 1953, California received $13 billion in prime defense contracts, overtaking New York as the leading recipient of defense funding. That surge abated with cuts initiated by Wilson. Stuart W. Leslie, "The Biggest Angel of Them All: The Military and the Making of Silicon Valley," in *Understanding Silicon Valley: The Anatomy of an Entrepreneurial Region*, ed. Martin Kenney (Stanford, CA: Stanford University Press, 2000), 48–70.

pg. 131, "turned out to be spectacularly wrong"—See Schumpeter, *Capitalism, Socialism, and Democracy*, in particular, p. 162. The full quote offering this prediction is as follows:

> I shall not stay to repeat how objective and subjective, economic and extra-economic factors, reinforcing each other in imposing accord, contribute to that result. Nor shall I stay to show what should be obvious and in subsequent chapters will become more obvious still, viz., that those factors make not only for the

destruction of the capitalist but for the emergence of a socialist civilization. They all point in that direction. The capitalist process not only destroys its own institutional framework but it also creates the conditions for another. Destruction may not be the right word after all. Perhaps I should have spoken of transformation. The outcome of the process is not simply a void that could be filled by whatever might happen to turn up; things and souls are transformed in such a way as to become increasingly amenable to the socialist form of life. With every peg from under the capitalist structure vanishes an impossibility of the socialist plan.

pg. 131, "work in predictable ways"—For a time, at least, Schumpeter was exactly right. From the 1950s to the 1980s, the major corporate laboratories—such as Bell Laboratories, Xerox PARC, and the Thomas J. Watson Research Center—led in the creation of new products and process, not just in the United States, but globally. (My father's first job after graduate school in the mid-1950s was making promotional and training films for IBM about how that company's new technologies were changing the world. The general theme is a popular one in my family.)

pg. 131, "cashing their biweekly paychecks"—Lewis Branscomb and Philip Auerswald, *Taking Technical Risks: How Innovators, Managers, and Investors Manage Risk in High-Tech Innovations* (Cambridge, MA: MIT Press, 2002).

pg. 132, "That is what has gone wrong."—Tyler Cowen, *The Great Stagnation* (New York: Penguin, 2011), location 61.

pg. 133, "one of the best"—David Leonhardt, "The Depression: If Only Things Were That Good," *New York Times*, October 9, 2011. See http://www.nytimes.com/2011/10/09/sunday-review/the-depression-if-only-things-were-that-good.html.

pg. 134, "its performance in the past"—Schumpeter, *Capitalism, Socialism, and Democracy*, 111. Schumpeter's own refutation of this argument is worth quoting in full:

Technological possibilities are an uncharted sea. We may survey a geographical region and appraise, though only with reference to a given technique of agricultural production, the relative fertility of individual plots. Given that technique and disregarding its possible future developments, we may then imagine (though this would be wrong historically) that the best plots are first taken into cultivation, after them the next best ones and so on. At any given time during this process it is only relatively inferior plots that remain to be exploited in the future. But we cannot reason in this fashion about the future possibilities of technological advance. From the fact that some of them have been exploited before others, it cannot be inferred that the former were more productive than the latter. And those that are still in the lap of the gods may be more or less productive than any that have thus far come within our range of observation. Again this yields only a negative result which even the fact that technological "progress" tends, through systemization and rationalization of research and of management, to become more effective and sure-footed, is powerless to turn into a positive one. But for us the negative result suffices: there is no reason to expect slackening of the rate of output through exhaustion of technological possibilities. (118)

pg. 134, "fundamentally new economic combinations"—This conjecture found expression in a graduate seminar on entrepreneurship, technology, and globalization that I cotaught with my colleague David Hart at Harvard's Kennedy School of Government in the spring of 2001.

pg. 135, "technological innovation slows or ceases"—Another panelist, Jim Adams, presented a paper which reported that the average team size for published scientific papers increased 50 percent from 1981 to 1999. James D. Adams et al., "Scientific Teams and Institutional Collaborations: Evidence from U.S. Universities, 1981–1999," *Research Policy* 34 (2005): 259–85.

pg. 135, " around economies of collaboration"—Tim O'Reilly, "Government as a Platform," *Innovations: Technology, Governance, Globalization* 6, no. 1 (2011): 13–40.

pg. 136, "new seed ideas into usable forms"—Martin L. Weitzman, "Recombinant Growth," *Journal of Economics*, 113, no. 2 (May 2011): 333. See also Bill Gates, "Address at Harvard: Commencement," *Innovations: Technology, Governance, Globalization* 2, no. 4 (Fall 2007): 3–9.

pg. 137, "a challenge to entrepreneurial capitalism"—Western idealization of an Asian model of development is not new. Over two centuries ago, referring specifically to imperial China, Simon-Nicolas Henri Linguet argued that "Asian despotism" was actually an effective system of governance: "Asian despotism . . . does not at all favor tyranny contrary to what many think; it imposes on the kings obligations that are narrower than the so-called dependence in which some would like to place them in relation to their own vassals. [The ideal system] does not advise them to be just; it forces them to be so." A despot is unlikely to govern poorly, according to this logic, since doing so is not in the despot's best interests. Because the government effectively owns the entire country, it will act in the best interests of the entire country.

pg. 137, "readily absorb surplus labor"—See Byeong-Cheon Lee, "Developmental Dictatorship and the Park Chung-Hee Era: The Shaping of Modernity in the Republic of Korea" (New Jersey: Homa & Sekey Books, 2003). Likewise, how did China go from being one of the world's poorest countries with a stagnating economy to the world's leading creditor nation and a global economic powerhouse? Yes, entrepreneurship played a critical role, as I argued in chapter 3. But I also acknowledged that the Chinese government has directly and indirectly compelled its people to save at an astoundingly high rate, and noted that it has used those savings to undertake massive infrastructure improvements and other investments. After a long interval during which the role of China's government in the economy gradually diminished, it has recently shown a slight resurgence. See Michael Wines, "China Fortifies State Businesses to Fuel Growth," *New York Times*, August 30, 2010.

pg. 138, "there is more to steal"—Olson, *Power and Prosperity*, 3.

pg. 138, "as an altruistic government"—Ibid., 11: "A stationary bandit has an encompassing interest in the territory he controls and accordingly provides domestic order and other public goods. Thus, he is not like the wolf that preys on the elk, but more like the rancher who makes sure his cattle are protected and given water." Societies that experience such a transition from outright predation to (metaphorical) animal husbandry become better off. However, according to Olson, the mechanism by which this occurs has nothing to do with good intentions or beneficence.

pg. 138, "obtaining majority support"—Ibid., 15. Where democratically elected leaders differ from autocrats is in one seemingly simple matter: democratic leaders must take into account the burden of various tax rates on the particular constituencies they serve. As a direct consequence, democratically elected leaders will tend to select lower tax rates than autocrats. By a similar logic, if there is substantial inequality in a society, democratic leaders representing the rich will, having done the simple arithmetic of the advancement of interests, set redistributive tax rates lower than would a democratic leader representing the poor. After all, a flat tax rate set on all members of society will, by definition, direct more money from the haves to the have-nots. Conversely, from the standpoint of the status quo, extreme and widespread inequality has the effect of converting the majority of a country's population into boosters of criminality: when continued destitution is certain, the uncertainty of a revolution may not look like a bad alternative. When the poor who constitute a significantly negligible share of national income are not represented by the political leadership, their interest in the continued survival of the nation is accordingly limited. Taken to an extreme, this same simple calculus explains the French Revolution, the ascendancy of the Communist Party in China, and other large-scale, class-based insurrections.

pg. 139, "for the efficiency of the society"—Olson, *Power and Prosperity*, 22.

pg. 139, "could be carried out effectively"—Dani Rodrik, Gene Grossman, and Victor Norman, "Getting Intervention Right: How Korea and Taiwan Grew Rich," *Economic Policy* 10, no. 20 (1995): 53–107.

pg. 140, "before the behavioral cart"—President Park Chung-Hee's government used an array of tools to direct the economy, from allocating resources, to fixing prices, to owning and controlling enterprises directly. See David Waldner, *State Building and Late Development* (Ithaca, NY: Cornell University Press, 1999), chap. 6; Tony Michelle, *From a Developing to a Newly Industrialized Country: The Republic of Korea, 1961–82* (Geneva: International Labor Organization, 1988).

pg. 141, "to invest in public goods"—See Jeffrey Frankel, "The Natural Resource Curse: A Survey," HKS Faculty Research Working Paper Series RWF10-005, February 2010; Michael Ross, "Blood Barrels: Why Oil Wealth Fuels Conflict," *Foreign Affairs* (May/June 2008): 2–8; Iqbal Z. Quadir, "Foreign Aid and Bad

Government: Helping Entrepreneurs Is the Right Approach," *Wall Street Journal*, January 30, 2008. See also Paul Collier, *Plundered Planet* (Oxford: Oxford University Press, 2010).

pg. 141, "gives rise to checks and balances"—Iqbal Quadir, "Foreign Aid and Bad Government," *Wall Street Journal*, January 30, 2009; http://online.wsj.com/article/SB123327734124831471.html. It is largely thanks to Iqbal that I have developed my present appreciation for the work of Mancur Olson and its application to the understanding of the relationship between entrepreneurship and development.

pg. 142, "interests of society, considered broadly"—The numbers tell the story. Infusions of aid totaling about $120 billion flow every year from rich to poor countries. But, at the same time, poor countries annually hemorrhage $500 billion to $800 billion in illicit capital sent to rich countries—the spoils primarily of corruption, drug trafficking, and terrorist financing. As Raymond Baker and Eva Joly of the organization Global Financial Integrity have written, "This outflow of illicit money is the most damaging economic condition in the developing world. . . . Until development experts account for total capital going into and out of recipient countries, aid will continue to be offset by a much larger counterforce of fleeing capital." Raymond Baker and Eva Joly, "Illicit Money: Can It Be Stopped?" *New York Review of Books*, December 3, 2009, 61–64.

pg. 142, "to which they are misgoverned"—"The Outsider: An Entrepreneur Shakes Up the Political Landscape," *Economist*, October 1, 2011; Olson, *Power and Prosperity*, 59.

CHAPTER 10

pg. 149, "mere ornaments, are highly valued?"—Michel Foucault, *The Order of Things: An Archeology of the Human Science* (New York, NY: Vantage Press, 1970), chap. 6.

pg. 151, "proud that we are Americans"—Remarks of Robert F. Kennedy at the University of Kansas, March 18, 1968. Accessible at http://www.jfklibrary.org/Research/Ready-Reference/RFK-Speeches/Remarks-of-Robert-F-Kennedy-at-the-University-of-Kansas-March-18-1968.aspx.

pg. 152, "summarized alternative measures"—Joseph Stiglitz, Amartya Sen, and Jean-Paul Fitoussi, *Report of the Commission on the Measurement of Economic Performance and Social Progress* (Paris: Commission on the Measurement of Economic Performance and Social Progress, 2009), http://www.stiglitz-sen-fitoussi.fr.

pg. 153, "market to exchange in the first place"—The passage and sections from the following three pages derive from Philip Auerswald, "Creating Social Value," *Stanford Social Innovation Review* (Spring 2009): 51–55.

pg. 154, "fundamental theoretical synthesis"—The work by Hicks and his contemporary Lionel Robbins to establish the foundation of modern economics was preceded by that of William Stanley Jevons, Leon Walras, Vilfredo Pareto, and Alfred

Marshall; it was followed by that of Kenneth Arrow, Frank Hahn, Paul Samuelson, and Gérard Debreu.

pg. 154, "which have no such implication"—J. R. Hicks, *Values and Capital* (Oxford: Oxford University Press, 1933), 19.

pg. 155, "(and willingness to live)"—Amartya Sen, *Commodities and Capabilities* (Oxford: Oxford University Press, 1999).

pg. 156, "to end torture"—International Bridges for Justice; see http://www.ibj.org.

pg. 156, "to cure neglected diseases"—Institute for OneWorld Health; see http://www.iowh.org.

pg. 156, "British or indigenous, can accomplish"—Marshall was the author of *Principles of Economics*, among the foundational works in the field of economics. The original quote, from Marshall's correspondence, refers directly to the Tata companies. See Alfred Marshall and John King Whitaker, *The Correspondence of Alfred Marshall, Economist* (Cambridge: Cambridge University Press, 1996), 283.

pg. 158, "is a valuable privately held asset"—That the desire for reputation is a powerful human motivator is obvious. Classic studies by Robert K. Merton documented systems of incentives among scientists that apply equally to entrepreneurs—particularly social entrepreneurs. See Robert K. Merton, *The Sociology of Science: Theoretical and Empirical Investigations* (Chicago: University of Chicago Press, 1973).

pg. 158, "dominated by tobacco or oil companies"—Compensating differentials are well known to exist in a variety of labor markets. Another example is extra pay required to incur risk, or to undertake otherwise undesirable jobs.

pg. 160, *"Model List of Essential Medicines"*—Hale has since left the Institute for OneWorld Health to start Medicines360, a nonprofit pharmaceutical company dedicated to developing medicines for women and children, including pregnant women. Material for Hale's story is drawn from *Victoria Hale: An Uncommon Hero Eradicating Black Fever*, a video by the Skoll Foundation, http://www.youtube.com/watch?v=NVP24_KmJ-g; and Victoria Hale, *Innovations: Technology, Governance, Globalization* 2, no. 4 (Fall 2007): 59–71.

pg. 160, "supported by analytics"—See, e.g., Philip Auerswald and Deborah van Opstal, "Coping with Turbulence: The Resilience Imperative," *Innovations: Technology, Governance, Globalization*, special edition for the World Economic Forum, 2009. Accessible at http://www.compete.org/images/uploads/File/PDF%20Files/INNOVATIONS-Davos-2009_Auerswald-vanOpstal.pdf

CHAPTER 11

pg. 162, "Wael Ghonim"—Wael Ghonim, interview by Harry Smith on CBS News' *60 Minutes*, online-only outtakes. Posted February 14, 2011. Accessible at http://www.cbsnews.com/video/watch/?id=7349173n.

pg. 162, "better than the old, but it was not"—This quote and those that follow are from Ibrahim and Helmy Abouleish, "Garden in the Desert: Sekem Makes Comprehensive

Sustainable Development a Reality in Egypt," *Innovations: Technology, Governance, Globalization* 3, no. 3 (Summer 2008): 21–48.

pg. 165, "as well as of power and authority"—Sir John Steuart, "The General Consequences Resulting to a Trading Nation upon the Opening of an Active Foreign Commerce," quoted in Hirschman, *Passions and the Interests.*

pg. 165, "forms of private capital ownership"—Olson, *Power and Prosperity*, 116–18.

pg. 166, "born in the Least Developed Countries defined by the United Nations"—Michael Clemens, "A Labor Mobility Agenda for Development," Center for Global Development Working Paper 201 (January 2010), 1.

pg. 167, "founders of Silicon Valley's start-ups were foreign-born"—For a summary, see Vivek Wadhwa, "Open Doors Wider for Skilled Immigrants," *Business Week*, January 3, 2007.

pg. 169, "master these perfected means"—José Ortega y Gasset, *The Revolt of the Masses* (New York: W. W. Norton & Co., [1930] 1994), 90.

pg. 174, "Egyptian entrepreneurs in international fora"—See http://www.sekem.com/.

pg. 175, "the end of the regime of Hosni Mubarak"—Mike Giglio "The Facebook Freedom Fighter," *Newsweek*, February 13, 2011. Accessible at http://www.newsweek.com/2011/02/13/the-facebook-freedom-fighter.html.

pg. 176, "at a critical point in the protests"—Kareem Fahim and Mona El-Naggar, "Emotions of a Reluctant Hero Galvanize Protesters," *New York Times*, February 8, 2011. Accessible at http://www.nytimes.com/2011/02/09/world/middleeast/09ghonim.html.

pg. 176, "and communicate with, one another"—Ron Burt, *Structural Holes: The Social Structure of Competition* (Cambridge, MA: Harvard University Press, 1995).

CHAPTER 12

pg. 177, "world's wealthiest man"—Angus Whitley and Elisabeth Behrmann, "Mexico's Carlos Slim Says He'd Rather Create Jobs Than Donate to Charity," Bloomberg.com, September 29, 2010.

pg. 178, "mischievous glint in his eyes"—Christopher Washington, remarks at George Mason University.

pg. 180, "the right places at the right times"—Manpower Inc., *World of Work Trends Booklet* (Milwaukee, WI: Manpower Inc., 2010).

pg. 181, "current capabilities of their employees"—American Society for Training & Development, *Bridging the Skills Gap: How the Skills Shortage Threatens Growth and Competitiveness, and What to Do About It* (Alexandria: VA: American Society for Training & Development, 2006), 4.

pg. 182, "most of your life eking out a living"—Talk given at TEDx Silicon Valley, December 12, 2009. Accessible at http://www.tedxsv.org/?page_id=525.

pg. 182, "in all of human history to date"—UNESCO, *Education for All Global Monitoring Report 2010* (Paris: UNESCO, 2010).

pg. 183, "Fadi Ghandour and Iqbal Quadir"—Remarks at the annual meeting of the Clinton Global Initiative, Wednesday, September 22, 2011.

pg. 184, "could ever eliminate itself"—Schumpeter, *Capitalism, Socialism, and Democracy*, 69.

pg. 184, "trustified capitalism"—Trusts refer to powerful conglomerates, such those that dominated US business at the start of the twentieth century.

pg. 184, "where in fact it was the lightest"—Alexis de Tocqueville, *L'ancien régime et la révolution* (New York: Harper and Brothers, 1856), 38. The original text is as follows: "Une chose surprend au premier abord: la Révolution, dont l'objet propre était d'abolir partout le reste des institutions du moyen âge, n'a pas éclaté dans les contrées où ces institutions, mieux conservées, faisaient le plus sentir au peuple leur gêne et leur rigueur, mais, au contraire, dans celles où elles les lui faisaient sentir le moins; de telle sorte que leur joug a paru le plus insupportable là où il était en réalité le moins lourd."

pg. 185, "than the whole had ever appeared"—Ibid., 49.

pg. 185, "particularly important case of sectional unemployment"—Schumpeter's observations in *Capitalism, Socialism, and Democracy* on this particular paradox of higher education are so current to the plight of youth today—whether they are in Chicago or Cairo—that they are worth quoting in full:

One of the most important features of the later stages of capitalist civilization is the vigorous expansion of the educational apparatus and particularly of the facilities for higher education. This development was and is no less inevitable than the development of the largest-scale industrial unit, but, unlike the latter, it has been and is being fostered by public opinion and public authority so as to go much further than it would have done under its own steam. Whatever we may think of this from other standpoints and whatever the precise causation, there are several consequences that bear upon the size and attitude of the intellectual group.

First, inasmuch as higher education thus increases the supply of services in professional, quasi-professional and in the end all 'whitecollar' lines beyond the point determined by cost-return considerations, it may create a particularly important case of sectional unemployment.

Second, along with or in place of such unemployment, it creates unsatisfactory conditions of employment—employment in substandard work or at wages below those of the better-paid manual workers.

Third, it may create unemployability of a particularly disconcerting type. The man who has gone through a college or university easily becomes psychically unemployable in manual occupations without necessarily acquiring employability in, say, professional work. . . . Cases in which among a dozen applicants for a job, all formally qualified, there is not one who can fill it satisfactorily, are known to everyone who has anything to do with appointments—to everyone, that is, who is himself qualified to judge. (152)

pg. 186, "the correspond to current realities"—The University of Miami's Launch Pad initiative is an exception that proves the rule, and represents a model for the rest of the country: http://www.thelaunchpad.org/. For an understanding of how Launch Pad fits into the broader story of the future of collegiate education, see panel 4 of the Presidents' Symposium on the Future of Collegiate Education, a workshop held at the Association of Public and Land-Grant Universities on May 28, 2010, http://www.aplu.org/page.aspx?pid=1643.

pg. 186, "among the relatively advantaged"—A January 2011 *New York Times* profile of Mohamed Bouazizi—the Tunisian street vendor whose suicide sparked that country's revolution—offers a vivid description of this phenomenon. Bouazizi himself was not a college graduate, but the circumstances of his peers in his hometown of Sidi Bouzid reflect Schumpeter's predictions: "There are jobs at a toy factory, one of the two biggest plants in town, but they pay only about $50 a month. People with college degrees head for the more affluent coastal cities or settle for less. Wassim Lassoued, who has a master's degree in physics, works part time in an Internet cafe. 'Five years ago, lots of money was sent here to establish new businesses,' he said. 'That money disappeared.'" Karim Faheem, "Slap to a Man's Pride Set Off Tumult in Tunisia," *New York Times*, January 22, 2011, http://www.nytimes.com/2011/01/22/world/africa/22sidi.html?pagewanted=1&_r=1.

pg. 188, "at least one attempt at an answer"—At the time I was finishing this book, Christopher Washington had picked up on his original vision and was working to launch a venture in Ghana informed by his experience with large-scale urban agriculture in the Washington, DC metro area.

CHAPTER 13

pg. 193, "call forth moral allegiance"—Schumpeter, *Capitalism, Socialism, and Democracy*, 142.

pg. 194, "on the cable news feed"—The Federal Bureau of Investigation, Terrorism 2002–2005 (Washington, DC: Federal Bureau of Investigation), p. 1: "In keeping with a longstanding trend, domestic extremists carried out the majority of terrorist incidents during this period." http://www.fbi.gov/stats-services/publications/terrorism-2002-2005/

pg. 195, "fighting against Islamic fascism"—Kari Huus and Tom Curry, "The Day the Enemy Became 'Islamic Fascists,'" MSNBC.com, August 11, 2006. Accessible at http://www.msnbc.msn.com/id/14304397/ns/politics/.

pg. 196, "impacts through exaggerated responses"—Philip Auerswald, "The Irrelevance of the Middle East," *American Interest* 2, no. 5 (May/June 2007): 19–37.

pg. 196, "category of 'the greatest risk'"—Falkenrath stated: "Of all the various remaining civilian vulnerabilities in America today, one stands alone as uniquely deadly, pervasive, and susceptible to terrorist attack: toxic-inhalation hazard (TIH) of industrial chemicals, such as chlorine, ammonia, phosgene, methylbromide, hydrochloric and various other acids." Statement before the United States

Committee on Homeland Security and Governmental Affairs, Washington, DC, April 27, 2005.

pg. 198, "creative spirit that drive entrepreneurs"—Philip Auerswald et al., *Seeds of Disaster, Roots of Response: How Private Action Can Reduce Public Vulnerability* (Cambridge: Cambridge University Press, 2006).

pg. 199, "continued poverty for much of the world"—Michael Atiyah and Frank Press, "Population Growth, Resource Consumption and a Sustainable World," *Interdisciplinary Science Reviews* 17, no. 2 (June 2002): 100–102.

pg. 200, "to deal with this important question"—John Tanton, "International Migration as an Obstacle to Achieving World Stability," *Ecologist* 6:6 (July 1976): 222. Accessible at http://www.johntanton.org/articles/mitchell_essay_immigration.html.

pg. 201, "if they are to bloom at all"—John Tanton, "End of the Migration Epoch? Time for a New Paradigm," *The Social Contract*, 4, no. 3 (Spring 1994).

pg. 201, "detain illegal immigrants"—NumbersUSA was founded in 2002 by Roy Beck, a former journalist and public policy analyst, while he was working for Tanton as the Washington, DC, editor of *The Social Contract*.

pg. 202, "rental price of their housing"—Gianmarco Ottaviano and Giovanni Peri, "The Economic Value of Cultural Diversity: Evidence from U.S. Cities," NBER Working Paper 10904, November 2004. See also "Rethinking the Gains from Immigration: Theory and Evidence from the U.S.," NBER Working Paper 11672 (2004).

pg. 202, "and employed 450,000 workers"—Vivek Wadhwa, "Our Best Imports: Keeping Immigrant Innovators Here," *Democracy: A Journal of Ideas*, no. 21 (Summer 2011), http://www.democracyjournal.org/21/our-best-imports-keeping-immigrant-innovators-here.php. See also re-search published by the Kauffman Foundation's program "Immigration and the American Economy," http://www.kauffman.org/research-and-policy/immigration-and-the-american-economy.aspx.

pg. 203, "family abandonment rate"—Michael A. Clemens, "Economics and Emigration: Trillion-Dollar Bills on the Sidewalk?" *Journal of Economic Perspectives* 25, no. 3 (Summer 2011): 89. For a comprehensive survey of the mechanisms by which the actions of diaspora populations affect, and benefit, home countries, see Kingsley Aikins and Nicola White, *Global Diaspora Strategies Toolkit: Harnessing the Power of Global Diasporas* (Dublin: Diaspora Matters, 2011), http://www.diasporamatters.com/download-the-diaspora-toolkit/2011/.

pg. 203, "capital movement in the world"—Lawrence MacDonald, "Migration and the Trillion Dollar Bills on the Sidewalk: Michael Clemens," Center for Global Development blog, September 7, 2011. See http://blogs.cgdev.org/global_prosperity_wonkcast/2011/09/07/migration-and-the-trillion-dollar-bills-on-the-sidewalk-michael-clemens/.

pg. 204, "regardless of ethnicity, religion or background"—Amy Chua, *Day of Empire: How Hyperpowers Rise to Global Dominance—and Why They Fall* (New York: Doubleday, 2007), xxxiii.

pg. 204, "diverse interests for collaborative success"—An interesting affirmation of this principle is found in a letter Tanton himself sent to the *New York Times* in response to the profile of him that the paper ran on its front page in June 2011: "Regarding my penchant for working with all sides of the political, ethnic, philosophic, economic, racial, religious and other spectra, that is how one forms a coalition that has political meaning and power. Forming a coalition from people who agree on all issues simply does not work." See http://www.johntanton.org/answering_my_critics/letter_2011apr18_jt_new_york_times.html.

pg. 204, "serving to keep opportunity out"—For policy proposals to reverse that trend, see Carl Shramm, "Rolling Out the Welcome Mat for Entrepreneurs," *McKinsey & Company: What Matters*, July 18, 2011, http://whatmatters.mckinseydigital.com/job_creation/rolling-out-the-welcome-mat-for-entrepreneurs.

pg. 204, "to be in the US illegally?"—I am referring to Arizona's Senate Bill 1070; see http://www.azleg.gov/legtext/49leg/2r/bills/sb1070s.pdf.

pg. 205, "nation is roused to action"—James Fallows, "How America Can Rise Again," *Atlantic* (January/February 2010).

pg. 206, "planting any perennial border"—Jane Garmey, "The Natural Look, with Much Effort," *New York Times*, September 10, 2008, F1. Accessible at http://www.nytimes.com/2008/09/11/garden/11meadow.html.

pg. 206, "suppress invasive weeds"—Ibid.

CHAPTER 14

pg. 207, "human relations in his business"—Charles P. McCormick, *The Power of People* (Baltimore, MD: McCormick & Company, [1949] 1952), xvi.

pg. 208, "manager of a multimillion-dollar business"—Ibid., 12.

pg. 209, "to give advice about it"—Ibid., 28–29.

pg. 209, "clear to everyone in the system"—W. Edwards Deming, *The New Economics for Industry, Government, Education* (Cambridge, MA: MIT Press, [1994] 2000), 50.

pg. 209, "unknown or unknowable"—W. Edwards Deming, *Out of the Crisis* (Cambridge, MA: MIT Press, [1982] 2000), 121.

pg. 209, "The Builder learns from them."—Umair Haque, "The Builders Manifesto," *Harvard Business School* blog, December, 18, 2009. Accessible at http://blogs.hbr.org/haque/2009/12/the_builders_manifesto.html. See also Umair Haque, *Betterness: Economics for Humans* (Cambridge, MA: Harvard Business School Press, 2011).

pg. 210, "as a curb to economic power"—John Kenneth Galbraith, *American Capitalism: The Concept of Countervailing Power* (New Brunswick, NJ: Transaction Publishers, [1952] 2008), 113. This subsection parallels Auerswald and Acs, "Defining Prosperity."

pg. 210, "defined the American political system"—See, for example, Baumol et al., *Good Capitalism, Bad Capitalism*, 194. Galbraith observed a transient form of economic organization linked directly to the technological and organizational realities of the mid-twentieth century and took it to be the end point of a nation's development. American capitalism is nothing if not dynamic, but Galbraith's framework is fundamentally static. It is hard, for instance, to imagine writing a book today on the topic of American capitalism that contains, as Galbraith's does, only two uses of the word "entrepreneur." While Galbraith alludes to the important role in economic life of technology and innovation, he states that both of these emanate from large corporations and thus only serve to reinforce the economic status quo.

pg. 210, "which they were supposedly arrayed"—Auerswald and Acs, "Defining Prosperity."

pg. 211, "the viability of automakers"—See http://www.npr.org/templates/story/story.php?storyId=104527823&ft=1&f=1001.

pg. 211, "Left? Right?"—Alluding to the same apocryphal quote, columnist William Kristol wrote at the time the auto bailout packages were being debated: "Whichever party can liberate itself from its well-worn rut to propose policies that help both American businesses and workers has a great opportunity. That party's leaders could begin by offering management and labor at the Big Three a little more sympathy and heaping upon them a little less calumny. Where's Charles Wilson when we need him?" "Left and Right, Piling On," *New York Times*, December 15, 2008, A31.

pg. 211, "helps you change a culture"—Bill Vlasic, "Culture Shock: G.M. Struggles to Shed a Legendary Bureaucracy," *New York Times*, November 13, 2009, B1.

pg. 211, "For decades."—Floyd Norris, "U.S. Teaches Carmakers Capitalism," *New York Times*, November 20, 2009, B1. Available at http://www.nytimes.com/2009/11/20/business/20norris.html.

pg. 212, "have spelled trouble?"—Dane Stangler, "The Insurgent Spirit and Messy Capitalism," RealClearMarkets.com, November 25, 2008, http://www.realclearmarkets.com/articles/2008/11/the_insurgent_spirit_and_messy.html.

pg. 214, "better or worse than the original one"—Ronald H. Coase, "The Problem of Social Cost," *Journal of Law and Economics* 3 (October 1960), 34.

pg. 215, "recurrent themes in this book"—See also Peter Orzag, "As Kaldor's Facts Fall, Occupy Wall Street Rises," Bloomberg.com, October 19, 2011.

pg. 215, "notably health and education"—Michael Spence, "The Impact of Globalization on Income and Employment: The Downside of Integrating Markets," *Foreign Affairs* (July/August 2011): 28–41.

pg. 215, "current standard but at far lower cost"—W. B. Arthur, "The Second Economy."

pg. 216, "occasionally suggested is the case"—In March 2009, Nobel laureate Paul Krugman posted to his blog a chart of US industrial production from 1929 to 1930 (the first thirteen months of the Great Depression), comparing it to the interval from 2007 to 2009 (the first thirteen months of what Krugman referred to as the

"Great Recession"). Noting that the drop in industrial production at the start of the Great Depression was about double that experienced in 2007–2009, Krugman concluded: "At this point we're sort of experiencing half a Great Depression. That's pretty bad." "The Conscience of a Liberal: The Great Recession versus the Great Depression," *New York Times* blog, March 20, 2009. Accessible at http://krugman.blogs.nytimes.com/2009/03/20/the-great-recession-versus-the-great-depression/.

Of course Krugman was hardly alone in trumpeting the severity of economic fallout from the global financial crisis. Analogies between the recession and the Great Depression proliferated in the winter of 2009. Yet that wasn't the first time Krugman rang alarm bells about another Great Depression. In 1998, during the Asian financial crisis, he expressed an equally dire outlook in a cover story for *Fortune* magazine: "Never in the course of economic events—not even in the early years of the Depression—has so large a part of the world economy experienced so devastating a fall from grace." Without a drastic intervention, "we could be looking at a true Depression scenario—the kind of slump that 60 years ago devastated societies, destabilized governments, and eventually led to war." "Saving Asia: It's Time To Get Radical," *Fortune,* September 7, 1998, accessible at http://money.cnn.com/magazines/fortune/fortune_archive/1998/09/07/247884/index.htm; cited in Fareed Zakaria, "Capitalist Manifesto: Greed Is Good (To a Point)," *Newsweek*, June 13, 2009. Accessible at http://www.newsweek.com/2009/06/12/the-capitalist-manifesto-greed-is-good.html. What actually happened? The interventions Krugman advocated were not, in fact, enacted. Calamity did not ensue.

pg. 217, "that most of the world still envies"—Fallows, "How America Can Rise Again." A reasonable counter to the argument I make here is that—even if we all agree that levels of human well-being matter in the way I am suggesting that they do—people nonetheless are well known to make assessments of their well-being based on the their relative standing in society, rather than in absolute terms. Furthermore, people tend to compare themselves to their most immediate peer group. As a consequence, improvements in human well-being are far more elusive than the foregoing argument would suggest. The evidence supporting such context-based assessments of well-being is strong. I would simply say that, compared with watching your child die in your arms of an easily preventable disease, the anxiety of "keeping up with the Joneses" is, itself, a rather significant luxury. As a consequence, it is not my primary concern.

pg. 218, "will be forced on them"—Ram S Tarneja, "My Friend Naval," Tata group website, 2004. Accessible at http://www.tata.com/aboutus/articles/inside.aspx?artid=SufsIy078IY=.

pg. 218, "asserts itself and there is a change"—McCormick, *Power of People*, 1.

pg. 218, "The people liberate themselves."—Statement in Mexico, 1958.

pg. 218, "by management and government"—McCormick, *Power of People*, 2.

pg. 218, "being of service to others"—Ibid., 2–3.

pg. 219, "leaders today, tomorrow, and forever"—Ibid., 3.

CHAPTER 15

pg. 220, "Asa Bowen Smith"—Clifford Merril Drury, *The First White Women over the Rockies: Diaries, Letters, and Biographical Sketches of the Six Women of the Oregon Mission Who Made the Overland Journey in 1836 and 1838* (Glendale, CA: Arthur H. Clark Company, 1963), 157.

pg. 221, "the embracing of true religion"—Thomas Harriot, *A Brief and True Report of the New Found Land of Virginia* (London, 1588), 25.

pg. 221, "We are a separate people!"—Colonel Tatham, *The Annual Biography and Obituary for the Year 1820*, vol. 4 (London: Longman, Hurst, Rees, Orme & Brown, 1820), 163–64. Original source located via Corntassel.net.

pg. 222, "limits to our onward march?"—"Annexation," *United States Magazine and Democratic Review* 17, no. 1 (July–August, 1845): 5–10. O'Sullivan used the term in reference to alleged European efforts to impede the westward expansion of the United States, which he claimed were "in a spirit of hostile interference against us, for the avowed object of thwarting our policy and hampering our power, limiting our greatness and checking the fulfillment of our manifest destiny to overspread the continent allotted by Providence for the free development of our yearly multiplying millions." In an earlier essay he had introduced the idea of manifest destiny, but did not employ that precise term; see John O'Sullivan, "The Great Nation of Futurity," *United States Democratic Review* 6, no. 23 (November 1839): 426–30. Accessible at http://digital.library.cornell.edu/cgi/t/text/text-idx?c =usde;cc=;view=toc;subview=short;idno=usde0006-4.

pg. 222, "competition with the Soviets"—Alexis de Tocqueville's reference to the United States as "exceptional" in *Democracy in America* (New York: Vintage, 1990) illustrates one way in which that term might be interpreted in this context:

> The position of the Americans is therefore quite exceptional, and it may be believed that no democratic people will ever be placed in a similar one. Their strictly Puritanical origin, their exclusively commercial habits, even the country they inhabit, which seems to divert their minds from the pursuit of science, literature, and the arts, the proximity of Europe, which allows them to neglect these pursuits without relapsing into barbarism, a thousand special causes, of which I have only been able to point out the most important, have singularly concurred to fix the mind of the American upon purely practical objects. His passions, his wants, his education, and everything about him seem to unite in drawing the native of the United States earthward; his religion alone bids him turn, from time to time, a transient and distracted glance to heaven. Let us cease, then, to view all democratic nations under the example of the American people. (36–37)

pg. 222, "affairs of the contemporary world"—William Pfaff, "Manifest Destiny: A New Direction for America," *New York Review of Books*, February 15, 2007.

pg. 224, "new and growing businesses?"—Tim Kane, "The Importance of Startups in Job Creation and Job Destruction," *Kauffman Foundation Research Series:*

Firm Formation and Economic Growth (Kansas City, MO: Kauffman Foundation, July 2010).

pg. 225, "twenty-first competitive advantage"—For insightful further analysis of the just-cited job-creation statistic, see Dane Stangler and Paul Kedrosky, "Neutralism and Entrepreneurship: The Structural Dynamics of Startups, Young Firms, and Job Creation," *Kauffman Foundation Research Series: Firm Formation and Economic Growth* (Kansas City, MO: Kauffman Foundation, September 2010).

pg. 225, "all corners of the global brain"—Anne-Marie Slaughter, "America's Edge: Power in the Networked Century," *Foreign Affairs* (September/October 2009): 103–4.

pg. 225, "quickly test these new combinations"—I thank Sandy Maxey for suggesting the use of the term "civic infrastructure" in this context.

pg. 226, "radical innovators must redraw"—Umair Haque, "Google Buzz and the Five Principles of Designing For Meaning," *Harvard Business Blog*, February 12, 2010. Accessible at http://blogs.hbr.org/haque/2010/02/google_buzz_revolution_evoluti.html .

pg. 227, "there is my country"—O'Sullivan, "Great Nation of Futurity," 429.

pg 228, "to create platforms for innovation"—Tim O'Reilly, "Government as a Platform," in *Open Government: Collaboration, Transparency, and Participation in Practice*, eds. Daniel Lathrop and Laurel Ruma (Sebastopol: O'Reilly Media, 2010): 12–39.

pg. 228, "This is a model for the future."—I thank President Clinton for sharing this observation with me. One application, which I have discussed with my Kauffman Foundation colleague Bob Litan, is the creation of a globally accessible platform for the registration of property rights. This innovation would bring into the digital age the rights-inclusiveness strategy that has long been championed by Peruvian economist Hernando de Soto.

pg. 228, "any of them lie fallow"—Richard Florida, *The Great Reset: How New Ways of Living and Working Drive Post-Crash Prosperity* (New York: Harper: 2010); Edward Glaeser, *How Our Greatest Invention Makes Us Richer, Smarter, Greener, Healthier, and Happier* (New York: Penguin Press, 2010); The Brookings Institution Metropolitan Policy Program, *Restoring Prosperity: The State Role in Revitalizing America's Older Industrial Cities* (Washington, DC: Brookings Institution, 2007).

pg. 229, "We have to make sure that happens."—Anya Kamenetz, *DIY U: Edupunks, Edupreneurs, and the Coming Transformation of Higher Education* (White River Jct., VT: Chelsea Green, 2010); Philip Auerswald, "First Newspapers, Now Universities: It's Transformation Time," WashingtonPost.com, June 8, 2010, http://views.washingtonpost.com/leadership/guestinsights/2010/06/first-newspapers-now-universities-its-transformation-time.html.

pg. 229, "strategies of diaspora engagement"—Aikins and White, *Global Diaspora Strategies Toolkit*. The US State Department deserves credit for not only having recognized the important role of diaspora communities resident in the US but also for having taken significant initial steps to mobilize America's collaborative advantage (see http://www.diasporaalliance.org/). However, realizing the full potential of a strategy of diaspora engagement in the US will require not only a far more broad-based effort within the federal government but also the implementation of creative new approaches by states, cities, and educational institutions across the country.

pg. 229, "everyone a changemaker world"—William Drayton, "Everyone a Changemaker: Social Entrepreneurship's Ultimate Goal," *Innovations: Technology, Governance, Globalization* 1, no. 1 (Winter 2006): 80–96; Thomas Kalil, "Innovation, Education, and the Maker Movement," Remarks at the New York Hall of Science, September 29, 2010, published in *O'Reilly Radar*, October 4, 2010, http://radar.oreilly.com/2010/10/innovation-education-and-the-m.html; Anya Kamenetz, "Why Education Without Creativity Isn't Enough," FastCompany.com, September 14, 2011, http://www.fastcompany.com/magazine/159/indian-engineers-education.

pg. 230, "America's best days lie ahead"—Warren E. Buffett, Letter to the Shareholders of Berkshire Hathaway Inc., February 26, 2011, http://www.berkshirehathaway.com/letters/2010ltr.pdf.

pg. 231, "It is an idea."—For an eloquent elaboration on this theme, see Anne-Marie Slaughter, *The Idea That Is America: Keeping Faith with our Values in a Dangerous World* (New York: Basic Books, 2007).

INDEX